THE EVERYTHING Family Guides

New York City, 3rd Edition

Dear Reader,

Welcome to our city! Be prepared for a unique experience.

You may have heard that New York is a rude, even cold place. But take it from this city kid that nothing could be further from the truth—in the local dialect, "fuggedaboudit." With all the people around, New Yorkers respect your privacy. But pierce that veil, and a local who has the time will go out of their way to help you. We want you to have a good time, be impressed, and carry away that positive impression.

New York is in a perpetual state of change. The wonderful thing about our city is that it keeps renewing itself. New York has a way of making what's old new again and what's new a welcome part of New York life.

The sheer desire to experience new sensations and absorb the latest fad in a mad dash to reward busy lives and hard work forces this city to renew itself with increasing speed and agility. That's what makes it the center of the world for me.

There is more than a lifetime of interesting things to do in the Big Apple because New York has eight million of its own to please. No matter what excites you and your family, you will find it here, usually in multiples. Don't be afraid to experiment, to ask, to lose yourselves. And don't be intimidated. New York isn't called "Fun City" for nothing. Really, "Omnotkidden!"

Jesse J. Leaf

THE EVERYTHING® Series

The handy, accessible books in this series give you all you need to tackle a difficult project, gain a new hobby, or even brush up on something you learned back in school but have since forgotten. You can read cover to cover or just pick out information from the four useful boxes.

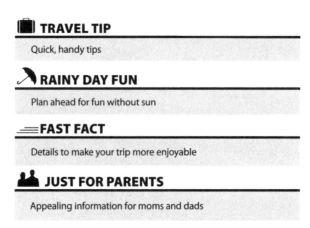

TRAVEL TIP

Quick, handy tips

RAINY DAY FUN

Plan ahead for fun without sun

FAST FACT

Details to make your trip more enjoyable

JUST FOR PARENTS

Appealing information for moms and dads

When you're done reading, you can finally say you know EVERYTHING®!

DIRECTOR OF INNOVATION Paula Munier

EDITORIAL DIRECTOR Laura M. Daly

EXECUTIVE EDITOR, SERIES BOOKS Brielle K. Matson

ASSOCIATE COPY CHIEF Sheila Zwiebel

ACQUISITIONS EDITOR Lisa Laing

DEVELOPMENT EDITOR Elizabeth Kassab

PRODUCTION EDITOR Casey Ebert

Visit the entire Everything® series at *www.everything.com*

THE EVERYTHING

FAMILY GUIDE TO

NEW YORK CITY

3rd Edition

All the best hotels, restaurants, sites,
and attractions in the Big Apple

Jesse J. Leaf

Avon, Massachusetts

This book is dedicated to the eight million individuals who give New York its heart and soul and make it the greatest city in the world. I especially dedicate it to those New Yorkers who are closest to me—Mindy, Joanna, Jason, and Alison—my family.

. . .

An Everything® Series Book.
Everything® and everything.com® are registered trade-marks of F+W Publications, Inc.

Published by Adams Media, an F+W Publications Company
57 Littlefield Street, Avon, MA 02322 U.S.A.
www.adamsmedia.com

ISBN 10: 1-59869-490-1
ISBN 13: 978-1-59869-490-1

Printed in Canada.

J I H G F E D C B A

Library of Congress Cataloging-in-Publication Data
is available from the publisher.

This publication is designed to provide accurate and authoritative information with regard to the subject matter covered. It is sold with the understanding that the publisher is not engaged in rendering legal, accounting, or other professional advice. If legal advice or other expert assistance is required, the services of a competent professional person should be sought.
—From a *Declaration of Principles* jointly adopted by a Committee of the American Bar Association and a Committee of Publishers and Associations

Many of the designations used by manufacturers and sellers to distinguish their products are claimed as trademarks. Where those designations appear in this book and Adams Media was aware of a trademark claim, the designations have been printed with initial capital letters.

*This book is available at quantity discounts for bulk purchases.
For information, please call 1-800-289-0963.*

Contents

Top Ten Things to Do in New York City

1. Take the family to Times Square, ride in the Toys Я Us Ferris Wheel, take in a Broadway show, and buy T-shirts afterward.

2. Go to the top of the Empire State Building and ride the Skyride.

3. Take the ferry to the Statue of Liberty and visit the Tenement Museum and Katz's Deli on the way back.

4. Spend a day in Central Park. Take pictures at the *Alice in Wonderland* and Balto statues, ride the carousel, float a wooden boat, ride a hansom cab, and eat lunch at Tavern on the Green.

5. Go to the American Museum of Natural History and the Metropolitan Museum of Art.

6. Have a meal in Chinatown and stroll the streets examining the trinkets.

7. Go shopping at Macy's or Bloomingdale's, in Greenwich Village, or along Fifth or Madison avenues.

8. Catch a professional sports game.

9. In the wintertime, go ice skating at the rink at Rockefeller Center or at least have lunch at the Rock Center Café and watch New Yorkers skate. Get up early on Thanksgiving morning, bundle up, and get a good spot on the Macy's Thanksgiving Day Parade route (usually along the Upper West Side).

10. Splurge and take one of the ten-minute helicopter rides over lower Manhattan.

Acknowledgments

I wrote this book on the shoulders of two other New Yorkers. Richard Mintzer laid the foundation with the excellent first edition. Lori Perkins continued with the task of wrestling the tumultuous energy of the Big Apple between two covers. It was now my turn.

As big as it is, New York is a city with a human dimension. I depended on the kindness of strangers as I spoke with literally hundreds of unsung workers in the hospitality industry who man the telephones, computers, and desks of hotels, restaurants, attractions, airports, train stations, and tourist offices. Members of NYC & Company, the Metropolitan Transit Authority, the Mayor's Office, maitre d's, tourist guides, park rangers—every single one reaffirmed my belief that New Yorkers are the greatest people in the world.

Two big thanks to my editors Lisa Laing and Elizabeth Kassab and to my agent June Clark for their patience, understanding, and generosity, helping me during an extended period of illness. I have never met such wonderful people in forty years in the business.

And finally, my son Jason, a third-generation New Yorker with the pulse of the city in his veins. Thanks, Jason, for the nights you roamed the streets with a cell phone in hand reporting on the activity and for the miles of city concrete you covered on your bike helping out the old man.

Introduction

The book you're holding is what you get when you ask a native New Yorker to write about the city he loves. This isn't a dry travel listing of abstract places. This is a love letter to you from a living city. I want you to love my city as much as I do, as much as eight million other folks do. I was born in and raised on the streets of New York (too) many decades ago. I know its buildings and its people intimately. Yet I still am as excited as a first-time visitor every time I go out. It is a city of infinite interest, experience, and surprise.

This should not be news to any urbanite. A city is built as a tool, playground, and refuge for its inhabitants. It is designed by them, and it exists for them. What makes New York a different—some may think alien—place are the same things that make it unequaled as a family tourist destination. It's the variety, the facilities, and the locals.

As a native New Yorker, I'm here to tell you that my fellow Gotham-ites are a great and warm people—most of them, most of the time. Ask a New Yorker for directions and you'll happily (if sometimes hastily) get them. Ask for a good restaurant or restroom close by, and they'll be proud to show off their knowledge and their city. Ask a New Yorker a question, and chances are you'll get a life story. In writing this book, talking to people took maybe three times as long as it would have because you just can't shut some "landsman" off. On more than one occasion, I've had to call back because I was so engrossed in schmoozing (a local leisure activity) that I forgot to ask the question I called about.

Tourists are sometimes overwhelmed by New York. No wonder. It is superlative in every way. There are between 18,000 and 20,000 restaurants in the city. There are more than 150 museums. It is the theater, art, financial, fashion, and sports capital of the world, and, well, you get the picture. No matter who you are or where your inter-ests lie, you'll find something in the Big Apple to win your heart.

Use Chapters 6 and 7 to help with the must-sees. Then explore all the rest that New York has to offer. As an important art center, it offers breathtaking museums and fabulous architecture. No visitor should miss the Metropolitan Museum of Art, which rivals the Louvre as one of the world's greatest museums. Add the Guggenheim, the Whitney, and the Museum of Modern Art, and you'll be sure to see the greatest in contemporary painting and sculpture. And don't forget the small galleries, where the cutting edge lies, either.

In the premier city for both serious and popular theater and other performing arts, you can always see the best of ballet, opera, and musical performances. But there is also off-off-Broadway and the small dance company workshops too. As a culinary capital, you can partake of the finest cuisine in the world in the most exquisite settings (Tavern on the Green and the 21 Club), but it offers some of the most offbeat and familiar food as well (Chinatown, hot dog street vendors, delis, and family pizzerias). Price icons for restaurant listings clue you in as to how much you can expect to pay:

$15 or less: ($)
$16–$30: ($$)
$31 or more: ($$$)

New York is rich in living American history. You can visit Revolutionary and colonial homes, the preserved mansions of America's robber barons, a turn-of-the-century tenement, and some of the finest examples of corporate architecture. On top of that, New York is a college town with four major universities of its own and many more in the surrounding suburbs. New York is also home to every major professional sport—men's and women's.

Because there is so much to see and do (and so many new museums and attractions opening every year), many people make New York a rotating spot on a variable list of vacation places and see a different side of the city each time they visit.

For families with children, New York is an oasis and a playground. Aside from the most obvious kid-pleasing attractions like the Bronx Zoo and the American Museum of Natural History, there are many other one-of-a-kind experiences. These range from the Museum of Television and Radio to Madame Tussauds wax museum to the Police and Fire Department museums. Kids who love the subway are always mesmerized by the Transit Museum, and don't forget that the Brooklyn Museum has the country's finest collection of Egyptian art (think mummies). No kid can resist a day in Central Park where there's fun to be had riding the carousel, sailing wooden boats, climbing on the *Alice in Wonderland* statue, and visiting the Central Park Zoo! Likewise, a trip to Times Square is a lifetime memory.

Whether it's your first visit to New York City or your twenty-first, read through this guide, make a list of things that intrigue you and your family, do some planning, and hit the phone or the Internet. Plan ahead and make reservations, but leave some time for serendipitous discovery.

CHAPTER 1

Welcome to New York

TO VISIT NEW YORK is to soak up the ambiance of a modern world-class metropolis. The city's history mirrors the history of the nation; every visitor can relate to it. To savor the full experience, read up on the events that contributed to the city's growth as one of the most financially, architecturally, and culturally significant places in the world. Many of the sights you will visit are part of the city's rich history; others are named for famous explorers, settlers, governors, and statesmen who helped define what the city became.

How It All Began

Cities owe their place and fortune to geographical luck. They spring up around harbors, crossroads, rest stops, and trade routes. New York is no exception. From day one, it was the first place many travelers encountered as they headed west from Europe. The first people to lay eyes on what would become New York were Native Americans. It was the Lenape who greeted Italian explorer Giovanni da Verrazzano, the first European to enter New York's harbor. The Verrazano-Narrows Bridge bears his name. He stayed long enough to name the place New Angoulême, then turned around and sailed back to Europe. The year was 1524.

English explorer Henry Hudson kick-started the city's development when he arrived on a commercial mission for the Dutch East India Company in 1609. Hudson sailed up the mighty river to the west of Manhattan and through the glorious valley; both the Hudson River and Hudson Valley are named for him.

The Dutch were the first Europeans to settle what they called Nieuw Amsterdam, but don't believe the colorful story that Peter Minuit pulled a fast one and bought the island from a local tribe for $24 worth of beads. File that away with fictitious tall tales like Washington and the cherry tree. The city flip-flopped between English and Dutch control in the 1660s and 1670s before the English claimed it for good (or at least until the Revolutionary War) in 1674.

≡ FAST FACT

The Dutch colony had lots of problems with the Native Americans who lived in the area and the British who coveted their colonial territory. In 1653, the governor, Peter Stuyvesant, ordered the construction of a wall in lower Manhattan to guard against a possible attack. By 1700, the wall had been torn down, but Wall Street keeps its place today.

New York was an important center during the American Revolution, and battles were fought all over the city. You can still find colonial bullet casings in parts of lower Manhattan, Queens, and Long Island. The first declarations calling for independence and the first intercolonial congress were drawn up in New York. In 1789, George Washington was inaugurated president in Federal Hall, the nation's first Capitol, on Wall and Nassau streets. New York City was the nation's capital before giving way to Philadelphia and eventually to Washington, D.C.

The City Grows and Prospers

In the early nineteenth century, New York developed as a center of fashion. Printing became a major industry, and the young book publishing pioneers were joined by newspapers like the *New-York Evening Post* (founded by Alexander Hamilton in 1801 and now the oldest daily in the country) and the *New York Tribune* (whose spirit survives in today's *International Herald Tribune*).

Business, industry, and commerce grew rapidly, and modern New York began to take shape. Wall Street became the nation's financial center, Central Park became the city's place to play, and baseball became the game to watch.

A City of Immigrants

Throughout the nineteenth century, European immigrants flocked to the city. Many settled on the Lower East Side near the newly constructed Brooklyn Bridge. Poverty, poor living conditions, disease, and corruption led to the formation of gangs throughout the city. The flood of immigrants continued unabated well into the twentieth century.

Larger-than-Life Construction Projects

The city wasn't a cohesive unit until 1898, when the five boroughs were consolidated into what was then the world's largest metropolis with a population of more than three million. Now that the boroughs were legislatively united, the challenge was to physically connect them. Starting with the Brooklyn Bridge, the early twentieth century ushered in the era of bridge building.

Mass transit also took on new life. In the first decade of the twentieth century, city workers were busy building the underground maze of railways that would become the New York City subway system. By 1910, there were more than eighty miles of subway below the New York City streets.

Significant building projects such as Pennsylvania Station, which opened in 1910 after six years of construction, and the New York

Public Library on Forty-second Street, which cost some $9 million, solidified New York's place as a modern architectural haven.

Fun and Games

What did New Yorkers do for entertainment when they weren't frequenting the popular taverns and saloons? They went to see the Ziegfeld Follies, New York's dancing girls, or to watch the early silent films, many of which were shot in New York and shown in a New York invention: the motion picture theater. It was the beginning of a new era of spectacular entertainment. The early twentieth century also saw the establishment of major league baseball, and New York boasted three teams: the Yankees, Giants, and Dodgers.

≡FAST FACT

The Brooklyn Dodgers went by five names in their seventy-three-year history. They entered major league baseball in 1884 as the Brooklyn Bridegrooms. They played as the Trolley Dodgers, Superbas, and Robins before finally becoming the Dodgers in 1932. Perhaps most famous as the team with which second baseman Jackie Robinson broke baseball's color barrier in 1947, the Dodgers moved to Los Angeles in 1957.

Growing Pains

New York's population topped the two million mark in the second decade of the twentieth century, but those years also saw their share of tragedy. In 1912, families waited in vain for the arrival of the greatest ocean liner ever built, the *Titanic*, which sank on its maiden voyage across the Atlantic Ocean. In 1915, the British liner *Lusitania* set sail from New York, but it too never reached its destination as it was the victim of a German submarine attack. In 1916, a tragic subway crash killed 102 people.

A suspicious fire at the Triangle Shirtwaist Factory in 1911 resulted in the deaths of 146 young women workers. The building where it all started, at Greene Street and Washington Place, near Washington Square Park, still stands and is part of New York University; a plaque on its side commemorates the tragedy.

Roaring Twenties and the Depression

The postwar era of Prohibition and speakeasies was a time of new hairstyles, nightclubs, flappers, jazz, and fun. The arts flourished during the Harlem Renaissance of the 1920s, and Harlem became the hub of jazz in the city. Duke Ellington, Louis Armstrong, and Paul Whiteman and his thirty-piece band, the Kings of Jazz, drew crowds uptown. Establishments like the Cotton Club (still operating), Roseland (also alive and well), and the Savoy Ballroom flourished.

Broadway shows were all the rage, and the classic *Showboat* opened in 1927. The New York Yankees were the talk of the world, with a newfound hero, Babe Ruth, picked up from the rival Boston Red Sox. The Yankees won twenty-five world championships throughout the century, far more than any other major league baseball team.

≡FAST FACT

Very quietly, without any great fanfare, a small experimental television station, the world's first—W2XAB—was set up in 1928.

Bottomed Out

The fun, dancing, and revelry that marked the Roaring Twenties came to a crashing halt with the stock market crash of 1929. The city fell into the Great Depression. The government funded public projects that required lots of workers. As a result, the 1930s saw another construction boom.

When the Empire State Building was completed on April 11, 1931, it was the world's biggest office building. Soon after, work began on Rockefeller Center and the Waldorf-Astoria.

However, while the city surged in some areas, such as development, it was still losing money. By 1932, New York was nearly $2 billion in arrears, a debt not matched by the rest of the country put together. Some 164 bread lines were not enough to feed the troubled city's hungry.

Mayor LaGuardia Steps In

The city needed a take-charge mayor, and in 1934, cuddly, unorthodox Fiorello LaGuardia (known as "Little Flower") stepped into the office he would hold for eleven years. Despite his appearance, he was tough and ready to turn around the city he loved.

LaGuardia inherited a $30 million deficit, with only $31 million left from a federal government loan that was set to run out just eight months after he took the office. LaGuardia instituted sales tax and utility tax programs, the first of a series of measures that would pull the city out of its financial crisis over the coming years. He also cracked down on crime, starting with the arrest of the city's most notorious mobster, Lucky Luciano.

LaGuardia cleaned up the city and put welfare recipients to work. LaGuardia Airport is fittingly named after the man who argued for a commercial airport within the city limits. A statue of LaGuardia stands sentinel over a street in Greenwich Village that also bears his name.

☂ RAINY DAY FUN

E. L. Doctorow, a Pulitzer Prize–winning author and native New Yorker, wrote a novel about New York titled *World's Fair*. Robert Caro's classic tale of New York politics, *The Power Broker: Robert Moses and the Fall of New York*, details the career of New York's legendary parks commissioner.

Construction Projects Continued

Despite the financial difficulties of the early 1930s, construction never stopped. Thousands of families moved into new housing projects, the subway lines expanded, and construction of New York City Municipal Airport, later renamed LaGuardia, began.

Helping to build the city was the ever-aggressive and highly controversial Robert Moses, a parks commissioner with a mission. Moses drew criticism for ousting tenants from their land to build 5,000 acres worth of parks, and he set up more than 250 playgrounds. One of the parks, Flushing Meadows in Corona, Queens, was created from a garbage dump for the fabulous 1939 World's Fair. To help make Queens and the World's Fair more easily accessible, the Triborough Bridge and Midtown Tunnel were constructed, and New York City Municipal Airport opened. The fair was a huge economic boon for the city.

Surviving World War II

The pall of war hung over the 1939 World's Fair. Czechoslovakia and Poland fell to German aggression in that year, Italy invaded Albania, and the Japanese expanded their Pacific empire. The United States entered the war after the Japanese attacked Pearl Harbor on December 7, 1941. In New York, security was increased on all bridges, tunnels, factories, and other significant points.

During the war, the lights of Broadway and the spectacular New York City skyline went dark or were dimmed. While the mayor moved north into Gracie Mansion (originally built in 1804 and redesigned by Robert Moses), the people of the city watched and waited for news from overseas.

The jubilant celebrations that swept through the five boroughs on V-J Day were immortalized in one photograph of a sailor and nurse kissing in Times Square. After the city welcomed its war heroes home with a rousing parade, New York continued the building expansion of the prewar era.

Among the new construction projects was a massive complex along the East River. After World War II, the United States invited the newly created United Nations to build its headquarters in an American city. The U.N. considered a number of possibilities before settling on New York. John D. Rockefeller donated money to purchase the site, and the city of New York gave more land to the U.N. as a gift. The eighteen acres that comprise the U.N. complex are considered international land.

≡FAST FACT

A Nazi assault on the United States during World War II was never a feasible option. Nevertheless, Joseph Goebbels, Hitler's propaganda minister, dreamed of destroying the city that represented the "medley of races" that clashed with the Nazi ideal.

The Boom of the 1950s and 1960s

By the second half of the 1950s, New York City had nearly eight million inhabitants. Postwar New York saw a return to manufacturing, led by the successful garment industry. Another industry—television—joined the mix, and early shows were produced in the city.

Yet America was changing. People were abandoning the big cities of the Northeast and seeking a better life in the sunny West. New Yorkers were horrified as they lost two of their three baseball teams in the same year; the Giants left for San Francisco and the Dodgers were relocated to Los Angeles in 1957.

The city entered the 1960s with new roadways, including the Throgs Neck Bridge, the Verrazano-Narrows Bridge, and the new second level of the George Washington Bridge. The New York Mets entered the scene, taking the uniform colors of the recently departed Giants and Dodgers, but it gained neither the trust nor the enthusiasm of those teams' old fans.

Lincoln Center, the most advanced and spectacular showcase for the cultural arts in the world, opened on Manhattan's Upper West

Side, but it had to overcome protests over its displacement of much-needed housing. The city also hosted the 1964 World's Fair, the second in twenty-five years at the same location, Flushing Meadows Park in Queens. Most exciting—to teenagers at least—was the American debut of the British phenomenon, the Beatles, who appeared on *The Ed Sullivan Show* and later at a relatively new venue in the city, Shea Stadium.

In the summer of 1964, riots rocked Harlem after a white police officer fatally shot an African American teenager. Unrest simmered in the rest of the city, and protests, sit-ins, walkouts, and strikes—including a newspaper strike that lasted for months and a transit strike that cost the city nearly a million dollars in revenue—set the city on a downward spiral. Much of the tension came to a head when Columbia University students occupied school buildings on the Upper West Side of Manhattan to protest university policies. Police were called in to forcibly remove the students, resulting in hundreds of arrests.

At the end of the decade, the New York Jets pulled off an improbable Super Bowl upset, and the hapless Mets emerged from the depths to win the World Series. The United States had sent a man to the moon, but New York was still in trouble.

≡FAST FACT

Subway tokens debuted in New York City in 1953. The fare was fifteen cents. The MetroCard replaced tokens in the 1990s and can be purchased in vending machines in the stations. You can pay for each ride separately or choose from an array of unlimited-ride MetroCards.

From Bad to Worse

While the tensions in the city eased somewhat in the early 1970s, the financial situation worsened. Much like the opening of the Empire State Building during the Great Depression, the new World Trade Center now towered over Manhattan, a symbol of optimistic indulgence, while officials searched their pockets and the treasuries for enough money to keep the city from bankruptcy. By 1974, the Big Apple had hit rock bottom. The city was broke.

"Fear City"

From newspaper employees to garbage collectors to doctors at city hospitals, the city was on strike, angered by New York's dismal financial situation. The police, who at one point also went on strike, issued warnings to tourists to stay away from "Fear City." Crime was up, and the city was falling apart—literally. In 1973, a truck fell through the West Side Highway, which was sorely in need of road repair. People abandoned New York in record numbers, and real estate prices hit rock bottom.

≡ FAST FACT

Gerald Ford was the first president to be mocked on *Saturday Night Live*. Chevy Chase's portrayal of the president sparked an enduring tradition of parodying national political figures. In 1976, Ron Nessen, Ford's press secretary, became the first political figure to host the show.

Finally, when even the state could not bail out the city, New York turned to Washington, D.C., and asked President Ford for help. The president snubbed New York, prompting the famous *Daily News* headline "Ford to City: Drop Dead."

A Slow Comeback

The city began to put itself back on track with more responsible fiscal management. The decade ended on a somber, chilling note as John Lennon was killed outside his Central Park West home, the Dakota.

Another feisty, irreverent mayor, Ed Koch, led the city into the 1980s, and tourists returned. Financially, New York was booming again, and the city resumed its place as a center for art and music.

A City Triumphant

New York experienced another stock market crash in late 1987, only to re-emerge in the dot-com boom of the 1990s under the leadership of Mayor Rudy Giuliani. A product of its times, the city became hard-nosed against crime and proactive toward business. It became one of the safest big cities in America. The economy boomed, and things looked rosy.

Then came September 11, 2001. New York, an icon of successful capitalism and the American Way, was the target of a terrorist attack. Terrorists piloted two hijacked commercial airliners into the World Trade Center in what was meant to be a four-pronged attack on the United States. The Twin Towers collapsed, killing more than 2,700 people. New York's resilience exerted itself, and the city emerged from the attacks united in its resolve to heal the emotional and physical scars of the tragedy. Ambitious plans for the rebuilding of the World Trade Center site are well underway with the construction of the Freedom Tower, a soaring, ebullient statement of hope, defiance, and élan.

JUST FOR PARENTS

Before you leave for New York, you might want to discuss the terrorist attack on the World Trade Center with your children. For older children who watched this attack on television, visiting the site—which is currently under construction—might help bring a sense of security as they witness how the city is being rebuilt.

New York has emerged triumphant, and the beat goes on. So coveted is living in the city that real estate prices have soared into the stratosphere. The boom in Manhattan has spread to the outer boroughs and even across the river to New Jersey. New York's appeal speaks to visitors as well. According to NYC & Company, the local convention and visitors' bureau, New York City is by far the number one visited city in the United States, safe for visitors and brimming with creativity and harmony.

CHAPTER 2

Planning Your Trip

NEW YORK OFFERS plenty of things to do 365 days a year, twenty-four hours a day. The key to having a successful family vacation lies largely in the planning. Determine the activities and sights your family will want to experience and figure out what time of year to visit. Start out on the right foot by deciding what mode of transportation you'll use to get to New York and how you will get from your point of arrival to your hotel or other first destination.

When to Go

There is no wrong time to visit New York City, but your experience will vary depending on when you make your trip. New York in the winter is so special that many families visit every year, and spring in the city can be as beautiful as it is in Paris. Summer is an endless street fair, and fall is a season of marathons and fashion.

The Weather

From ample snowfall to sizzling summer heat, New York is a city with very distinct seasons and a wide range of temperatures. You can expect summer temperatures in the eighties, but factor in high humidity in July and August. September and October are perfect walking months, with a range of temperatures from the low fifties into the midseventies. Temperatures drop below the midfifties from

November to March; below-freezing temperatures and snow are not uncommon in the winter months, and the wind chill makes it feel even colder. The city thaws out by April and May, which are pleasant and mild months with temperatures in the fifties, sixties, and seventies.

 TRAVEL TIP

The chilly temperatures of January and February may dissuade some travelers, but the hotel rates are lower during those two months, and there is always plenty to see and do. If there's snow, major streets are cleared immediately, the subway is unaffected, and the city's lights sparkle even brighter.

New York sees an average of forty inches of rain annually, with no particular rainy season. Annual snowfall is often around twenty to twenty-five inches, but the city has been known to get significantly more or less—for instance, nearly fifty inches of snow fell in the winters of both 2003 and 2004, yet there were no heavy storms until well into 2007. Good snowstorms wreak havoc on arrivals and departures, but if one hits New York in the middle of your stay, venture out to Central Park to play in the winter wonderland.

The Holiday Season

December is a joyous time in New York, with the glow of the huge tree at Rockefeller Center, the annual Radio City Christmas Spectacular, and the traditional performance of *The Nutcracker,* not to mention the incredible department store windows. The festivities end with the world-famous New Year's Eve party in Times Square. This is the peak tourist season, with high-priced hotel rooms that fill up fast. Following the holidays, tourism slumps a bit, which makes it easier to get great Broadway tickets or reservations at the best restaurants.

 TRAVEL TIP

You may be thrilled at the deals that you find at Internet discounters like Travelocity or Expedia, but don't stop just yet. The hotels themselves will often match what you find and possibly offer other packages and promotions.

Spring and Fall

Spring and fall may be the best times to visit the city if your schedule permits. You still have the opportunity to enjoy most activities in the buffer months, and there are many festivals and special city events. Hotel rates are somewhere in between their highest and lowest points and tend to fluctuate from year to year.

Make It a Road Trip

Once you've decided the time of your visit, consider your options for getting to the Big Apple. Driving to New York City will save you the cost of airfare and is certainly a popular choice when coming from nearby cities.

If driving seems like a good option, be sure you have a plan for what to do with your car once you arrive. Parking is at a premium in the city, so driving in means paying for garages. The average hotel parking fee runs $25 to $45 a day. If you plan to use public transportation once you arrive, which is advisable—if not mandatory—in Manhattan, you can find a parking lot with a weekly rate, which will save you money.

Driving in and out of the City

Whether you're coming from Connecticut, New Jersey, or upstate New York, your options for entering the boroughs are the George Washington Bridge, Lincoln Tunnel, and Holland Tunnel. If you don't have an E-ZPass tag (for electronic toll collecting), be sure to bring enough cash for the tolls.

The George Washington Bridge, which opened in 1931, has two levels of two-way traffic connecting Manhattan to Fort Lee, New Jersey, from 179th Street. Primary routes to the bridge are the Henry Hudson Parkway on the west side along the Hudson River and Harlem River Drive, which becomes FDR Drive, along the East River.

☂ RAINY DAY FUN

Whether you fly or drive, before you head off for the city, let the kids draw a map of the route. Point out the landmarks you'll be passing through or over on the way: states, bodies of water, landmarks such as the George Washington or the Brooklyn Bridge, Manhattan Island. These may be their first, and therefore most memorable, glimpses of the city.

The Alexander Hamilton Bridge connects the Cross Bronx Expressway directly with the George Washington Bridge, crossing into Manhattan. The GW Bridge stands 200 feet above the Hudson River and is one of the most traveled bridges in the world. It connects easily with the Palisades Parkway, Interstate 80, the New Jersey Turnpike, and other major New Jersey roadways. You can also walk or bicycle across the bridge on outer walkways. The $6 toll is charged only to traffic entering Manhattan.

The Lincoln Tunnel connects Manhattan from West Thirtieth to Thirty-second streets with Weehawken, New Jersey and, like the George Washington Bridge, intersects with most major New Jersey routes. The tunnel has three connecting tubes that were completed in the late 1950s. Follow the signs for the Lincoln Tunnel carefully, as the lanes have been divided for use by trucks and cars. Some lanes are closed to passenger cars. Nearly forty million cars, trucks, and buses use it every year. The toll is $6, charged only to traffic entering Manhattan.

🧳 TRAVEL TIP

With the E-ZPass, a prepaid toll card you mount on your car windshield, you can zip through the tollbooths in several states instead of waiting in line to pay. If you don't have the pass, make sure you go through the Cash Only lanes. If you make a mistake and go through an E-ZPass lane (marked by a purple and white sign), the system will trace you through your license plate and send you a bill. Info at *www.ezpassny.com*.

The Holland Tunnel connects Lower Manhattan from Canal Street to Jersey City and provides easy access to I-78, the Pulaski Skyway, the New Jersey Turnpike, and Routes 1 and 9. The granddaddy of underwater travel, this tunnel dates back to 1927. There is a $6 toll for traffic entering Manhattan.

Vehicle traffic between Manhattan and Staten Island flows through Brooklyn via I-278 over the Verrazano-Narrows Bridge and through the Brooklyn Battery Tunnel. You can no longer take your car on the Staten Island Ferry; they were banned after a deadly accident in 2004 killed thirteen people.

═FAST FACT

Gas is significantly cheaper in New Jersey than in New York City, and finding a gas station in Manhattan is not an easy task. If you're driving through the Garden State, fill your tank before you cross the border. If you find yourself running low in Manhattan, look for gas stations on the far west side, near access to the Westside Highway, or the east side off FDR Drive.

If you're traveling from Queens into Manhattan or vice versa, you can take the Queensboro Bridge, also known to locals as the Fifty-ninth Street Bridge (Simon and Garfunkel sang about it in "Feelin' Groovy"), which connects Long Island City in Queens with First and Second avenues in Manhattan at Fifty-seventh and Sixty-ninth streets. Although the bridge has two levels, it has been undergoing restoration for a decade and chances are you'll encounter construction delays somewhere, sometime, until 2009. Nonetheless, the bridge is toll free! It provides easy access to Queens Boulevard, Northern Boulevard, and, via Van Dam Street, the Long Island Expressway in Queens.

The Queens Midtown Tunnel is at the west end of the Long Island Expressway. The tunnel deposits you in the east thirties in Manhattan, between First and Second avenues. The tunnel toll is $4.50 in both directions and traffic is very busy during rush hour.

The Triborough Bridge connects Queens from Grand Central Parkway to Manhattan at 125th Street, where you can easily go south onto FDR Drive or north onto Harlem River Drive. The elaborately designed bridge also connects Queens with the Bronx, and the Bronx (from the Bruckner Expressway) with Manhattan. There is a $4.50 toll in all directions.

📰 TRAVEL TIP

If you want to leave Manhattan for a multistop trek to one of the four outer boroughs—the Bronx, Brooklyn, Queens, or Staten Island—it's probably best to go by car. Use the main parkways and expressways to get to your chosen section of the borough, and carefully follow local street directions once you've exited.

The Bronx connects with Manhattan at the Triborough Bridge and at other bridges, including the Willis Avenue Bridge, which connects the Harlem River Drive with the Major Deegan in the Bronx. The Willis Avenue Bridge (off the Harlem River Drive), Third Avenue Bridge (at 129th Street), the Madison Avenue Bridge (at 138th Street), and the Macombs Dam Bridge (at 155th Street) also connect the Bronx with Manhattan.

On Manhattan's west side, you can take the Henry Hudson Parkway north past the Cloisters and connect with Riverdale (part of the Bronx), which goes directly into the Henry Hudson Bridge. There is a $2.25 toll in both directions. The road becomes the Saw Mill River Parkway and heads north to Westchester, where you can catch the New York State Thruway and the Hutchinson River Parkway.

TRAVEL TIP

The city has privatized its low-cost municipal parking lot system. Muni-Meters in every borough accept quarters, dollar coins, credit cards, and prepaid New York City parking cards. The city has also planted single-space meters that accept credit cards in all boroughs. For more information, go to *www.nyc.gov* and search for "municipal parking."

There are four routes connecting Brooklyn with lower Manhattan. The famed Brooklyn Bridge will take you from Cadman Plaza or the Brooklyn Queens Expressway (BQE) into Manhattan with easy access to FDR Drive or Park Row by City Hall. The Manhattan Bridge connects Flatbush Avenue and Grand Army Plaza in Brooklyn with Canal Street in Chinatown. The Williamsburg Bridge connects Metropolitan Avenue and the BQE with Delancey Street in Manhattan. All of these bridges are free.

The Brooklyn Battery Tunnel connects West Street in Manhattan to the Gowanus and Prospect Expressways in Brooklyn. The tunnel is easily accessible from the FDR Drive or Henry Hudson Parkway. The tunnel toll is $4.50 in both directions.

Be Prepared

The best way to plot your course, both in getting to the city and once you are there, is with an online mapping service like Maps On Us (*www.mapsonus.com*), Mapquest (*www.mapquest.com*), Expedia (*www.expedia.com*), Google Maps (*http://maps.google.com*), or mul-timap.com (*www.multimap.com*). Many of New York's streets are one-way or have limited access, especially with new traffic laws during weekday work hours that restrict turns in midtown Manhattan between Sixth and Park avenues. Internet maps will show you the best way of reaching your destination and will give you directions based on the address. Another option is to contact the Automobile Association of America (AAA), which provides maps and driving directions to members, both hard copy and online (*www.AAA.com*).

If You Prefer to Fly

Since New York City is truly a city that never sleeps, you can fly into one of the three major airports (LaGuardia, in northern Queens, JFK, in southern Queens, and Newark, in New Jersey), get a cab, and check into a hotel at any hour. Make sure the hotel knows ahead of time when you plan to arrive; otherwise, it may make you wait for your room, which can be exhausting when you are traveling with kids. Flying at night is a good way to avoid crowds at the airports and traffic en route to Manhattan.

 **TRAVEL TIP**

Follow the Transportation Security Administration's 3-1-1 guidelines. All liquids must be carried in 3-ounce bottles in a 1-quart clear plastic resealable bag. Each passenger is allowed one bag. The only exceptions to the 3-ounce rule are prescription medications, baby formula, breast milk, and juice; you must declare these items to a security official. Check *www.tsa.gov* for more information.

All three city airports are varying distances from Manhattan. LaGuardia is the closest, but not by much. If you're staying in Brooklyn, Queens, or the Bronx, Newark Airport would be a less desirable choice, since the other two airports are located close by. Otherwise, let the cheapest airfare guide you.

Airport Guidelines

Give yourself plenty of time to get to the airport, check in for your flight, and get through security. Generally, you must arrive an hour ahead of time for a domestic flight and two hours early for an international flight, but some situations add an hour to both. Airlines bump tardy passengers from overbooked flights, so be aware of that.

At the security checkpoint, children and adults alike must remove belts and shoes when going through the metal detector, so make sure your family dresses accordingly. All passengers are expected to have photo ID at check-in.

 TRAVEL TIP

Save money on a flight to New York by flying into one of the lesser-known airports—White Plains Airport (HPN) in Westchester County or Long Island MacArthur Airport (ISP) in Long Island. There are often seats available during the more crowded times since fewer people know about them. However, this only saves you money if you are renting a car or have someone to pick you up at the airport. Otherwise, a cab ride to midtown will run you $100 to $120.

Make sure all bags have zippers or clasps that can be closed for security. Remember to label all bags so that they are easily identifiable at the airport luggage carousel. If you plan to carry bags onto an airplane, security rules at the time of this writing limited you to one carry-on to fit in an overhead and a purse, briefcase, laptop computer, or small backpack. There are also additional items that do not count toward your carry-on allowance, including a child car seat, infant diaper bag, collapsible umbrella-type stroller, coat, camera, medical devices, and reasonable reading material. Check with your airline and the TSA (*www.tsa.gov*) before traveling for the latest regulations.

Major Airlines

New York is a major hub. Every major airline and most of the smaller ones offer frequent flights into and out of the city. Depending on where home is, you should have an opportunity to choose among several carriers to find the best deal.

Air Canada

✆ 1-888-247-2262

✉ www.aircanada.com
Service fee: $15 per passenger, $37 maximum per booking (four-hour Canadian stopover required)

American Airlines

✆ 1-800-433-7300

✉ www.aa.com
Service fee: $10 per ticket, $15 for award tickets

Continental Airlines

✆ 1-800-523-3273

✉ www.continental.com
Service fee: $10 per ticket

Delta Airlines

✆ 1-800-221-1212

✉ www.delta.com
Service fee: $10 per ticket

JetBlue Airways

✆ 1-800-538-2583

✉ www.jetblue.com
Service fee: None

Midwest Airlines

✆ 1-800-452-2022

✉ www.midwestairlines.com
Service fee: None

Northwest Airlines

✆ 1-800-225-2525

✉ www.nwa.com
Service fee: $10 per ticket

Southwest Airlines

✆ 1-800-435-9792

✉ www.southwest.com
Service fee: None, but prices may be $10 cheaper online

United Airlines

✆ 1-800-864-8331

✉ www.united.com
Service fee: $15 per ticket

US Airways

✆ 1-800-428-4322

✉ www.usairways.com
Service fee: $10 per ticket

Try to make your reservations as far ahead of time as possible. Airlines may give you a better deal if you book at least twenty-one days in advance, but the old rule that you'll get a better airfare if your stay includes a Saturday night isn't true anymore. Check prices on various airlines, and look for advertised specials. If you're planning your visit around a major holiday, you need to book even further in advance. Tickets go quickly during the Thanksgiving and year-end holidays.

TRAVEL TIP

Farecast (*www.farecast.com*) helps you pinpoint the optimal time to purchase airfare. It uses historical data to tell you whether prices for a particular flight are likely to rise or fall in the next few weeks.

Always push for a better price; you have nothing to lose. Computer pricing has allowed airlines to fine-tune seat pricing to the smallest degree, so airfares vary widely depending on your departure point, the type of seats you are purchasing, and when you purchase them. On an airplane, everyone on board may have paid a different ticket price.

JFK International Airport (JFK)

✆ 718-244-4444

⌨ *www.panynj.gov*

JFK International Airport is one of the world's busiest. Opened as Idlewild International Airport in 1948, its name was changed in the 1960s to honor President John F. Kennedy. All major carriers land at JFK. Transportation information counters are located on the lower level near baggage-claim carousels, and taxis, buses, shuttles, and limousines pull up just outside. Car rental facilities are also nearby and can be reached by rental company shuttle buses.

Although the airport is located some fifteen miles outside of Manhattan in Queens, travel by taxi to Manhattan takes about fifty to sixty minutes—longer during busy times. Taxis charge a flat rate of $45 plus tolls and tips. The tip should be roughly 15 percent depending on service.

Shuttles run from the airport to all areas of the city: Grand Central, Penn Station, and the Port Authority on Forty-second Street, as well as to midtown hotels and other locations. During the day and early evening, this is a good way to save on cab fare. However, if you are traveling with a large family, an SUV cab might be cheaper because you'll pay a flat fee rather than a per-person charge, as you would on a shuttle.

LaGuardia Airport (LGA)

✎ 718-533-3400

✎ www.panynj.gov

Smaller than JFK, the 680-acre LaGuardia Airport handles all of the primary carriers and offers mostly domestic flights. Originally opened commercially in 1939 as New York City Municipal Airport, the name was later changed in tribute to former Mayor Fiorello LaGuardia. Located less then ten miles from Manhattan, the trip from this Queens-based airport can be anywhere from thirty to forty-five minutes. Taking a cab that charges by the meter will cost around $35 plus tolls and tips. Cabs are easy to find at any number of taxi stands.

💼 TRAVEL TIP

Taxi drivers are not allowed to solicit fares in the airport. Always wait in the taxi stand line and let the dispatcher or the cab line do the work. If a cab driver or anyone else meets you in the terminal and offers you a ride—even at a low rate—refuse it. So-called "gypsy cab" drivers are not legal and are not authorized by the city.

Newark Liberty International Airport (EWR)

☎ 973-961-6000

✍ www.newarkairport.com

In nearby Newark, New Jersey, Newark Liberty International Airport is some thirty to forty minutes from Manhattan (more during rush hour) by car or bus. New Jersey's largest commercial airport, Newark has enjoyed major renovations over the years, including monorail service from terminal to terminal. If you're heading to the west side of Manhattan, you might consider flying into Newark. Also, Newark is generally less crowded than Kennedy or LaGuardia. Taxis cost $55 to $65 plus tolls and tip.

Airport Transportation

If you think a cab isn't a great option for your family, there are plenty of alternatives. For information about ground transportation from any of New York's three major airports, call the Port Authority Ground Transportation Hotline at 1-800-247-7433.

Bus or Shuttle

New York Airport Service buses go directly to Manhattan's major destinations. Fare from JFK is $15 per person, and a roundtrip ticket costs $27. The fare from LaGuardia is $12 per person, and a roundtrip ticket costs $21. One child under twelve is free for every full-fare adult. Senior and student discounts are available at the Grand Central office. Call 718-875-8200 or find information online at *www.nyairportservice.com*.

Airlink is another van shuttle service that offers door-to-door service. The fare is $17 from JFK and $15 from LaGuardia or Newark. Find more information at 1-800-490-3229 or *www.airlinknyc.com*.

Super Shuttle provides a blue van on twenty-four-hour call to all destinations in Manhattan. Charges are based on zip code and range from $13 to $22, with discounts for additional family members. For more information, call 212-964-6233 or visit *www.supershuttle.com*.

Driving from JFK

If you rent a car, you can get to Manhattan from JFK by taking the Van Wyck Expressway to the Long Island Expressway. Head west to the Midtown Tunnel, which will deposit you in the east thirties in Manhattan. You can also take the Grand Central Expressway and proceed over the Triborough Bridge—but watch the signs because the bridge also goes to the Bronx—and follow the signs for Manhattan/FDR Drive. You can also take the Belt Parkway around Brooklyn to the Brooklyn/Queens Expressway and go over the Brooklyn Bridge to Lower Manhattan. Alternately, follow signs to the Gowanus Expressway and take the Battery Tunnel into Lower Manhattan, but be ready to pay a toll.

Driving from LaGuardia

If you rent a car, you can get to Manhattan from LaGuardia by going west on Grand Central Parkway, which will take you to the Triborough Bridge—but watch the signs, because the bridge also goes to the Bronx! Look for the sign for Manhattan/FDR Drive. If you're going to lower Manhattan, you can also get the Brooklyn/Queens Expressway from Grand Central Parkway and head to the Williamsburg or Brooklyn Bridge.

Driving from Newark

If you rent a car, you can get to Manhattan from Newark by following the airport exit signs to the New Jersey Turnpike (I-95) north. Take the turnpike, following signs for the Holland Tunnel, the Lincoln Tunnel, or the George Washington Bridge. The Holland Tunnel goes into lower Manhattan, the Lincoln Tunnel goes into midtown Manhattan, just south of Forty-second Street, and the George Washington Bridge enters the city near the upper tip of Manhattan, around 178th Street.

AirTrain JFK

AirTrain JFK is a cheap, relatively efficient way to get around the airport and into midtown via the New York subways and buses or the Long Island Rail Road. It is free to use within the airport to connect between terminals. When you leave the airport, a $5 fee can be taken off New York's subway MetroCard. Children under five are free. During rush hours, it is definitely the way to go. It runs twenty-four hours, seven days a week, and is heated in the winter and air-conditioned in the summer. For more information, call 1-877-535-2478 or visit *www .panynj.info/airtrainjfk.*

TRAVEL TIP

A few tips for driving in New York: Unless a sign specifies otherwise (a rarity), you cannot make right turns on a red light in New York City. People frequently cross against the light in Manhattan, so watch out for pedestrians. Do not leave your car unattended unless it is parked and locked with valuables out of sight. Remember to retract your radio antenna.

AirTrain Newark

If you prefer public transportation, take AirTrain Newark, an elevated train that loops around the airport and connects with Amtrak and New Jersey Transit. This will get you quickly into midtown or the Northeast Corridor. Use is free within the airport to connect between terminals, hotel shuttles, and rental cars. When you buy a ticket for Amtrak or Jersey Transit, the fare is included. It runs twenty-four hours, seven days a week, and is heated in the winter and air-conditioned in the summer. For more information, call 1-888-397-4636 or visit *www.panynj.info/airtrainnewark.*

Private Coach

Olympia Trails Newark Liberty Airport Express buses leave for the Port Authority, Bryant Park, and Grand Central every fifteen to thirty minutes from 4 A.M. to 1 A.M., 365 days a year. The cost is $14 one way, $23 roundtrip; seniors, disabled, and students ages twelve to sixteen are $7; kids under twelve ride free with an accompanying adult. Call 908-863-9275 or visit *www.coachusa.com/olympia.*

Take the Bus

If you don't live very far away, taking the bus is an affordable option. Greyhound, Trailways, and other carriers offer service to the Port Authority Bus Terminal on Eighth Avenue between Fortieth and Forty-second streets in Manhattan.

TRAVEL TIP

On the east coast, several companies have bus networks that connect the Chinatowns in New York, Boston, Washington, D.C., and Philadelphia. Fares from any of these cities to New York can be as low as $12 one way. These buses are quite popular and can be very crowded, so get to the station early to make sure you get a seat. Check out *www.chinatown-bus.com* for more information.

The following bus companies offer service to New York City:

Adirondack Trailways
  1-800-776-7548
  www.trailwaysny.com

Greyhound Lines
  212-971-6300
  1-800-231-2222
  www.greyhound.com

Martz Trailways
  1-800-233-8604
  www.martztrailways.com

New Jersey Transit
  973-491-7000
  www.njtransit.com

Peter Pan Bus Lines
  1-800-343-9999
  www.peterpanbus.com

Short Line Bus
  1-800-631-8405
  www.coachusa.com/shortline

To contact the Port Authority Bus Terminal, call 212-564-8484 or visit *www.panynj.gov.*

Ride the Train

Amtrak is the leading rail carrier of passengers to and from points across the country in and out of New York City. It usually has some kind of deal or promotion going. For Amtrak information, call 1-800-USA-RAIL (872-7245) or visit the Web site at *www.amtrak.com*.

Trains pull into Pennsylvania Station on the west side of Manhattan between Seventh and Eighth avenues just below Thirty-fourth Street. From there you'll easily be able to take a taxi or bus to your hotel. Penn Station is very busy and crowded, so be sure to keep an eye on your children and personal property at all times. Cabs are easily found on surrounding streets.

The Metro-North Railroad services areas in northern New York state and Connecticut. It departs from the Grand Central Terminal on East Forty-second Street at Park Avenue. For schedules and information, call 212-532-4900 or 1-800-638-7646, or visit *www.mta.info*.

RAINY DAY FUN

The world's largest underground museum of art is the Metropolitan Transit Authority Arts for Transit program. For two decades, as subway and commuter rail lines are rehabilitated, a portion of the funds has been allocated for the installation of permanent works of art. Major artists are commissioned to execute a wide array of works in ceramics, glass, bronze, terracotta, steel, aluminum, and stone. The best way to see the works is to buy a One-Day Fun Pass for unlimited use of the system. For more information, call 212-878-7250 or log onto *www.mta.info*.

PATH (Port Authority Trans-Hudson) is a rapid-transit link between New York and New Jersey. It's really an interstate subway, and the final stop is located a block from Penn Station. The fare is $1.50, seniors $1, and kids under five are free.

Planning the Perfect Vacation

You have the choice of putting a vacation package together yourself, buying a prepackaged deal over the Internet, or hiring a travel agent to work for you. It all depends on your comfort level with each method.

Making Travel Arrangements

Using the Internet is impersonal and might raise questions that can't be answered. You can always start that way and use the phone or e-mail to resolve questions. You might prefer the personal touch and expertise of a travel agent. With the help of his or her connections and knowledge of the industry, a travel agent can often put a package together for less money. This can save you both time and cash. You also have flexibility to add to or subtract from your itinerary, and you have an advocate should something go amiss.

TRAVEL TIP

Manhattan is the only borough that uses the 212 and the new 646 area code. The Bronx, Brooklyn, Queens, and Staten Island all require you to dial 718 or the new 347. The 646 area code can also be used for a cell phone, but 917 is the most frequently used area code for mobile New Yorkers.

However you do it, start by researching your trip. Make a list of what you want and don't want, and decide what level of amenities you desire (for example, the kind of hotel room, transportation, or entertainment you expect). This will affect many of your decisions, from the amount of cash you carry to the clothes you pack. Also find out ahead of time what to do if you are dissatisfied with the accommodations and need to change them.

Once you've researched potential accommodations and narrowed your list, ask the travel agent, search the Internet, or call the hotel about rates or discounts at those specific locations.

🧳 TRAVEL TIP

If you aren't used to walking, start building up your stamina a few weeks before you go on vacation. Walk around your neighborhood and park your car at the back of the parking lot to get yourself to walk farther. You won't have to stop and rest as often, and you can spend more time seeing and experiencing New York City.

However you plan, be careful of too-good-to-be-true deals advertised on the Internet or anywhere else. To check on a travel agent, log on to the American Society of Travel Agents' Web site at *www .travelsense.org*, which will lead you to a member travel agent. Even if you don't choose a travel agent, the site has some good travel advice. Establish a good rapport with your agent or get a referral from someone you know and trust.

Packing Tips

First and foremost, bring comfortable clothes and shoes. The primary means of getting around Manhattan is walking, so be prepared. A good pair of walking shoes can make the difference between a fun-filled, action-packed day and an all-out exhausting one.

Be prepared for varying temperatures during swing seasons. Wearing layers of light and warm clothing will help keep you comfortable and happy while touring the city. Watch the Weather Channel, use the weather resources of the Internet, or check the weather section of the paper to get an idea of the climate as you plan for your trip. It's a good idea to have at least one small folding umbrella, since there's always the chance of a shower—particularly a late-afternoon thundershower, if you're visiting in the summer months. But don't worry, at the very first drop, umbrella street vendors spring out of the pavement like flowers in the desert. Don't pay more than a couple of bucks.

If you plan to stay in New York City for ten days or less, it's to your advantage to bring two weeks' worth of clothes, since having laundry done in Manhattan hotels can be expensive. Midtown Manhattan does not have many laundromats, although they are plentiful once you leave the midtown area for Chelsea or the Upper West Side.

JUST FOR PARENTS

While the finer restaurants may require jackets and even a tie for men, most restaurants, especially those with family fare, do not have dress codes. But as a nice change, you might consider packing a dressy outfit or two along with your casual attire. Incidentally, all restaurants with a strict dress code will have loaner jackets and ties for the men.

If you forget something at home, don't worry! The multitude of shops, chain pharmacies, and twenty-four-hour stores in New York City will allow you to buy whatever you might need. Although the city can be pricey, the locals shop here for their necessities during a hurried lunch hour or after work, so there are plenty of reasonably priced stores around to meet your needs.

Stay Safe

Tuck any activities away before you land so you're not carrying anything but your suitcases. Keep cameras stowed out of sight until you are settled in your hotel. Unfortunately, there are some people in every major city who will try to take advantage of tourists, so be alert and don't accept offers of rides, tours, currency exchanges, or anything else from anyone you just happen to meet at the baggage claim area or on the streets of the city. Don't play street games like Three-Card Monty—they are rigged and you can't win. Do not trust anyone to hold or guard your things for you.

Go over your itinerary and any travel rules you have with your children. Make sure they know what to do if they get separated from you. Traveling in New York City is a lot of fun for the whole family, but as with any destination, exercise common sense at all times.

CHAPTER 3

Getting Around the City

WHEW! YOU'RE IN New York City! Now how do you get from your hotel to the Empire State Building? The Metropolitan Museum of Art? Yankee Stadium? Jones Beach? Don't worry, the worst part of your trip is over. If you are staying in Manhattan, it's simple—you use mass transit, take a taxi ("cab it," as New Yorkers say), or walk. Outside of Manhattan, you can drive, take a commuter train, or an express bus.

The Street System

Manhattan is pretty easy to figure out. The island is laid out on a grid, with numbered cross streets running east and west and avenues running north to south. The numbered streets start with First Street in lower Manhattan and end with 220th Street at the top of the island, right before the Bronx starts. Avenues start at the East River and count upward going west to the Hudson River. There are a few named fill-ins where the island bulges, but that's pretty much it.

Avenues

Here are the primary avenues on the east side, starting at the East River and going west (to keep traffic at a modicum of tolerability, most are one way):

- York Avenue runs both ways between Fifty-third Street and Ninety-sixth Street.
- First Avenue runs north.
- Second Avenue runs south.
- Third Avenue runs north, with two-way traffic below Twenty-fourth Street.
- Lexington Avenue runs south to Twenty-second Street.
- Park Avenue runs both ways.

≡FAST FACT

The Bronx continues Manhattan's numbered streets—from 221st Street until 260th Street, where Yonkers (a different municipality) begins. Broadway runs from Lower Manhattan through the Bronx and into Yonkers in a meandering line that creates those famous squares of New York—Madison, Herald, and Times—as well as Columbus Circle.

Fifth Avenue, which runs south, is the line that divides the east and west sides of Manhattan. All cross-street addresses are designated "East" or "West," and they march away, in ascending order, from Fifth Avenue. Therefore, 12 East Fifty-ninth Street will be just east of Fifth Avenue, and 12 West Fifty-ninth Street will be just west of Fifth Avenue. Always specify east or west when taking down an address on numbered streets. A handy gauge for distance is the fact that twenty north-south streets equal a mile.

Here are the primary avenues on the west side:

- Sixth Avenue (although formally named the Avenue of the Americas, New Yorkers never call it that) runs north to Central Park.
- Seventh Avenue (also saddled with the formal Fashion Avenue, which nobody ever uses) runs south from Central Park.

- Eighth Avenue runs north and changes to Central Park West at Fifty-Eighth Street.
- Ninth Avenue runs south and becomes Columbus Avenue above Fifty-ninth Street (Columbus Circle).
- Tenth Avenue runs north and becomes Amsterdam Avenue above Fifty-ninth Street.
- Eleventh Avenue runs two ways above Forty-second Street and south below it; above Fifty-ninth Street it becomes West End Avenue.
- Twelfth Avenue runs north and ends at Fifty-ninth Street.
- Riverside Drive runs both ways from Seventy-second Street to the George Washington Bridge (between 178th and 179th streets). When the Henry Hudson Parkway is congested, Riverside Drive is often the best alternate route.

Franklin Delano Roosevelt Drive (always called "the FDR" by New Yorkers) runs along the East River. It becomes the Harlem River Drive above the Triborough Bridge. On the west side is the West Side Highway, which turns into the Henry Hudson Parkway as you head north from lower Manhattan. It runs the length of the island, with great views of the Hudson River, the George Washington Bridge, and the New Jersey Palisades.

≡FAST FACT

Lucy and Ricky Ricardo's address in the *I Love Lucy* TV show was 623 East Sixty-eighth Street, which would have put them in the middle of the East River!

Both the FDR Drive and West Side Highway run uptown and downtown with narrow entrance and exit ramps. When not crowded, they are the quickest ways of getting uptown or downtown, but watch out for potholes!

 **TRAVEL TIP**

When the Rockefellers donated the land in Upper Manhattan on which the Cloisters was built, they also donated the land across the river in New Jersey. They stipulated that no commercial development ever be made, leaving an unobstructed view of the New Jersey Palisades from upper Manhattan, much like Henry Hudson might have seen hundreds of years ago.

Exceptions to the Rule

When navigating Manhattan, the grid of numbered cross streets and primary avenues runs from Greenwich Village to Harlem and is relatively easy to follow, as you'll see on any city map. Washington Heights, at the far northern end of the island, is the narrowest part of the city. It's easy to navigate because you're never too far from either the Harlem River Drive to the east or the Henry Hudson Parkway to the west.

All bets are off, however, once you get into the oldest parts of the city, from Battery Park at the southern tip of the island north to Greenwich Village (the widest part of Manhattan), which were laid out before the grid system came to be. This is particularly true in the West Village, where narrow streets cross and turn in all directions. The East Village, also known as Alphabet City, brings you to avenues A, B, C, and D in a new grid leading to the Lower East Side.

The Lower East Side, SoHo, TriBeCa, Little Italy, Chinatown, and the financial district, which are all part of lower Manhattan, require careful navigation and good directions and/or map-reading skills. Church Street, Center Street, Broadway, and Bowery (you'll hear people call it "the" Bowery, referring to the neighborhood) are your primary north/south avenues; major cross streets include Houston (it's pronounced HOWS-ton in this neck of the woods), Canal, Delancey, and Church streets (in the financial district). The world-famous Wall

Street is in this area, but you'll be surprised to find it's pretty wimpy trafficwise, not a major thoroughfare at all.

≡FAST FACT

The Avenue Q in the Tony Award-winning musical of the same name does not actually exist. The musical's authors invented it. Although the musical features fuzzy puppets reminiscent of Sesame Street characters, it deals with adult issues like sex that may be inappropriate for children.

Car Rentals

Renting a car in New York City is expensive. If you are flying in, your best bet is to pick up a car at the airport and try to get a package air/car deal. Also try the Internet for rates. From about $70 a day to $400 a week (prices vary greatly with the day of the week and date, size of car, location, and add-ons such as GPS and infant seats), a car in the city can be costly, with tolls, gas, and parking costs added to your rental expense. There is also insurance to worry about, which can run an additional $15 to $20 per day if you are not covered under your own policy or the credit card you rent the car with. And finally, there is a 13.375 percent tax on car rentals.

Knowing that driving in the city can be difficult and that parking is hard to come by, you might consider renting a car for only part of your stay if you want to venture outside of Manhattan. Make those rental arrangements before you arrive, and use the Internet, AAA, or any other memberships for discounts on rental cars. You should also book in advance, and be careful to reserve your pickup for a time you are fairly sure you can make—many Manhattanites don't have cars, so they rent on weekends, which means that New York City car rental companies do not hold cars past the scheduled pickup time, especially on weekends in the summer. Be sure to choose a major rental company with a good reputation and a good service record. Here are a few suggestions:

Alamo Rent A Car
📞 1-800-327-9633
🖥 www.alamo.com

Enterprise Rent-A-Car
📞 1-800-261-7331
🖥 www.enterprise.com

Avis Rent A Car
📞 1-800-331-1212
🖥 www.avis.com

Hertz
📞 1-800-654-3131
🖥 www.hertz.com

Budget Rent A Car
📞 1-800-527-0700
🖥 www.budget.com

National Car Rental
📞 1-800-227-7368
🖥 www.nationalcar.com

Dollar Rent-A-Car
📞 1-800-800-4000
🖥 www.dollar.com

Thrifty Car Rental
📞 1-800-847-4389
🖥 www.thrifty.com

 **TRAVEL TIP**

If you are a member, you can rent a Zipcar in New York City. Zipcar (which recently merged with Flexcar) is a car-sharing network in more than a dozen cities in the United States and Canada. It is available in cities and college towns where people want to be able to drive but don't want to deal with the hassles of owning or leasing a car, paying for insurance, and finding parking. For information, visit www.zipcar.com.

You must be at least eighteen to drive a car in New York City. Many rental companies will either not rent to anyone under twenty-five or will add a surcharge to drivers under that age, so call to check on this policy. You also need a major credit card. Children under five or under forty pounds are required to ride in car seats, which you can rent from the rental car company (usually $10 extra per day). Have your reservation number ready when you get to the rental car window at the airport or at the rental car office. Don't let them talk you into a host of unnecessary extras.

If you can, fill the gas tank in advance (if the deal offered is a good one) rather than agreeing to the traditional "return the car with a full tank" routine, since finding gas stations in Manhattan is difficult. If you plan to pick up the car at one location and deposit it at another, arrange this with the rental car company ahead of time, particularly if you are traveling to another city. Sometimes there are drop-off charges.

Limos and Car Services

Limo services provide style and convenience, and New York, not surprisingly, has a gazillion limousine services that offer a range of transport options, from sedans to stretch limos and Hummers to vans, with rates to match. You can find a car for as little as $35 an hour for standard cars, but rates vary widely so call ahead and pick your price range. There is usually a minimum time requirement, and a 20 percent gratuity is added. Make sure the company gives you a waiting-time grace period if there is an airport pickup, and ask for a nonsmoking car if you want one. Here's a sampling of some major limousine and car services in the city that post their rates on the Internet:

Altour Limousine
📞 212-897-5123
📞 1-888-839-0300
✑ www.altourlimo.com

Bermuda Limousine International
📞 212-647-8400
📞 1-800-223-1383
✑ www.bermudalimo.com

Carmel Car and Limousine Service
📞 212-666-6666
📞 1-800-9CAR-MEL (922-7635)
✑ www.carmellimo.com

Mirage
📞 718-937-6600
📞 1-800-464-7243
✑ http://miragelimousine.com

New York Limousine Service
📞 1-800-447-1955
✑ www.nylimocoach.com

New York Luxury Limousines
📞 718-251-2525
📞 1-800-228-3050
✑ www.newyorkluxurylimo.com

Regency Limousine International
📞 1-866-302-2201
✑ www.regencylimo.com

Tel Aviv Car & Limousine Service
📞 212-777-7777
📞 1-800-222-9888
✑ www.telavivlimo.com

Vega Transportation
📞 718-507-0500
📞 1-888-507-0500
✑ www.vegatransportation.com
Vega Transportation specializes in luxury wheelchair transport.

You can usually charge these trips on a credit card—in fact, many companies prefer it. Either way, if a gratuity is not included—although it usually is—always tip your driver 20 percent. Also be sure to ask the company whether it has limousines if that is what you are looking for. Some companies are limo services and others provide cars. It is not always implied by the title.

Mass Transit

The New York City subway system runs throughout four out of five boroughs (Staten Island is out of the loop), and buses run everywhere the trains don't. Both the subway and the bus system are operated by the Metropolitan Transit Authority (MTA). You can find information about fares as well as maps and suggested routes at the MTA's Web site *(www.mta.info)*.

In Manhattan, the quickest way to travel is by subway. Buses, while slower, will get you where you want to go while giving you some views of the city. Bus and subway fares are $2 per person.

TRAVEL TIP

Don't leave the hotel without a subway map you can carry in your purse or pocket. You can always ask for one at a change booth or pick one up at one of the NYC & Company offices—there's one at 810 Seventh Avenue (between West Fifty-second and West Fifty-third streets). You can also request a map by calling 1-800-NYC-VISIT (692-8474) or 212-484-1222 (in town). Some hotels have the maps too.

Get MetroCards for Everyone

You'll need a MetroCard to ride the subway and bus. The fare for a single ride is $2. Buses take exact change; paper money, half-dollars, and pennies are not accepted. Unlimited-use MetroCards are the best deal, and there are several kinds. A single-day unlimited card—the Fun Pass—is $7.50; a seven-day pass is $25. You can also buy a Pay-Per-Ride card. The MTA adds an extra 15 percent to the card for every $7 you put on it.

MetroCards allow for free transfers between the subways and buses within two hours from the time the fare is paid. You will need a MetroCard for each member of the family—there are no discounts for students, and every person over the age of five pays full fare. If you have a Medicare card, you can get a reduced-fare MetroCard; show your card to the booth attendant. MetroCards can be purchased at subway vending machines, where you can use cash or credit card, or at more than 4,000 merchants citywide. The MetroCard will also get you discounts in some museums, restaurants, and shops.

≡FAST FACT

New York buses don't take paper money; it's not to be annoying, but because of technology. By far the largest transit system in the country, it has to empty the thousands of cash boxes with large vacuum hoses. This would shred paper currency.

Taking the Bus

New York City has the largest accessible fleet in the world (more than 4,500), all equipped for passengers with disabilities. Before you get on a bus, read the sign on the front that tells you where it is going. It's easy to get on the wrong bus, so ask if you are not sure. New Yorkers will be helpful. Drivers, although sometimes curt, will usually answer if you ask where the bus is going or at least point to the sign.

The concierge at your hotel or someone at the front desk can help you plan your route for the day and tell you which bus or subway will take you where you are headed. Also, watch for "limited" buses in Manhattan. These are buses that stop only at major intersections. If you find yourself at an express bus stop, you're in luck. When there is no traffic, a limited bus can get you where you want to go in a hurry, provided it stops near your destination. "Limited" buses are designated as such in the front window.

If you are traveling between 10 P.M. and 5 A.M., you can request the driver let you out anywhere along the route, so long as the driver thinks it's safe.

The Subway System

The New York City subway system is an intricate maze of underground tracks covering 660 miles in passenger use (and 840 miles total), zigzagging under four of the five boroughs. Initially constructed in the early 1900s, the subways carry more than 4.9 million passengers daily in some 6,200 subway cars that stop at 468 stations along 26 routes. It is the quickest, easiest, and cheapest way to get around the city.

Transferring from one train to another is free, provided the two trains connect at some point. Subway maps tell you the stations where multiple trains stop. During morning and evening rush hours (6–10 A.M. and 5–7 P.M.) the trains are very crowded, so try to travel at other times.

 TRAVEL TIP

Security is a concern across the country. If you are using any New York public transport, heed the advice of authorities: "If you see something, say something." Call 1-888-NYC-SAFE (692-7233). Check the MTA's Web site for more information: *http://www.mta.info/mta/security/seesomething.htm*.

You can plan numerous connections to take you where you want to go. Be aware, and follow the signs carefully. Finding your connection can be confusing at busy stations such as Forty-second Street or Union Square (Fourteenth Street) in Manhattan. Subway entrances often indicate "uptown only" or "downtown only," meaning you need to cross the street and look for the train going in the other direction. If you pay attention, you won't join the many visitors (and locals, for that matter) who have taken the wrong train—it happens.

 RAINY DAY FUN

A visit to the New York City Transit Museum is a unique experience for anyone who really loves trains. It tells how the 100-year-old system was built through displays of great antiques and artifacts. It also has one of the best museum shops in town, where you can get the signature subway map on a tie, a shirt, or even a shower curtain. Subway token jewelry is also available. For a preview, visit the museum Web site at *www.transitmuseumstore.com.*

New York's Subway Lines

New York City subway lines are designated with either a letter or a number and a color. They cover four of the five boroughs; Staten Island has its own Staten Island Railway system. Here are some popular destinations and the subway routes you can take to get there:

- Brooklyn Bridge, South Street Seaport, or City Hall—take the A, C, J, M, Z, 2, 3, 4, or 5 train
- Central Park West and the American Museum of Natural History—B or C train
- Grand Central Terminal or East Forty-second Street (closest to the United Nations)—4, 5, 6, 7, or S (crosstown shuttle) train
- Lincoln Center—1 train
- Macy's, Thirty-fourth Street area—B, D, F, N, Q, R, V, or W train
- Metropolitan Museum of Art—4, 5, or 6 train and walk two blocks west
- Rockefeller Center—B, D, F, or V train
- Shea Stadium—take the 7 train from Grand Central, or pick it up at Queensboro Plaza (not Queens Plaza)
- Times Square—N, Q, R, S (crosstown shuttle), W, 1, 2, 3, or 7 train
- Upper East Side of Manhattan or East Harlem—4, 5, or 6 train

- Upper West Side of Manhattan or Washington Heights—1 or C train
- Yankee Stadium—B, D, or 4 train

Keep in mind that you can transfer for free at stations where the lines intersect. A complete and updated map is provided on the inside cover of this book.

Going on Foot

One of the best ways to get around in Manhattan is to walk. Whether it's window shopping along Fifth Avenue or strolling the narrow streets of Little Italy, walking is a marvelous way to enjoy the sights and sounds of New York City. It also beats sitting in traffic.

One thing you must remember when walking is to look very carefully when stepping off a curb. Just because the light has changed does not mean a cab driver is going to stop—many take red lights as a mere suggestion. Bicycle messengers do not adhere to traffic laws and have been known to hit pedestrians. Always wait a moment before crossing, or follow the crowds of people at a busy intersection. Jaywalking is a fine art to New Yorkers, who spend years honing their skills.

If you have the luxury of not having to get somewhere on time, walking through New York City can be exhilarating. Times Square, Greenwich Village, Broadway, Fifth Avenue, Wall Street, the Upper East or West Sides—they all offer a host of stores, restaurants, street vendors, and excitement found nowhere else in the world. People watching is often half the fun. From a film crew to an A-list star to a clown or mime, you can spot just about anything and anybody on the streets of New York.

The city is an architectural paradise, effortlessly mixing cultures and periods. An ornate nineteenth-century church standing next to a sleek black-glass skyscraper, the outlines of a demolished "ghost building" on the outer wall of a standing structure, or a skyscraper wrapped around a small building whose owner wouldn't sell (Macy's on West Thirty-fourth Street is a famous example) are not at all uncommon—and great fun for the kids to look out for.

TRAVEL TIP

Although New York has made great strides in safety, it's generally not advised to ride the subways past 11 P.M., particularly if you're alone. If you are at a rather quiet, unoccupied subway station, once you enter through the turnstiles stand near the station booths or in the yellow designated waiting area toward the center of the platform. The city does have transit cops; however, there are more stations than cops, and more often than not the transit cops are busy watching the turnstiles rather than the platform.

Taking a Taxi

The best thing about taxis is that they are plentiful, at least in Manhattan, where more than 12,000 cabs drive zealously in pursuit of their next fare. They are available at all hours and get you places quickly. Taxi fares currently begin at $2.50 and increase $0.40 for every ⅕ mile when the cab's speed exceeds six miles per hour; otherwise the fare increases $0.40 every two minutes. There is a $1.00 surcharge for rides beginning between 4 P.M. and 8 P.M., and a $0.50 surcharge added between 8 P.M. and 6 A.M.

How to Hail a Cab

Outside of Manhattan, you need to call to get a taxi or car service. In Manhattan, however, you can get a taxi through the concierge at your (or any) hotel, at a taxi stand, or, most commonly, by standing on the corner and signaling with your arm up. When you hail a cab, make sure the vehicle that responds is a yellow medallion cab. Do not get into a cab that is not licensed by the Taxi and Limousine Commission.

Be aggressive when hailing a cab, particularly in busy areas. Watch how New Yorkers do it; it's an art. The toughest times to get a taxi are during rush hour, in the rain, or at 4 P.M., which is shift change for cab drivers. Many of them are anxious to get home after a twelve-hour day and will not pick up passengers. Their lighted Off Duty signs mean just that.

When a cab stops to pick you up, do not tell the driver where you are going until you are seated and the door is closed. Once inside, the cab driver cannot turn you away. If a cab driver attempts to turn you away, take down his number and report him to the Taxi and Limousine Commission, or call a police officer to intervene.

Clearly explain to the driver where you are going. Giving street coordinates, such as "Thirty-fourth Street and Fifth Avenue, please" is usually the best way to get where you want to go, better than giving a street address. If you are going to a well-known building, you can say so, such as "I'm going to Macy's." As you would in any other car, make sure you and your children are secured in seat belts.

JUST FOR PARENTS

New York offers some hybrid taxis, and the entire fleet is scheduled to go green by 2012. The hybrid vehicles will cut the fleet's carbon emissions in half over the next decade and will represent thousands of dollars of savings in fuel costs.

At the End of the Ride

Have your money ready as you approach your destination. The driver gets the amount on the meter plus a tip (usually 15 percent). He or she may not ask for more, except for tolls incurred. Rules and rates are posted clearly in the back of the cab.

Watch carefully when getting out of a cab; the driver may leave you in a busy area, and bike messengers think nothing of zipping past a taxi on the passenger side. Look before getting out.

Check to make sure you take your belongings. When you pay, you should ask for a receipt—not only for your travel expense records, but also so you'll have the taxi ID number in case you leave something behind in the cab. Call the New York City Taxi and Limousine Commission at 311 or 212-639-9675 (or go online at *www.nyc.gov /html/tlc*) if you need to track down a lost article left in a taxi or lodge a complaint.

≡ FAST FACT

SUV cabs have been introduced to the city. Still yellow, and still the same price, they carry up to six passengers. By law, regular cabs can only carry four passengers, and one of those has to sit in the front with the driver.

For People with Disabilities

New York, like the rest of the country, has become more and more accessible for people in wheelchairs. All newer buildings and many of the older ones are wheelchair accessible, and city buses pick up wheelchair passengers at the curb by lowering the steps in the back-door stairwell.

Most hotels, major tourist sites, and theaters provide access for wheelchairs or anyone who cannot climb stairs. It is advisable to call ahead and ask where the entrance is and how to navigate once inside. Facilities like Madison Square Garden and other arenas, theaters, and stores have elevators. When booking your hotel, you should inquire about accessibility as well as in-room facilities such as hand railings in the shower or bathtub. Newer hotels are more likely to meet the needs of people with disabilities than older ones.

One significant program that is designed to assist travelers with disabilities is called the Access Project. It is associated with Big Apple Greeters, a volunteer program that connects visitors with residents of the city for three- or four-hour personalized visits/tours (see page

64). The Access Project works in conjunction with the New York Convention and Visitors Bureau and the Mayor's Office for People with Disabilities, the MTA, and other organizations to provide information and easy access to the sights, hotels, theaters, and transportation of New York City to people with a wide range of disabilities and mobility problems. The Access Project at Big Apple Greeter makes New York accessible to all visitors and can be reached at 212-669-3602, TTY 212-669-8273.

Other resources for travelers with disabilities include the following:

MTA (subway and bus) Travel Information Center
☎ 718-330-1234

MTA Information for People with Disabilities
☎ 718-596-8585
TTY☎ 718-596-8273

TA NYC Transit, Access-a-Ride, Paratransit
☎ 877-337-2017 (local)
☎ 718-393-4999 (out of town)
TTY☎ 718-393-4259

The Lighthouse (national service organization for the blind)
☎ 212-821-9200
TTY☎ 212-821-9713
✍ www.lighthouse.org

JUST FOR PARENTS

There are two weekly publications for New York parents. You might want to call and ask for a copy of *Big Apple Parent* (212-315-0800) or *New York Family* (212-268-8600) before you leave, especially if you have young children. Issues of the publications can usually be found free in banks and kid-related stores once you arrive.

Able newspaper
📞 516-939-2253
🖥 www.ablenews.com

New Mobility magazine
📞 215-675-9133

Mayor's Office for People with Disabilities
📞 212-788-2830
TTY📞 212-788-2838
🖥 www.nyc.gov/mopd

The Andrew Heiskell Braille & Talking Book Library
📞 212-206-5400
TTY📞 212-206-5458
🖥 www.talkingbooks.nypl.org

Disability Rights
📞 1-800-514-0301
TTY 📞 1-800-514-0383
🖥 www.ada.gov

Ambulette services

Papi's Ambulette Service
📞 212-662-4094

Mobile Wood & Ambulette
📞 212-926-6210

Wheelchair Getaways
📞 1-800-379-3750
📞 718-375-0171
🖥 www.wheelchairgetaways.com
/franchise/newyork_brooklyn

Vega Transportation
📞 718-507-0500
📞 1-888-507-0500
🖥 www.vegatransport
ation.com

Tripway Services Ltd.
📞 212-777-1277

CHAPTER 4

New York Tours

IT SHOULD BE no surprise that a city with as much to offer as New York will have just as much a variety of tours to cover it all. No matter what your interest, method of touring, and level of adventure, there are at least several choices for you. While bus tours are probably the most popular, especially the hop-on/hop-off variety, there are walking tours, customized tours, ethnic tours, food tours, multilingual tours, water tours, bike tours, and even helicopter tours available.

Bus Tours

There are two major companies that offer bus tours of New York City. Both have various packages depending on what you want to see and how much you want to spend. You can do a standard drive around the city or you can opt for a more extensive package that includes a boat tour or other perks.

CitySightsNY

▤ 47-25 27th Street, Long Island City

✆ 212-812-2700

✆ 1-866-964-8700

✆ www.citysightsny.com

Those bright blue and yellow double-decker, hop-on/hop-off buses you see around town are part of a large multiservice company called CitySightsNY. Its signature offer is the All Around Town Tour, which takes about seven and a half hours and can be spread out over forty-eight hours. It is a combination of the Downtown, Uptown Treasures and Harlem, and Nights Tours and comes with free admission to the Museum of the City of New York and a free two-hour Liberty Harbor Boat Cruise. The price is $49 for adults, $39 for children five to eleven, and children under five are free.

In addition, the company has a long list of other tour possibilities and combinations of land-, water-, and air-based tours. The double-decker buses only use the top for best visibility and run 365 days a year. In inclement weather you'll get a poncho or the deck will be covered by a transparent cover. The buses are heated and leave from various parts of Manhattan. Free specialty guide books are part of the deal. Tickets are sold in several places around town, by phone, or online (tickets are e-mailed).

Gray Line New York Sightseeing Tours
🖃 777 8th Avenue
✆ 1-800-669-0051
✉ www.graylinenewyork.com

In business since 1910, Gray Line is the grande dame of bus-tour sightseeing. It offers a host of tours and combinations that will save you money. Its Super Saver Special is a three-day hop-on/hop-off adventure that will take you uptown, downtown, to Brooklyn, and on a night-lights tour, a heritage tour, and a harbor cruise. Free twelve-hour parking is included. The Internet price is $104 for adults, $80 for kids five to eleven. No tours December 25 or January 1.

The main offices of this busy and popular bus-tour operation are at 777 Eighth Avenue between West Forty-seventh and West Forty-eighth streets. Another branch is located at street level inside the Port Authority at West Forty-second Street and Eighth Avenue. It's a good idea to drop in and see what is available. You can always visit the Gray Line's Web site, but the brochures and displays will give you a better overview, and the personnel will tell you where to pick up buses and at what time.

TRAVEL TIP

News reports that keep up on traffic and weather are very important in this crowded city. Turn your radio dial to 880 or 1010 AM. There is also a weather and traffic channel on every local cable system. Ask your concierge for the channel in your hotel, as there are different systems in different parts of the city.

Boat Tours

Manhattan is an island, which makes boat touring a natural adjunct to the bus tours. You have several options to choose from, from straightforward tourist cruises to specialty tours.

Circle Line Tours
- West 42nd Street and 12th Avenue, at Pier 83
- Take any subway line to the 42nd Street station, then the west M42 bus to the Circle Line Pier (ask the driver)
- 212-563-3200
- *www.circleline42.com*

For more than fifty years, Circle Line has been sailing the waters around Manhattan, pointing out the sights along the way. Its most popular cruise is a three-hour circumnavigation of the island under the tutelage of an experienced guide who will point out key attractions. It passes the Statue of Liberty, Ellis Island, the World Trade Center site, Yankee Stadium, and many other sights of the city as you sail under the Brooklyn Bridge, George Washington Bridge, and past the piers and South Street Seaport. Take a sweater or jacket as it can get breezy. Three-hour sightseeing tours are $29 for adults, $24 for seniors, and $16 for children under twelve.

Various other tours are offered, including music and DJ tours, a Seaport Liberty Cruise, Semi-Circle Cruises (shorter versions of the Circle Line full tour), cruises to Bear Mountain, holiday cruises on the Fourth of July and New Year's Eve, fall foliage tours, and combo tours partnering with major attractions. Food and drink, including snacks, sandwiches, and hot dogs, are available on board. Ships sail from West Forty-second Street and Twelth Avenue, at Pier 83.

TRAVEL TIP

For those who want some excitement with their sightseeing, Circle Line offers The Beast, a speedboat that takes up to 145 passengers on a thirty-minute, fun-filled ride around the harbor at about forty-five miles per hour. The kids will love it. Adults pay $17, and children under twelve pay $11; note there's a forty-inch (100 cm) height restriction.

Chelsea Screamer

⌨ Pier 62 at Chelsea Piers, on West 23rd Street and the Hudson River

🚌 Take any subway line to 23rd Street, then the M23 bus west to Chelsea Piers

📞 212-924-6262

✎ www.chelseascreamer.com

The Screamer speedboat takes you on an exhilarating wind-in-your-hair trip around lower Manhattan, past the Statue of Liberty, and then up the Hudson for a look at the *Intrepid* (the floating seaside museum). Much smaller than *The Beast*, Chelsea Screamer speedboats run from May through October and cost $20 for adults and $15 for children under twelve; children under three are free.

Classic Harbor Line

⊞ Pier 59 at Chelsea Piers, West 18th Street at the Hudson River

🚊 Take any subway line to 14th Street station, then the M14D bus west to Chelsea Piers (make sure it says "Chelsea Piers")

📞 646-336-5270

🖰 www.sail-nyc.com

If the kids loved *Pirates of the Caribbean* and you were entranced by *The Great Gatsby*, this is the company for you. Two historic sailing vessels take you around New York Harbor for an excitingly (for the youngsters) romantic (for guess who) afternoon in classic elegance or under billowing sails. The newly built *Manhattan* is a 1920s-style luxury motor yacht. Cruise prices range from $40 to $155. The *Adirondack* is an all-wooden, 1890s-style pilot schooner built in 1994. Cruise prices range from $40 to $50. The schooner *Imagine* is the company's newest addition to its fleet. It offers cruise packages with prices ranging from $40 to $50.

Spirit Cruises

⊞ Pier 61, at 23rd Street

🚊 Take any train to the 23rd Street station, then the M23 bus west to Chelsea Piers (last stop) and walk to Pier 61

📞 212-727-2789

📞 1-866-399-8439

🖰 www.spiritcruises.com

No time for a transatlantic cruise? Here's a good alternative. You can set out on one of two kinds of ships for lunch or dinner cruises around lower Manhattan. The three-deck, 600-passenger *Spirit of New York* is a recently remodeled cruise ship that looks like a more manageable transoceanic cruiser.

The European-inspired *Bateaux New York* is an upscale experience with fine wines, gourmet food, and live musicians. The glass ceiling and walls of this vessel allow for breathtaking views of the city. A long list of dancing and entertainment cruises, theme cruises, and packages is offered from about $45 to $125 per person, depending on sailing date and ship. There are discounts for seniors (sixty-five and older) and children on lunch sailings only.

≡FAST FACT

The *Adirondack* has won the Mayor's Cup twice. The annual race in Plattsburgh, New York, has drawn vessels from the United States and Canada for more than thirty years.

New York Waterways

📞 1-800-533-3779

✉ www.nywaterway.com

New York Waterways offers sightseeing cruises, specialty tours, and commuter ferries. Food is available on board, so you can combine lunch and a sea trip and get on with your sightseeing. Adults are $16; seniors $14, students with ID $12, kids under twelve $11, and kids under three are free.

Adults over twenty-one (ID required) can unwind on the ninety-minute Happy Hour Cruise for $20. Drinks are two-for-one, and snacks are free. The company also runs ninety-minute and two-hour day and night cruises and cruise-sightseeing combinations. During baseball season, you can cruise to a New York Yankees game in the *Yankee Clipper*. The company also goes to several points in New Jersey and upstate New York.

🧳 TRAVEL TIP

Unlike the bus tours, you cannot simply hop on and off the boat tours. Make the boat ride an interactive experience for your family. Ask your children to pick out the attractions they want to see the most and why. Factor their answers into how you plan the rest of your stay.

Shearwater Sailing

⬚ North Cove Yacht Harbor & Marina at the World Financial
Center Battery Park City Esplanade (directly in front of the
Winter Garden)

🚆 World Trade Center station (E train)

✆ 212-619-0907

✍ *www.shearwatersailing.com*

You can follow one of Donald Trump's winning *Apprentice* teams
by sailing on the *Shearwater*, an 82-foot double-masted schooner
built in 1929. Daylight sails are $45, sunset and evening sails $55; kids
$25. Sunday brunch sails are $65, children $35. There is also a Fourth
of July special event sail, and private charters are available as well.

TRAVEL TIP

Boat tours give you an unparalleled view of New York City. They are
an experience in themselves, and they can be an entertaining way to
learn more about the city while you kick up your feet and relax. Keep
in mind that the tours are not ferries. To visit attractions like Ellis
Island and the Statue of Liberty, you'll need to take specific ferries.

World Yacht Dining Cruises

⬚ Pier 81 (West 42nd Street at the Hudson River)

🚆 Take any subway line to the 42nd Street station, then the west
M42 bus to the Circle Line Pier (ask the driver)

✆ 212-630-8100

✆ 1-800-498-4270

✍ *www.worldyacht.com*

Since 1984, World Yacht has been setting sail with its offerings
of luxurious, romantic dining experiences at sea. As the ship sails
the Hudson River, you'll go under the Brooklyn Bridge and past the
Statue of Liberty and Ellis Island as musicians play and dinner is

served. It's a highly recommended, very special dining, sailing, and sightseeing experience for visitors and New Yorkers alike. Three-hour cruises depart at 7 P.M. (passengers board at 6 P.M.). Cruises cost about $90 per person Sundays through Thursdays, and $100 on Fridays and Saturdays. Jackets are required and ties recommended for men on the dinner cruises.

JUST FOR PARENTS

World Yacht's sunset dinner cruise or the Sunday-morning brunch cruise are romantic experiences, but they are not for children. Get a babysitter to look after the kids, and treat yourself to a memorable night out. Be sure to book ahead.

Brunch cruises also run during part of the year for about $60. Casual attire is permitted for brunch cruises, but jeans, shorts, and sneakers are always prohibited. There are special cruises for Valentine's Day, Mother's Day, Fourth of July, Thanksgiving Day, and December 31. The company sails year-round with an abbreviated schedule in the off season.

Helicopter Tours

This may very well be the ultimate New York experience. It's an undeniable thrill to look down at this great city while you fly over it, and you get a different perspective on the city as a machine.

Don't expect a *M.A.S.H.* chopper; these are all modern, roomy, and comfortable. Most tours must add modest fuel, security, and passenger fees. Although you can walk in, all companies strongly prefer you call ahead for information and reservations. Tours leave from one of two places: the Downtown Heliport and the VIP Heliport.

TRAVEL TIP

If you take a helicopter tour, absolutely make sure the Statue of Liberty is one of the sites included in the tour. The aerial view of Lady Liberty is truly awesome for adults and children alike.

Downtown Manhattan Heliport

Pier 6 (East River and South Street)

South Ferry station (1 train) or Whitehall Street station (R or W train)

VIP Heliport

West 30th Street and 12th Avenue

West 34th Street-Pennsylvania Station (A, C, or E train) then walk or take the M34 bus west to its last stop (Javits Center)

Helicopter Flight Services, Inc.

212-355-0801

www.heliny.com

You can take your pick from a variety of tour options. Per person, tours run $129 for fifteen minutes, $179 for twenty minutes (both are two-person minimum), and $275 for thirty minutes (four-person minimum). With luck, you may be upgraded. There's also a half-hour tour for $1,350 total for up to six people. Tours run Monday to Saturday, 10 A.M. to 6 P.M.; Sunday and holiday tours start at 11 A.M. Weekday tours leave from the Downtown Heliport, Sunday tours depart from the VIP Heliport.

 **TRAVEL TIP**

Chopper travel times may seem short, but you can cover a lot of ground in a few minutes. You won't have to deal with traffic or other delays, and the views of the city are beyond compare. Kids especially will enjoy the experience of swooping over the city's landmarks.

Liberty Helicopters

📞 1-800-542-9933

📞 212-967-6464

✍ www.libertyhelicopters.com

An award-winning company for helicopter safety, Liberty has a variety of tours (routes) available, ranging from five to fifteen minutes. Tours cover numerous sights and cost from $69 to $186 per person depending on length. A private helicopter can be had for $849 (about a fifteen-minute flight for up to four people). The company even has a two-minute run out of Jersey City, New Jersey, for $30. The Downtown Heliport is open Monday to Saturday from 9 A.M. to 6:30 P.M. (must have reservation); The VIP Heliport is open every day of the year from 9 A.M. to 9 P.M. (walk-ins welcome).

New York Helicopter Charter

📞 212-361-6060

✍ www.newyorkhelicopter.com

Another multiservice company, tours here range from $119 (ten to twelve minutes) to $275 (twenty to twenty-five minutes) per person. Flights depart from the Downtown Heliport Monday to Friday, 9 A.M. to 6:30 P.M., weekend tours depart from the VIP Heliport from 11 A.M. to 6 P.M.

Bike Tours

If you want to work off some of that great New York food, get on a two-wheeler and take a bicycle tour of the big town. You don't have to be an athlete, just comfortable riding a bike. If you're concerned about pedaling around the Big Apple, take solace in the fact that New York has been named one of the best cities in America to ride a bike.

≡FAST FACT

The springtime Five Boro Bike Tour takes bikers forty-two miles through all five boroughs. It has been an annual staple for more than thirty years and attracts more than 30,000 riders each year. Traffic is rerouted for this event, the largest biking event in the country.

Bike Central Park
📞 917-371-6267
✎ www.bikecentralpark.com

Bike Central Park offers three ways to see Central Park on wheels. You can rent a bike and cruise on your own, join or form a group and have a guide take you around, or (and this is most cool) relax in the padded seat of a pedicab while the tour guide tells you the story of Central Park and the sights as they pass by. Bike rentals run from $10 for an hour to $35 all day (10 A.M. to 6 P.M.). Free locks for all, and helmets are provided for kids under fifteen.

The guided tours leave at 10 A.M. and cover the whole park in two hours. There is a minimum of six people, but you can call and see if you can join a party. The pedicabs, big three-wheeled bikes with a padded seat in the back, hold three adults or two adults and two children. Tours are forty minutes long and cost $50.

☰FAST FACT

New York's streets are always clogged with vehicular traffic, but the city has a large population of ardent bikers. Occasionally hordes of bikers take to the streets to celebrate cycling and advocate for environmentally friendly transportation.

Bike the Big Apple
⊡ 1306 2nd Avenue
✆ 1-877-865-0078
✎ www.bikethebigapple.com

At last count, this company offered five interesting tours of New York. A seven-hour (rest stops included) old country tour covers Manhattan, Roosevelt Island, Queens, and Brooklyn for $75. Bike and Bite Brooklyn takes you to neighborhoods most tourists never see and lets you experience Brooklyn cuisine. This six-hour tour costs $65. The Park and Soul tour covers Central Park and Harlem, Secret Streets covers southern Manhattan, and a twilight tour takes riders to the Brooklyn Bridge at sunset.

All tour prices include the bike, helmet, reflective vest, front and back bike lights, and a guide. It isn't for younger kids, and no infant bike seats are available. Tours leave from two different midtown locations convenient to hotels. Call or log on to reserve and get locations.

Central Park Bicycle Tours
✆ 212-541-8759
✎ www.centralparkbiketour.com

A bike tour is a marvelous way to see a great park and get exercise at the same time. Two-hour tours are $40 for adults and $20 for children fifteen or younger, and prices include bike rental. Tours leave seven days a week at 10 A.M., 1 P.M., and 4 P.M.; 9 A.M. and 11 A.M.

tours are added in the summer. You can also rent bikes at a rate of $20 for two hours, $25 for three hours, or all day for $40. Rental includes a helmet, poncho, lock, and a map of Central Park. Credit cards are accepted.

Walking Tours

Walking is the most intimate way to get acquainted with Manhattan. There are an amazing number of walking tours conducted by a variety of people—from large companies to a single professor or writer talking about her specialty. These special-interest tours focus on a specific theme (such as a Seinfeld tour conducted by Kenny "the real" Kramer and one that covers knitting shops). Here is a representative sampling to get you started.

Amazing New York Tours
✆ 212-587-0321
✆ *www.amazenyc.com*

You can design your own tour or choose from a long list of suggestions. There is a $40 minimum for up to four people and $10 a person for every additional person. Of special note is the one-hour College Neighborhood Tour for $25 total for a family of up to five people. It's a great idea if you are considering one of New York's excellent schools.

JUST FOR PARENTS

Taking any kind of tour is the most efficient way to get to know a city, but choosing the right tour is important. You know your family better than anyone, and the wonderful thing about New York is the huge variety of tours offered. Shorter bicycle tours, individualized tours by Big Apple Greeters, self-guided tours using electronic devices, or tours by boat or helicopter may be good opportunities for your family.

Big Apple Greeters

✆ 212-669-8159

✐ www.bigapplegreeter.org

This organization is one of the things that make New York great! The idea is simple—real New Yorkers volunteer to take visitors around a neighborhood on a one-to-one basis. The service is free—no fees, no tipping allowed. You can choose the neighborhood or leave it to Greeter's choice. It's a marvelous way to get a feel for a neighborhood while enjoying a personalized experience, as opposed to a boiler-plate tour.

≡FAST FACT

Big Apple Greeter started in 1992 as a way to make New York City more accessible to visitors. It was intended to counter New York's perception as a tourist's worst nightmare—an overwhelming, over-powering, overpriced metropolis.

There are about 300 greeters who speak twenty-two languages (including signing). Visits take between two and four hours, more if you agree, and can accommodate one to six people, including children. You will get a private tour and will never share with another party. Visitors with disabilities are welcome.

Big Onion Walking Tours

✆ 212-439-1090

✐ www.bigonion.com

Big Onion has offered tours through historic and ethnic neighborhoods all around the city since 1991. Choose from a wide-ranging variety of tours. Adults $15, seniors $12, students with ID $10. There is a $5 extra charge for food on the Original Multi-Ethnic Eating Tour.

Knickerbocker's New York Tours

✆ 917-526-2518

✉ *www.nyknowledge.com*

Experienced guides will work with you to plan the perfect tour for your family. Tours are offered in ten languages, and guides are knowledgeable about a number of New York-centric topics. Just in case you're curious, the tours are not affiliated with the basketball team.

92nd Street Y

✆ 212-996-1100

✉ *www.92ndsty.org*

The 92nd Street Y (a New York cultural treasure in itself) offers a wide selection of walking tours of different areas of the city and outer boroughs. The tours include journeys to areas of historic, social, artistic, and cultural importance. Walking tours include Madison Square Garden, Grand Central Station, Lower East Side synagogues, Brooklyn Bridge, Prospect Park, Van Cortlandt Park, and a Gracie Mansion tea tour. The tours run from two to four hours and cost $15 to $25. Call for more information and to register.

▣ TRAVEL TIP

Just about any walking tour that involves food is a good value. You will get a tour of the city and a meal for a decent price. Your kids will enjoy the interactive experience, and the tastes and smells of the tour are more likely to stick with them than the trivia tidbits offered on a standard walking tour.

Susan Sez NYC Walkabouts

📞 917-509-3111

🖱 www.susansez.com

Susan Birnbaum goes where no man has gone before—well, almost. She takes you to neighborhoods that are usually neglected: City Island, the Bronx's Arthur Avenue, Astoria, Manhattan's crafts shops. But she also goes to the traditional places as well. Of interest are the neighborhood tours for people moving to the Big Apple. Tours are $18 to $40, except for the $75 knitting tour, which includes lunch and discounts on purchases.

TRAVEL TIP

If you arrive in New York without booking a tour beforehand, don't worry. You can find schedules for walking tours at visitor centers and local newspapers. Ask the concierge at your hotel for suggestions and recommendations.

Additional Options

New York is bursting with eclectic tour options. You can download an audio tour, see television and movie locations, or learn about hip-hop New York.

CityShow

📞 646-414-1100

🖱 www.cityshownyc.com

Rent a cool GPS device that knows where you are anywhere in the city, shows you on a map, and provides entertaining stories, photos, and music. The subway and restroom finders are invaluable. Rental is $49.95 a day or $129.99 for three days.

⟱ FAST FACT

Geocaching is a GPS phenomenon. It's a high-tech treasure hunt that can be a fun way to see some of New York's parks. You will need a GPS device and an account at the Geocaching Web site (*www.geo caching.com*).

Racon Tours

☏ 646-435-2798

✑ *www.racontours.com*

Download Racon Tours' audio tours at home onto your MP3 player, PDA, iPod, or Smartphone and you're ready to tour when you arrive in town with integrated audio, video, and interactive map. New devices are always added, so check online before you go. The cost is $14.95 per tour area.

Talking Street

☏ 1-877-870-TOUR (8687)

✑ *www.talkingstreet.com*

Use your own cell phone to listen to a native celebrity (Sigourney Weaver, Paul Sorvino, Jerry Stiller) talking about the sight you're looking at. Choose a stop, call a special number, and you get a private tour when and where you want it. Total cost is $5.95, and it's activated for seven days.

🧳 TRAVEL TIP

Self-guided tours, such as cell-phone tours, are a convenient way to see the city at your own pace. The only problem for families is supplying everyone with a cell phone, but these tours are a great way to get an interesting introduction to the city.

Doorway to Design

📞 212-229-0299

📞 718-339-1542

✍ www.doorwaytodesign.com

Doorway to Design offers tours of the fashion and art world, architectural tours, shopping tours to New York's wholesale district and private discount shopping in Manhattan, and tours covering the culinary arts, hot neighborhoods, antiques, and private homes and gardens, among others. Call for fees.

Hush Tours

📞 212-714-3527

✍ www.hushtours.com

Hush Tours provides walking and bus tours by pioneer rap artists. These artists will show you a hip-hop look at New York. You'll see celebrity homes, visit clubs, and listen to live music. Two-hour tours are $25; four-hour tours are $55.

≡ FAST FACT

Hush Tours was founded with the purpose of educating people about the roots of hip-hop. The company battles the negative stereotypes associated with the genre by focusing on hip-hop's contributions to art, entertainment, and culture.

Kramer's Reality Tour

📞 212-268-5525

📞 1-800-KRAMERS (572-6377)

✍ www.kennykramer.com

This unique tour is an all-Seinfeld multimedia experience that covers the people, places, and yada, yada, yada behind the show. All tours are hosted by Kenny Kramer, the "real" Kramer. Tickets for the three-hour bus tour are $37.50 plus $2 service charge. This tour is extremely popular, so reserve early.

On Location Tours

☎ 212-209-3370

✐ www.screentours.com

This tour includes sites in New York that have been used in movies and television. Some of the tours are dedicated to one production, like *Sex in the City*. Screentours also offers a walking tour of Central Park movie sites. Tours run three and a half hours and cost $32 to $36.

≡FAST FACT

Many films and television shows take place in New York City, and some of them film on location. The Law & Order franchise films all over the city, bringing in $50 million in revenue for the city each year.

Urban Park Rangers

✐ www.nycgovparks.org

The rangers are a part of the New York City Department of Parks. They provide free tours of the many parks in New York City, with an emphasis on plant life, bird watching, wildlife, and geology. Call 311, the general New York information number in town, 212-NEW-YORK (639-9675) from outside the city, or log on to the Web site and search "tours" for more information or to request a schedule.

Walkin' Broadway

📞 212-997-5004

📞 1-866-NYC-BWAY (692-2929)

🖰 www.walkinbroadway.com

This is a self-guided, in-depth tour of Broadway, with the added attraction of using an audio unit that plays original soundtracks and displays photos of historic places, plays, and people. Rental is $12.

Watson Adventures Scavenger Hunts

📞 1-877-9-GO-HUNT (946-4868)

🖰 www.watsonadventures.com

This company organizes teams for scavenger hunts of information in museums and other sites in town, including Central Park, the American Museum of Natural History, and Grand Central Terminal. Ask for rates on family hunts.

CHAPTER 5

The Neighborhoods of Manhattan

WHEN YOU LOOK at Manhattan from the air or across the Hudson or East rivers, you see a spectacular skyline, a noiseless landscape devoid of life. But when you're in the midst of it—walking, biking, driving, or touring the streets of Manhattan—you'll discover an energetic blend of distinctive neighborhoods, each with its own characteristics. You'll see the nooks and crannies, the parks, the playgrounds, and the architecture. You'll encounter the local merchants, read the signs, and see the storefronts that characterize the overall flavor of each neighborhood.

Home Is Where the Heart Is

New Yorkers define themselves by their neighborhoods. Each one is unique and rich with its own sites and history, cuisine, and lore. This is why Manny Ramirez always comes back to his roots in Washington Heights, why Spike Lee opened his store in Brooklyn and Rosie Perez still lives there, and why Yoko Ono hasn't moved from the Dakota.

New York is the quintessential melting pot, an immigrant city where cultures have blended and created some of the most incredible food and arts imaginable. Where else could you find Cuban Chinese food or kosher French, Italian, Indian, Japanese, pizza, nouvelle, Eastern European, Moroccan, vegetarian, vegan, Chinese, steakhouse, Cajun, and Persian restaurants?

There's a definite pulse in the subcultures that meld and merge from one part of town to another. Even the beat changes slightly, from the frantic pace of Chinatown to the slower saunter of Bleecker Street in the Village. With the exception of parts of midtown, you'll find residential buildings like brownstones, old brick apartment buildings, and sleek, modern, high-rise glass buildings. Historical sights, special events, and the people you pass on the street will tell you what part of town you're in. A Greenwich Village type wouldn't dream of living in Murray Hill, and an Upper Westsider looks with disdain at the more tony Upper East Side. Buildings from different eras often share the same block, and a ten-block stroll can take you into an entirely different socioeconomic and ethnic neighborhood.

 TRAVEL TIP

It should be no surprise that the shrine of the patron saint of immigrants, Mother Cabrini, can be found in New York City. The shrine of this founder of the Order of the Sacred Heart is in Upper Manhattan at 701 Fort Washington Avenue. The nearest subway stop is West 190th Street station (A train). Mother Cabrini's body is enshrined in a glass coffin just yards away from the Cloisters, where European saint reliquaries are on display as part of the Metropolitan Museum of Art's medieval collection.

You'll find a variety of manufacturing centers throughout parts of lower and midtown Manhattan. The upper west twenties, for example, is called the flower district; it leads to the fur district, around Thirtieth Street and Seventh Avenue. The west thirties are home to the garment industry, and in the west forties you'll find electronics on one block and jewelry on another in the diamond district. And these areas aren't subtle. You'll see a row of jewelry stores lining a city block on West Forty-seventh Street between Fifth and Sixth avenues.

Manhattan continues to evolve, and the boundaries between districts are never constant. As Manhattan has lost its manufacturing base, industrial lofts have been converted to high-priced residential lofts. Neighborhood labeling has taken on marketing value, so that the fur district in the west twenties has become part of desirable Chelsea when a real estate broker gets involved. New Yorkers, lovable rebels that they are, have also taken to downshifting, calling some of their neighborhoods by names of nearby edgier (read "seedier") neighbors to sidestep being branded yuppies.

A Quick Overview

Manhattan alone has more than twenty distinct neighborhoods. As a point of reference, here are the neighborhoods of Manhattan as they run from north to south:

- **Inwood**—from 220th Street to approximately 190th Street
- **Washington Heights**—the area from 155th Street to 190th Street
- **Harlem**—110th Street to about 151st Street
- **Morningside Heights**—the area around Columbia University
- **Upper East Side**—everything east of Central Park from Fifty-ninth Street to about Ninety-ninth Street
- **Upper West Side**—west of the park from Fifty-ninth to 104th Streets
- **Midtown**—from Thirty-fourth Street to Fifty-ninth Street (including the theater district of the west forties and Hell's Kitchen)
- **Murray Hill**—a residential area above Gramercy Park, from about Twenty-third to Thirty-fourth streets on the east side
- **Chelsea**—on the west side of town from Fourteenth to Thirtieth streets
- **Gramercy Park**—a private park on the east side in the twenties and the neighborhood that surrounds it
- **Union Square**—the neighborhood around Fourteenth Street and Fifth Avenue

- **Greenwich Village**—from Broadway to the Hudson River from about Fourteenth Street to West Houston
- **East Village**—Broadway to the east, from about Fourteenth Street down to First Street
- **SoHo**—the area South of Houston Street
- **TriBeCa**—the Triangle Below Canal Street
- **Chinatown**—the East River side of Canal Street
- **Little Italy**—the area around Mulberry Street
- **Lower East Side**—the far east side of Manhattan below First Street
- **Wall Street/Battery Park City**—everything south of Canal Street

New neighborhood names are being carved out in the real estate wars. The area centering around Fifth Avenue in the teens and lower twenties is being called the Flatiron district; the east twenties and thirties are known as Kips Bay; lower Manhattan around the Wall Street area is the financial district; and the area around the government buildings is called Civic Center. Then there's NoHo (NOrth of HOuston), NoLita (NOrth of Little ITAly) to its south, and . . . you get the idea. Hell's Kitchen, the area from West Fourteenth to West Fifty-ninth streets and between Eighth Avenue and the Hudson River, is trying hard to be called Clinton.

🧳 TRAVEL TIP

In New York City, signs that read Tow-Away Zone or other ominous warnings really mean business—your car will be towed if you leave it unattended. When you park, be sure to read the signs and pay the meter, if required. If your car is towed, you'll find it in the police lot on the west side of Manhattan. You'll have to pay a steep fine (from $60 to $180, plus a $165 towing fee) to get it back and spend valuable vacation hours in the process.

It would take an entire book to give you the history and an overview of each neighborhood. The rest of this chapter covers a few of the more commonly frequented neighborhoods in greater detail.

The Lower East Side

From 1892 to 1934, between twelve and twenty million men, women, and children took their first steps onto American soil at Ellis Island. The next stop from the tiny island for a great number of these immigrants was the small pocket of land near the Brooklyn Bridge along the East River, Manhattan's Lower East Side. In the early 1900s, the neighborhood was the most overcrowded in America.

On what had been farmlands, builders crammed three- and four-story row houses that barely fit on the narrow strips of land that had been sectioned off for single-family dwellings. These Lower East Side tenements were quickly filled and then overcrowded, housing more people than they were designed for. Many ethnic groups lived together in the area, including an enormous Jewish population, immigrants from Eastern Europe, and large contingencies from Ireland and Italy.

Many New York celebrities grew up on the Lower East Side, including Robert DeNiro, Zero Mostel, James Cagney, George Burns, and Jimmy Durante. The Marx Brothers, George Gershwin, and others honed their skills in its burlesque houses, Yiddish theaters, and (in later years) the settlement houses there. One of New York's most famous gangsters of the 1930s, Lucky Luciano, and one of the city's most renowned mayors, Fiorello LaGuardia (who would later put Luciano behind bars), were also born in the neighborhood.

Today the population of the neighborhood is in transition. Latino and Chinese immigrants have settled in waves, but professionals are slowly gentrifying the neighborhood. The boutiques and bistros have inevitably followed, but discount shopping stores along Orchard Street still draw clients.

A Brief Itinerary

To get to the Lower East Side, take the subway to Delancey-Essex Street (F, J, M, or Z train). Stroll along Orchard, Delancey, and Grand streets to find bargains on vintage clothing, hip-hop wear, designer clothes, shoes, and inexpensive packs of underwear, linens, and housewares. For many years, vendors took their wares out to the streets on Sunday along these popular shopping locales. Some still do so today, although most of the old storefronts are home to trendy boutiques.

Visit the Lower East Side Tenement Museum (page 164) for a guided tour through an 1863 tenement at 108 Orchard Street, between Delancy and Broome streets. The furnishings give you an idea of the daily existence of the thousands of immigrants who lived there. The unique museum is a tribute to urban housing.

Get a bite to eat at either Ratner's Restaurant or Katz's Delicatessen, where the portions are big, the décor isn't fancy, and the traditional Jewish-style food is still first rate.

⸗FAST FACT

If you expect deli fare like you order at home, be prepared to be dazzled. New York is the birthplace of delicatessen, so don't miss the authentic: pickles straight from a barrel, homemade coleslaw, potato salad, and pickled peppers. Get pastrami on rye, a knish or two, the matzo ball soup, a hot dog with sauerkraut, and a blintz with applesauce. Seltzer goes with everything.

Stop by and tour the beautiful Eldridge Street Synagogue (12 Eldridge Street), the nation's first Eastern European Orthodox synagogue, built in 1887. It has been restored and converted into a cultural center and gift shop.

Streit's manufactures matzos, as they have since 1925, at 148 Rivington Street. You can visit this working bakery and watch as the different kinds of matzos bake in the ovens. A family member (founder Aron Streit's great-grandchildren) might even give you a tour. This is the only family-owned and operated matzo company in America.

Chinatown

Chinatown and Little Italy are neighbors, located just blocks from the city's courthouses, City Hall, the municipal buildings of lower Manhattan, and the Lower East Side. To get to Chinatown, cab it or take the subway to the Canal Street station (A, C, E, J, M, N, Q, R, W, or 6 train).

For years, Chinatown has been the place to go for New York's best Chinese food, but it is much more than a neighborhood of restaurants. The interest in Chinatown is the cultural ambiance—there aren't many traditional touristy sights. Since the early settlers came to the neighborhood from China in the 1870s, the area has exploded beyond its original boundaries into Little Italy and even across Canal Street.

For years, immigrants worked in factories, restaurants, and local shops. Many locals still do. The neighborhood houses garment factories and numerous shops. Many of these establishments sell food, and the kids will love seeing roasted ducks hanging in shop windows. Noodles, seafood, and vegetables are abundant inside and outside the jam-packed little shops that line the tiny streets.

Clothing, electronics, souvenirs, and all sorts of goods are for sale here beneath Chinese signs. You'll even see a few pagoda-style roofs, but the area is not a Disney tribute to Chinese culture; it is an authentic and very busy neighborhood that moves at a frantic pace. If you stroll the main business streets, Canal and Mott, you'll find yourself smack in the middle of the frenzy.

A visit to Chinatown should include a stop at the Museum of Chinese in the Americas. Also shop the stores on Mott Street, and be sure to stop by the shops frequented by the local residents. It will give the kids a fascinating view of a unique culture. Once you've worked up an appetite, check out the recommendations in Chapter 17 and have lunch and/or dinner at one of the 300 restaurants in the neighborhood.

 RAINY DAY FUN

Drop into the Museum of Chinese in the Americas at 70 Mulberry Street (212-619-4785). It will be moving to 174 Lafayette Street (between Canal and Howard streets), so call for the current location. Founded in 1980 as the New York Chinatown History Project, the museum was chartered in 1992. It is currently the only nonacademic museum on the East Coast dedicated to documenting and interpreting the history and culture of Chinese Americans. Included in the exhibits are photos, documents, sound recordings, textiles, and more.

Another option is to stop at Fung Wong's on Mott Street to buy rice cakes, roast pork buns, egg rolls, and other delights to take back to your hotel. Definitely visit the Chinatown Ice Cream Factory on Bayard Street by Mott for a taste of lychee, papaya, and other exotic flavors of ice cream.

The Chinese New Year is celebrated in grand style in Chinatown, with dragon parades and all sorts of festivities. It's very crowded, but if you're in town during the Chinese New Year, you might head on down and check out the excitement.

Little Italy

Fractionally smaller and calmer than Chinatown, Little Italy has narrow streets and turn-of-the-century buildings with restaurants and shops below. In the early twentieth century, many of the city's half-million Italian immigrants lived in this area. In the past fifty years, however, neighborhoods in the other boroughs, such as Bensonhurst (in Brooklyn), Belmont (in the Bronx), and the suburbs of New Jersey now house the lion's share of Italian Americans.

The neighborhood is still home to a bevy of old-fashioned Italian restaurants and bakeries, along with some trendy newer shops mixed in. To get there, take the subway to the Broadway-Lafayette Street station (B, D, F, or V train), the Spring Street station (6 train), or the Prince Street station (N, R, or W train).

E. Rossi & Company is still at Grand and Mulberry, selling everything from embroidered postcards to pasta makers. Also in the area you'll find Old St. Patrick's Cathedral on Mulberry Street and San Gennaro Church on Baxter Street, which hosts one of the city's best festivals.

A visit to Little Italy should include a stop at Ferrara's (108 Mulberry Street, between Canal and Hester) to buy pastries, especially cannoli. Have a pick-me-up or dessert at Rice to Riches (37 Spring Street, between Mulberry and Mott, *www.ricetoriches.com*) where the only thing on the menu is rice pudding in an astounding variety of flavors and toppings. Refer to Chapter 17 for a list of dining establishments to try during your visit.

If you happen to be in town during the second week of September, take the family to the Feast of San Gennaro that lines Mulberry Street from Canal to Grand. The smells from the street venders are delicious, but you can also sit outside and have a meal at one of the fine Italian restaurants as the throngs pass you by. The street teems with outdoor games, music, and fun.

JUST FOR PARENTS

If your kids liked the street-vendor zeppoli at the San Gennaro Festival, you can make them at home. Heat about an inch of oil in a large skillet. Take frozen crescent-roll dough and make it into balls. Drop the balls into the oil and fry them for about a minute or two. When they're brown, remove them from oil and blot dry on a paper towel. Roll the zeppoli in confectioner's sugar.

If you have the time, visit the new Little Italy in the Belmont neighborhood of the Bronx, centered on Arthur Avenue near the Bronx Zoo and the New York Botanical Garden. Take the subway to the Fordham Road station (D or 4 train, then the #12 bus heading east) or Pelham Parkway station (2 or 5 train, then the #12 bus heading west), or the Metro-North Harlem River line to Fordham Road, then take the shuttle bus to Belmont and Bronx Zoo.

Greenwich Village

Greenwich Village and its close neighbor, the East Village, are located below Fourteenth Street. If you're planning to meander around the Village, it's best to get down there by public transportation. Greenwich Village is very popular, and parking is at a premium.

Go to the West Fourth Street-Washington Square station (A, B, C, D, E, F, or V train) or Christopher Street-Sheridan Square station (1, 2, or 3 train). The nearest subway stop in the East Village is the Astor Place station (6 train).

A Little History

The Dutch settlers of New Amsterdam ventured north in the early 1600s and discovered a large area of land where they could plant crops. Until then, the land had been inhabited by Native Americans. When the English took over in the later 1600s, the neighborhood became a country setting—a suburb of sorts. By the 1700s, the West Village by the Hudson River was a major area for fishing and growing produce. Room was set aside for a public gallows in the center of the city, which is now Washington Square Park.

In the early 1800s, more and more settlers moved north to escape the epidemics—smallpox, yellow fever, and cholera—that plagued the city. They moved primarily to the area below Houston Street. Farms, shops, markets, and various businesses sprang up in the Village. Finer, more fashionable homes were built, particularly at the foot of Fifth Avenue around Washington Square Park. The luxurious townhouses remain, mostly now serving as offices of New York University.

≡FAST FACT

Electric Lady Studios at 52 West Eighth Street is a Village landmark that musicians flock to. This was the first recording studio ever owned by a recording artist. It was founded in 1970 by Jimi Hendrix and has been used by David Bowie, the Beastie Boys, and many other artists from the 1970s to the present. In 1997, its signature curved brick arch was demolished and replaced with a glass front.

The nineteenth century also saw the birth of New York University and the emergence of galleries and establishments for the literary community. An upscale community throughout much of the nineteenth century, the neighborhood began to change toward the turn of the century. The elite moved further north, and a more bohemian culture settled into the area. Small theaters and galleries opened, and local publishers distributed diverse local magazines and irreverent books.

Greenwich Village blossomed into New York City's home of up-and-coming writers, artists, and musicians. Edgar Allan Poe, Walt Whitman, and Mark Twain lived in Greenwich Village in the 1800s, and Sinclair Lewis, Eugene O'Neill, Jackson Pollock, and Norman Rockwell were among the many to be part of the Village in the twentieth century. The Beat poets of the 1950s gave way to the folk singers of the early 1960s, including Bob Dylan, Arlo Guthrie, and Peter, Paul, and Mary. By the late 1970s, the East Village was home to punk rock.

Whatever the artistic trend, the Village captures it in art and music. Outdoor art shows flank the park twice a year, and clubs like Webster Hall present the hottest up-and-coming and established performers. Off-Broadway and avant-garde theater became part of the local artists' own brand of self-expression many years ago, and it remains a significant part of Village culture today. Stores and galleries have displayed the latest trendy paraphernalia of each new generation, and the fads and fashions are evident in the area around Washington Square Park.

Demographically, the stereotypical starving artist and writer have fled to ever-more outlying boroughs of the city and even New Jersey. Previously dirt-cheap walkup tenements have been reincarnated as highly prized condos.

≡ FAST FACT

Movements and social causes have been an important part of Village life, from the antiwar protests of the 1960s to activities championing the rights of gays and lesbians in recent decades. The Village has become a place where the gay and lesbian community can thrive and flourish.

In terms of aesthetics, little has changed in Greenwich Village over the past thirty years. Redbrick townhouses with cozy little courtyards still line the streets. Restaurants, shops, and galleries are still busy at night; only the latest merchandise changes with the times.

The East Village

The neighboring East Village was a drug-infested, seedy neighborhood in the 1970s. Today it has joined the city's economic and social boom. Dozens of relatively inexpensive Indian restaurants can be found on East Sixth Street (between First and Second avenues), theaters featuring rising talent are busy on East Fourth Street, and trendy shops are in vogue on St. Marks Place. The East Village has emerged as the alternative to the alternative, especially for those interested in escaping the more commercial Greenwich Village. Don't be fooled, however—some of the East Village shops have Fifth Avenue prices.

A Quick Itinerary

Stroll through Washington Square Park, the Village's heart and soul. Note the Memorial Arch built in 1889 to celebrate the 100th anniversary of George Washington's inauguration. Watch street performers, chess and checker players, and artists drawing or sketching.

Go shopping on Eighth Street in the more popular mainstream stores, on Bleecker Street for trendy shopping, or on St. Marks Place in the East Village for even trendier shopping. Get great gourmet food at Balducci's on Sixth Avenue by Tenth Street or the absolute best pastries and desserts at Veniero's on Eleventh Street between First and Second avenues. If you want first-rate tea or coffee, try McNulty's Tea & Coffee Company on Christopher by Bleecker.

See a play at the Actor's Playhouse, Cherry Lane Theater on Commerce Street, the Minetta Lane Theater, or Astor Place Theater on Lafayette (East Village). Find out what is playing at the Joseph Papp Public Theater on Lafayette Street between Fourth Street and Astor Place, where musicals such as *Hair* and *A Chorus Line* had their first performances.

Check out the nineteenth-century houses of Grove Court between Bedford and Hudson streets or Gay Street between Waverly and Christopher. Blink and you'll miss 75 Bedford Street; only nine and a half feet wide, it was built in 1873. Its neighbor, 77 Bedford Street, is some 200 years old.

Browse the Forbes Magazine Galleries, featuring items from the Forbes personal collections, including hundreds of toy boats, thousands of toy soldiers, and numerous trophies and awards. There are also changing exhibits at the gallery on 62 Fifth Avenue (near Twelfth Street) in the Forbes Building.

Have a drink, or at least a look, at White Horse Tavern on Hudson Street at Eleventh Avenue. The 120-year-old saloon was the drinking home of poet Dylan Thomas and storyteller O. Henry, who has a booth named after him here, among other writers, poets, and artists.

JUST FOR PARENTS

Go to a concert at Webster Hall (formerly the Ritz) at 125 East Eleventh Street, where Duran Duran got its U.S. start. There's also the longtime home of folk music, the Bitter End, on Bleecker. You can also find plenty of jazz if you visit legendary clubs like the Blue Note, Village Vanguard, or Knickerbocker (a celeb favorite because of its food).

Stroll down narrow Minetta Lane and stop in to see the former speakeasy Minetta Tavern at Minetta and MacDougal. You might also stop at Le Figaro Café, a great people-watching locale and longtime favorite Village hangout on the corner of Bleecker and MacDougal.

Admire the Gothic Revival architecture of the Grace Church (1846) or the Church of the Ascension (1841), the Romanesque architecture of Judson Memorial Church (1892), or the more recent copper-domed St. George's Ukrainian Catholic Church (1970s).

Have dinner at one of the many village restaurants. Choose from the following suggestions or venture out on your own:

- Café Loup, on West Thirteenth Street between Sixth and Seventh avenues
- Ennio & Michael, on LaGuardia between Bleecker and West Third Street
- James Beard House, on Twelfth Street between Sixth and Seventh avenues
- Il Mulino, on Third Street between Thompson and Sullivan
- La Ripaille, on Hudson between Bethune and West Twelfth Street
- Westville East, on the corner of Avenue A and Eleventh Street
- Pearl Oyster Bar, on Cornelia between Bleecker and West Fourth Street

The spring and fall art shows are enjoyable, but the Village always has so much activity that it's easy to get caught up in the atmosphere that makes this New York City's most eclectic, yet earthy, neighborhood.

Times Square and Forty-second Street

Less than two miles north of the Village you'll find the bright neon lights, megahotels, and anything-but-subtle tourist shops and restaurants that define Times Square. Like the billboards that loom from the rooftops above, everything is grand and bright. All major transportation goes to Times Square and cabs are plentiful, but parking is not. Go to either the Times Square-West Forty-second Street station (N, Q, R, S, W, 1, 2, 3, or 7 train), the West Forty-second Street-Port Authority Bus Terminal station (A, C, or E train), or even the West Forty-second Street-Bryant Park station (B, D, F, or V train) a block to the east. Although it has been thoroughly cleaned up (cynics say sterilized), it's still a big city and discretion should be exercised when visiting late at night.

A Historical Overview

From as far back as the early part of the twentieth century, the area around Times Square has been home to numerous theaters. It was the place to go for entertainment, and as the city grew it became a focal point. The Manhattan subway has stopped at West Forty-Second Street since 1904. The nearby Port Authority bus terminal brought visitors to the city, and passenger ships docked at piers on the west side of town. In short, it was the first stop for numerous visitors to the city.

A central gathering point, advertisers saw it as a place for grand-style billboards, and theater owners made sure to have dazzling marquees. By 1904 it had become known as the Crossroads of the World. The tradition of dropping the ball on New Year's Eve began early in the twentieth century, decades before Dick Clark was even born.

≡FAST FACT

Along Seventh Avenue in the thirties, the streets are lined with bronze circles depicting the stars of the fashion world, a sort of garment district version of the Hollywood Walk of Fame. You'll find accolades to Donna Karan and Ralph Lauren. On West Thirty-ninth Street and Seventh Avenue, you'll also find a giant statue of a garment worker sewing on an old Singer sewing machine. This is a tribute to the generations of immigrant workers who made America's clothing right here (and still do). This is also the area to find designer sample sales.

Times Square and Forty-second Street went largely unregulated in many respects. Primarily a nonresidential neighborhood, the area around West Forty-second Street became a haven for anyone who could do business with the visitors coming into the city, from merchants to prostitutes. Always a home for the latest trend in cinema, Forty-second Street movie houses ran into competition as theaters were built in neighborhoods throughout the boroughs after World War II.

Times Square went through a decline that lasted through the late 1990s, but that all changed dramatically with the beginning of the new millennium. Disney has been a leader in completely rehabilitating the area. The neighborhood was radically overhauled with new stores, and the old historic theaters were revamped.

Walking around Times Square and Forty-second Street today, you'll see the usual big, bright, and brassy giant neon lights—the lights of Broadway. Don't stop and look up without stepping into an alcove, or you might get knocked over. Thousands of people work in the large office buildings around the area, including lots of media.

Times Square is where Broadway and Seventh Avenue cross as Broadway slants its way down the city from the west side toward the east side. Standing in Times Square (really a triangle), you can see a bevy of massive billboards, huge storefronts, major hotels, marquees, fast-food eateries, and hordes of people, not to mention constant traffic.

Suggested Itinerary

Times Square and Forty-second Street are always full of activity. There's a lot to do, so choose carefully. To start, visit the actual Times Square between Forty-second and Forty-seventh streets and Broadway and Seventh Avenue. Look up at the myriad immense billboards and watch your kids take in the experience. Look at the new Times Square Studio on Forty-fourth Street and Broadway. From behind those glass windows, *Good Morning America* is broadcast live every weekday morning. If you get there early enough, you can watch them do the show.

Get tickets to see a Broadway show. From West Forty-second to West Fifty-fourth streets, you'll find nearly forty shows at spectacular old and new theaters. You can stop at the TKTS booths (pronounced tee-kay-tee-ess) on West Forty-seventh Street and Broadway or at South Street Seaport, downtown, to purchase reduced-price tickets for many Broadway shows. Chapter 14 covers Broadway performances in greater detail.

 **RAINY DAY FUN**

The flagship Toys Я Us store on West Forty-fourth Street and Sixth Avenue (Avenue of the Americas) is a must-see for everybody. Young children should take a spin on the giant Ferris wheel, with its fourteen different cars modeled after famous toys, but there's also the roaring *T. Rex* from *Jurassic Park* and an entire Empire State Building made of LEGOs. There's a two-story Barbie dollhouse, and the life-size Candy Land candy store is always a big hit. The "R" Zone is filled with the latest electronics, from games to media.

Check out some of the remodeled, reopened theaters, such as the New Amsterdam on West Forty-second Street. The 1903 theater was the original home of the Ziegfeld Follies and was remodeled and reopened by Disney in 1997. The art deco facade was added in the 1940s and remains on this architecturally stunning theater. The New

Victory Theater, dating back to 1900, was restored a few years earlier. This was a former home to numerous productions in the early part of the twentieth century before becoming a popular burlesque house in the 1930s. For many years, these theaters were "dark" (with no performances) and did nothing but deteriorate amid the decadence that was Forty-second Street. Today they are worth seeing, at least from the outside, and if you are fortunate you'll get tickets for a show there. The New Victory Theater hosts many types of shows, often for kids, including acrobatic acts and other fun events.

Stop by the Hilton Theater (formerly the Ford Center for the Performing Arts), which opened in 1998. The building uses rescued architectural elements from two demolished New York landmark theaters, the Lyric and the Apollo, and is one of the biggest and most dazzling theaters in the city. Tours are available; call 212-556-4750. The cost is $12 per person, $10 for students.

Check out the New Forty-second Street Studios at 229 West Forty-second Street (between Seventh and Eighth avenues), a state-of-the-art, all-glass building housing rehearsal studios, the workshop/experimental theater the Duke, and the American Airlines Theater.

Teens will gravitate to the Hard Rock Cafe, Quicksilver (a skateboarder's paradise), and the space-age games at Lazar Park on West Forty-sixth Street by Seventh Avenue. Dad and the guys will want to stop in at the ESPN Zone, while the little ones will be enthralled by the Hello Kitty store. The whole family will love Madam Tussauds and the new Ripley Odditorium.

There's plenty of shopping to do here. Be forewarned that many of the smaller places sell overpriced junk; don't get suckered. There are lots of places to eat, including an Applebee's and the biggest McDonald's you'll ever see.

When it returns in 2008, you can head west and check out the Intrepid Sea, Air & Space Museum, off Pier 86 in the Hudson, or head east to Fifth Avenue and visit the incredible New York Public Library between Fortieth and Forty-second streets.

Take a stroll through Bryant Park, a seven-acre park that was recently renovated and now sports lovely gardens, interesting statues, plenty of chairs for outdoor concerts or fashion shows, and a grill. The park is situated behind the library (and over stacks of thousands of books stored underground) on Sixth Avenue between West Fortieth and West Forty-second streets.

RAINY DAY FUN

If it gets rainy and cold, take a break from the elements and check out some of the incredible hotels in the area, including the Marriott Marquis (only revolving rooftop restaurant in New York), W New York, The Muse, Millennium Broadway, the brand new Time Hotel, or the classic Algonquin.

If you have time, stroll down West 46th Street between Eighth and Ninth avenues and check out Restaurant Row (page 280), with its wide selection of first-rate dining (and entertainment in several of the establishments). Another option is to dine at the theater crowd's longtime favorite, Sardi's, on Forty-fourth between Broadway and Eighth Avenue.

Harlem

North of 110th Street, the neighborhood of Harlem covers some six square miles and has been one of America's preeminent African American communities for decades. Divided by Fifth Avenue into Harlem and East Harlem, the overall neighborhood, which also includes Spanish Harlem, has a long history that has seen its share of both high and low points. To get to Harlem, take the A, D, 1, or 9 train to 125th Street. The 2 and 3 also stop at Lenox Avenue.

═FAST FACT

Former president Bill Clinton opened his headquarters in Harlem at the Adam Clayton Powell Jr. State Office Building plaza in 2001. Clinton chose Harlem to show his support of the African American community, and community leaders welcomed him.

Harlem's Dutch Roots

Originally a Dutch settlement back in 1658 (called Nieuw Haarlem), the area grew into an affluent section of the city in the 1800s, with estates, farms, and even plantations. If they became successful, immigrants from the Lower East Side commonly moved north to this rapidly growing area.

It was thought that the new subway lines of the early 1900s would further the growth of this area by making Harlem more easily accessible from the rest of the city. With that in mind, developers began constructing more apartment buildings throughout the neighborhood. The buildings, however, did not fill up. A developer named Phillip Payton bought up many of these empty properties and began turning them over to hundreds of black families, hard pressed for housing in the city. By 1915, nearly a quarter of a million black families had moved in, and an equal number of white families had moved out.

By the 1920s, Harlem was the largest black community in the United States and gave birth to the Harlem Renaissance. Harlem was filled with popular nightspots, including the famous Cotton Club, which is still in business. Jazz greats could be seen and heard performing all over the neighborhood. White audiences traveled north to hear the likes of Count Basie, Duke Ellington, and Cab Calloway. Literary legends like Langston Hughes and James Baldwin also grew up in this thriving community.

Harlem's fortunes faltered after the stock market crash and the Great Depression. The area declined in the following decades, and the neighborhood became known for its high rates of crime and drug abuse. Recently, Harlem has begun to fight back and is once again emerging as a cultural center. The famed Apollo Theater returned, and restaurants, clubs, parks, and new housing finally began to crop up again in Harlem in the 1990s. Developers are going full tilt, and national retailers have established outlets where none existed before. Today, Harlem is a busy, growing community once again.

TRAVEL TIP

Harlem, Your Way! is a tour company with several fascinating offerings including daily walking and bus tours. It has gospel tours, gospel brunch visits, jazz tours, architecture tours by foot or bicycle, and others. It is located at 129 West 130th Street, 212-690-1687, *www.harlem yourwaytours.com.*

A Visit to Harlem

Stop at the classic Apollo Theater on 125th Street between Seventh and Eighth avenues. It's one of the neighborhood's greatest landmarks and has seen a long list of legendary performers in its nearly century-old history. Catch a show (particularly on amateur night) or take the tour. Another option is to see a production at the National Black Theater on Fifth Avenue between 125th and 126th streets (212-722-3800).

Browse the Studio Museum; it features a history of Harlem on Lenox Avenue between 125th and 126th streets. Stop at the New York Public Library's Schomburg Center for Research in Black Culture on Lenox Avenue at 135th Street.

Have a weekend gospel brunch at the new rendition of the old Cotton Club on West 125th Street ($32 per person), or enjoy the finest soul food in town at Sylvia's, on Lenox and 126th Street (see page 334).

🧳 TRAVEL TIP

Harlem has become a major shopping area, with branches of national chains such as Old Navy, Disney, Body Shop, and Modells stores lining 125th Street. Despite a crackdown, there are still some of the ever-popular street vendors offering music, books, incense, dashikis, and African sculpture. The Malcolm Shabazz Harlem Market, which features fabulous African wares, can be found at 52 West 116th Street off Lenox Avenue.

Take a trip west to Riverside Drive at 120th Street and visit Riverside Church, with its 400-foot carillon tower and a spectacular view looking out over the Hudson River.

Take a tour featuring the gospel music of Harlem.

CHAPTER 6

Must-See Attractions

WHERE TO GO, what to see. New York has so much to offer that the decision can seem daunting. Take it a step at a time. You probably have a short list in your mind of things you or the family want to see and do. Start with that, then go through the list of must-see and landmark attractions in this chapter and the next and decide what you can do in the number of days you have allotted for your visit. Of course, the ages and interests of your vacation party and the time of the year will determine some of your choices.

Central Park

- 🚇 59th Street entrance: West 59th Street-Columbus Circle (A, B, C, D, or 1 train)
- 🚇 All entrances between West 59th Street and West 110th Street: (B or C trains)
- 📞 311 (in N.Y.C.)
- 📞 212-NEW-YORK (639-9675) (out of town)
- ✉ www.centralparknyc.org

Central Park is the heart of Manhattan. For more than 150 years, it has provided sustenance to the mind, body, and spirit of the town and its inhabitants. This precious 843-acre plot is the green space and front yard to more than half the island's inhabitants, who come to run, walk their dogs, listen to free concerts, meditate, unwind, and watch their children play in the twenty-one different playgrounds. It truly is an oasis in the middle of the city, exactly what the designer, Frederick Law Olmsted, had in mind when he conceived the idea in the tradition of the great parks of Paris and London.

Chapter 8 covers Central Park in depth because there is so much to see and do in this green haven. Put aside at least an afternoon to tour it, no matter what time of year you visit.

TRAVEL TIP

Some of the most significant sights are the city's museums. If you plan to mix one or several of the major museums into your itinerary, you'll need to plan accordingly. For instance, the American Museum of Natural History will take at least three hours for the most basic of highlights, as will the Metropolitan Museum of Art. Try a mix: art followed by science. The fabulous Rose Center for Earth and Space adjoins the Museum of Natural History.

Young children will want to say hello to the *Balto* statue, the famous Alaskan sled dog; play on the giant *Alice in Wonderland* statue; float and race boats; and ride on the carousel. Everyone will want to visit the small zoo, famous for its polar bears, seals, and petting zoo. In the winter there's outdoor ice-skating, and in the spring and summer there are boat rides. True romantics will want to eat a meal at the fabulous Tavern on the Green or take a carriage ride through the park. There are also free concerts around the band shell in the summer and a Shakespeare in the Park series. No one can go through the park without passing Strawberry Fields, the green space Yoko Ono dedicated to her husband, John Lennon.

Location and Hours

The park is right in the middle of Manhattan, from West Fifty-ninth Street north to West 110th Street, and from Fifth to Eighth avenues. Even though the park is a wonder during the day, no one should enter after sunset unless there's a crowd going to an event. There are free daily walking tours throughout the park. Call the park for a schedule.

Ellis Island

🚇 South Ferry station (1 train), Whitehall Street station (R or W train), or Bowling Green station (4 or 5 train), then Circle Line Statue of Liberty ferry

📞 212-363-3200

✎ *www.nps.gov/ellis*

For sixty years starting in the early 1890s, Ellis Island was the first stop on American shores for nearly twelve million immigrants from all over the world. Their first stop was the federal immigration facility, now the Ellis Island Immigration Museum, a major tourist attraction. Located just north of the Statue of Liberty, the Ellis Island Immigration Museum combines photos and items from the past with modern technology, including computers that help visitors trace their heritage. Ellis Island attractions include the following:

- A live play with actors portraying events surrounding the immigration experience. The play changes periodically.
- Two small theaters feature the film *Island of Hope, Island of Tears*, which recounts the history of the famed island.
- A spacious gallery, Treasures from Home, houses photos and cherished objects from the homeland.
- The American Immigrant Wall of Honor contains the names of more than half a million immigrants, from the great-grandparents of George Washington to those of Jay Leno and maybe your own ancestors.

- The American Family Immigration History Center, a resource for immigration history, featuring state-of-the-art computer technology. Visitors can trace their roots and receive a print-out of their family's background information.
- An indoor/outdoor restaurant on the premises offers a breath-taking view of the New York City skyline.

Ellis Island should be part of your visit to the Statue of Liberty. They are right next to each other, just off the foot of Manhattan in the harbor between New York and New Jersey.

Location, Hours, and Fees

The park is open from 9 A.M. to 5 P.M. every day except December 25, with extended hours during peak seasons. A roundtrip ferry ride costs $11.50 for adults, $9.50 for seniors sixty-two and over, and $4.50 for children four to twelve; it's the only transportation to and from the island. The ferry leaves Castle Clinton Monument in lower Manhattan. Call 212-269-5755 for ferry information. You can also get to the island from Liberty State Park in New Jersey. There is far less of a crowd leaving from there.

Statue of Liberty

📧 Liberty Island
🚇 South Ferry station (1 train), Whitehall Street station (R or W train), or Bowling Green station (4 or 5 train), then Circle Line Statue of Liberty ferry
📞 212-363-3200
🖊 *www.nps.gov/stli*

After the terrorist attacks of September 11, the interior of the Statue of Liberty was closed to tourists for more than two years. But the public has been welcomed back for the unique experience of personally interacting with this national icon. New Yorkers grow up with the lady and think of her as family.

You can walk the lobby and the promenade, view the remarkable museum (a favorite with the kids who love the full-sized replicas of the statue's face and foot), see Fort Wood, and take in a spectacular view from the tenth-floor pedestal observation level. The torch and crown are closed to the public.

The History

The Statue of Liberty was officially dedicated in 1886. She towers some 305 feet above the Hudson River, and she has welcomed ships into the land of liberty for more than 100 years. In 1986, Lady Liberty received a full facelift and makeover, just in time for her 100th birthday.

Location, Hours, and Fees

The Statue of Liberty stands at the gateway to the harbor, just off the tip of Manhattan on Liberty Island, a stone's throw from neighboring Ellis Island. You'll have a tremendous sense of what America, freedom, and democracy are all about after spending a day visiting these two sites. Free ranger-guided tours are given throughout the day, and audio guides in several languages can be rented for $6.

A roundtrip ferry ride costs $11.50 for adults, $9.50 for seniors sixty-two and older, and $4.50 for children four to twelve; it's the only transportation to and from the statue. The National Park Service limits the number of people allowed into the statue and issues Time Passes. Passes are given out with your ferry ticket on a first-come, first-served basis. For advance ferry tickets, call 1-866-STATUE4 (782-8834) or go online at *www.statuereservations.com*. There is a $1.75 handling fee for advance tickets. The park is open from 9 A.M. to 5 P.M. every day except December 25, with extended hours during peak seasons. Ferry tickets can be purchased at the Castle Clinton Monument in lower Manhattan starting at 8:30 A.M. Ferries leave starting at 9:30 A.M. (8:30 A.M. during the summer months) and sail every twenty to thirty minutes. For current scheduling, call 1-866-STATUE4 (782-8834) or go online at *www.circlelinedowntown.com*.

≡FAST FACT

You can research your family's heritage for free online at *www.ellis island.org*. If your ancestors were immigrants and they are not listed, you can have them added and inscribed on the American Immigrant Wall of Honor on Ellis Island and carry on your family history for generations to come.

Because it draws huge crowds, it's a good idea to set out for the statue in the morning. Waiting in line can be very hot in the summer, so dress accordingly. Bring sunscreen, and wear a hat. If possible, go on a weekday rather than a weekend, when the lines are simply too long. You can also get to the island from Liberty State Park in New Jersey. There is far less of a crowd leaving from there.

Due to increased security measures, all bags and knapsacks are searched and there is a bit of a wait to get through security. Bring your camera for some terrific shots of the statue.

Empire State Building

- 350 5th Avenue (between 33rd and 34th streets)
- East 33rd Street station (6 train) or West 34th Street-Herald Square station (B, D, F, N, Q, R, V, or W train)
- 212-736-3100
- *www.esbnyc.com*

The famed Eighth Wonder of the World was first opened in 1931, and for many years it was the tallest building in the world. The Empire State Building is one of the city's icons, immortalized in dozens of films such as *King Kong, Sleepless in Seattle* (when Tom Hanks finally meets Meg Ryan atop its observation deck), and *Independence Day.* Its upper floors are adorned with lights that change colors for special occasions (such as red and green for the holidays), casting a glow over the vast skyline that surrounds it. The view from the top is one you'll never forget.

Nearly four million people visit this signature landmark annually, and more than 120 million have visited in its lifetime. The observatories, one on the eighty-sixth floor (1,050 feet high with indoor and outdoor viewing) and the other on the 102nd floor (1,250 feet high and glass enclosed), offer breathtaking views on a clear day.

The building houses a number of restaurants, retail stores, banks, several ATMs, a twenty-four-hour pharmacy, a currency exchange, and even a post office. Tickets are sold on the concourse level, just above the ornate marble lobby. The building's Web site has activities for children and a chance for them to win a free admission ticket.

The Skyride

✆ 1-888-SKY-RIDE (759-7433)

✆ 212-279-9777

✐ www.skyride.com

An additional attraction for children in particular in the Empire State Building is the New York Skyride, an interactive flight-simulated tour of New York City that has you flying over thirty famous New York sites. The fourteen-minute static shows and twelve-minute wild ride are located on the second floor. Pregnant women and children under three feet tall are not allowed on the ride.

Hours and Fees

Observatory prices are $18 for adults; $16 for seniors and youths between twelve and seventeen; $12 for children ages six to twelve; children five and under are free. Tickets for the 102nd floor are sold only at the Observatory ticket office on the second floor and cost $15 in addition to the regular ticket price. The Observatory is open 8 A.M. to 2 A.M., 365 days a year. The last elevator leaves forty-five minutes before closing.

The Skyride is open from 10 A.M. to 10 P.M., 365 days a year (shortened hours on January 1 and December 24, 25, and 31). Tickets cost $25.50 for adults, $18.50 for seniors sixty-five and older and youths twelve to seventeen, and $17.50 for children six through eleven. Five-year-olds and under are free, but they have to be over three feet tall.

Combination tickets are available for the Skyride and Observatory, and both the Observatory and Skyride are part of the CityPass package (see page 162 for more information on CityPass).

American Museum of Natural History and Rose Center for Earth and Space

   ⌨ West 81st Street and Central Park West
   🚇 West 81st Street-Museum of Natural History station (B or C train)
   📞 212-769-5100 (information)
   📞 212-769-5200 (ticketing)
   ✑ *www.amnh.org*

Founded by Theodore Roosevelt in the late 1800s, this museum is one of the city's gems. It's a must-see attraction for visitors of all ages, especially children. Currently it houses more than thirty-two million specimens and has a research staff of 200. It will take at least a half a day to hit the highlights of the museum with the new and improved Rose Center and Hayden Planetarium, the IMAX theater, and four floors of dinosaur bones, preserved animal specimens, gems, and scientific displays about life on this planet.

The most wonderful thing about this museum is how little and yet how much it has changed. You can show your kids your favorite exhibits, such as the nearly century-old model of a giant mosquito or the huge slice of a 1,300-year-old giant Sequoia tree—and yet there are always new discoveries, new wings, and new state-of-the-art exhibits. Look for the new Hall of Human Origins, which presents the most comprehensive evidence of human evolution ever assembled; the newly reorganized 3,700-specimen gem collection; and the newly refined shape of the ninety-four-foot giant blue whale suspended over the redone Hall of Ocean Life.

🧳 TRAVEL TIP

Remember to bring a student ID card or a card showing that you qualify for senior rates. Almost all sights have lower prices for seniors, and many do for students. There are often discounts for AAA members, and look for coupons in tourist brochures and on the Internet.

While exhibits change, some of the permanent exhibits to catch include the new Earth Event Wall, which broadcasts current news of earthquakes, volcanoes, storms, and other natural occurrences using live-action videos and computer animation. Also check out the Hall of Biodiversity on the first floor, where you can step into a rain forest and also see a twenty-odd-pound New Jersey lobster from the turn of the century while you learn about the changing environment and extinction. The museum's popular indoor butterfly exhibit opens in the winter months.

Other halls include African Mammals, Human Biology and Evolution, several fossil halls (including one on primitive mammals and two devoted to dinosaurs that are spectacular—*Jurassic Park* come to life), and Reptiles and Amphibians. Several exhibitions feature the peoples and cultures of the world, including halls of African, Asian, South American, and Pacific Peoples. For children ages five through twelve, there is the Discovery Room, where they can touch and re-create many of the objects they've seen in the museum itself. Some of the museum highlights include:

- A huge skeleton of the awesome *Tyrannosaurus rex,* with six-inch teeth in a four-foot jaw
- The Star of India, weighing 563 karats, the world's largest star sapphire
- The Cape York meteorite, the largest meteorite on display in the world (thirty-four tons)—so big that it has to be supported by beams planted in the bedrock beneath the museum

- An actual skeleton of a dodo bird, extinct for more than 300 years
- A fossilized dinosaur embryo and a dinosaur mummy, considered one of the greatest discoveries in the history of paleontology.

Rose Center for Earth and Space

For sheer awesomeness and goggle-eyed wow-ability, nothing beats the new Rose Center for Earth and Space adjoining the Museum of Natural History. This is a twenty-first-century rebuild of the legendary Hayden Planetarium, and it has propelled the museum into the space age with a vengeance. The kids (and you too) will go ga-ga over the exhibits, the interactive areas, and the planetarium show itself. There is something to enthrall every member of your family; even teens will get excited over *SonicVision*, a digitally animated alternative music show. A visit to the Rose Center is a must for any visitor to the city. The view of the building at night is awesome.

Eating Facilities

The museums have an unusually good selection of food. The Museum Food Court, on the lower level next to the subway entrance, is large with many stations serving all kinds of vittles, from barbeque to vegetarian. The Starlight Café in the food court is great for lighter fare: wraps, sandwiches, salads, snacks, drinks, and a kids' menu. It is directly accessible from both the museum and Rose Center. The new Café on One in the Great Gallery near the West Seventy-seventh Street entrance is similar. Café on 4 is a trip. It's a bistro that changes its identity according to the major exhibit. On the first Friday of the month, from 5:30 P.M. to 8 P.M., there is a tapas bar in the lower level of the Rose Center where you can munch on tapas and sip sangria, wine, or soft drinks while listening to live jazz.

There are many unusual shops in the museums: the Museum Shop, Dinostore, the Kiosk, the Butterfly Shop, the Planetarium Shop, and the Satellite Shop.

Hours and Fees

Admission to the museum is by a strongly suggested contribution of $14 for adults, $10.50 for seniors and students with ID, and $8 for children two to twelve. A combination ticket to the Rose Center is $22 for adults, $16.50 for seniors and students, and $13 for children two to twelve. There are several more packages offered involving the IMAX theater and special exhibitions. You can also use CityPass at the American Museum of Natural History (see page 162 for more information). Tickets may be purchased over the phone or online.

≡FAST FACT

The Willamette meteorite—at fifteen and a half tons, the largest meteorite ever discovered in the United States—was once an object of reverence for the Inuit Indians, who come to the museum annually for a private ceremony. It is believed to be four billion years old. You can see it in the Rose Center's Hall of the Universe.

Rockefeller Center

🔲 From West 47th to West 51st streets between 5th and 7th
avenues

🚈 West 47th–50th Street-Rockefeller Center station (B, D, F, or
V train) or 5th Avenue-53rd Street station (E or V train)

✆ 212-632-3975

✍ www.rockefellercenter.com

Since 1934, Rockefeller Center has stood amidst all of the change and growth of the city around it. The nineteen buildings that make up the eleven-acre complex house numerous corporations, including some of the leaders in media and communications. Recently renovated, Rockefeller Center remains one of the most popular tourist stops in New York City.

Named for John D. Rockefeller, who initiated the construction of what was originally designed as three office buildings and the Metropolitan Opera, the complex continued to grow. The focal point of Rockefeller Center, and the building most associated with it, is the GE Building, also known as 30 Rock.

≡FAST FACT

The Rockefeller family is one of the legendary New York dynasties. John D. Rockefeller Sr. founded the Standard Oil Company and amassed a fortune. In later life he became a philanthropist, donating money and resources to numerous causes through the Rockefeller Foundation. Nelson Rockefeller, John Rockefeller's grandson, was a four-time governor of New York and served as vice president under Gerald Ford from 1974–1977.

While touring 30 Rock and its neighbors, you'll find an abundance of fine art, including sculptures, murals, and mosaics. The designers developed a motif for the artwork, called "New Frontiers and the March for Modern Civilization," which expresses the vision behind the new venture.

You can go up to the newly opened Top of the Rock Observation Deck with truly spectacular indoor or outdoor viewing of New York from seventy stories up. It's open 365 days a year from 8 A.M. to midnight (last elevator at 11 P.M.). Reserved-ticket admission is $17.50 for adults, $16 for seniors sixty-two and older, and $11.25 for kids six to twelve. Get more information at 212-698-2000 or *www.topoftherock nyc.com*, where you can find various add-ons and promotions.

Outside the GE Building, take time to stroll the promenade from Fifth Avenue to the Channel Gardens, where nearly 20,000 varieties of plants can be found. Incidentally, the Channel Gardens were given their name by journalists, who noted that the promenade was set between the French and English buildings. Just before the gardens meet the skyscraper, you'll find the famed ice-skating rink, which by summer becomes the outdoor seating for the Rock Center Café and the Sea Grill Restaurant.

Overlooking the skating rink is *Prometheus*, an eighteen-foot-tall, eight-ton gilded bronze statue. The mythical Greek figure, kitschy but fun as it really seems to be flying, is shown stealing fire from the gods as a gift for man. Every year since 1936, from early December through early January, the famous Rockefeller Center Christmas tree is set up overlooking the rink. The tree-lighting ceremony, complete with a bevy of entertainers, draws thousands of onlookers. Thousands more visitors stop by to see the dazzling tree during the holidays.

The entire area is replete with stunning artwork and period architecture. Shops are also abundant around the GE Building, and there are more than forty restaurants, encompassing fine dining, fast food, and all points in between.

Below 30 Rock, underground walkways called concourses connect most of the buildings, allowing visitors and the nearly 300,000 people who work in Rockefeller Center to stay warm and dry during inclement weather.

 ## JUST FOR PARENTS

High atop 30 Rock sits the famous Rainbow Room restaurant. Opened in 1934, the Rainbow Room has long been a fashionable and romantic place for fine food and a spectacular view. A revolving dance floor, fabulous views through big glass windows, and an orchestra add to the ambiance. It is now open to the public on a limited basis—currently Friday and Saturday dinner and dancing, a grand Sunday brunch, and year-end holiday feasts. There's a strict dress code. Children are welcome with an adult. Call 212-632-5000 for reservations or log on to *www.rainbowroom.com*.

Guided Tours

There are three interesting and very worthwhile guided tours offered, and all leave from the NBC Experience Store. Rockefeller Center tours begin every day, except Thanksgiving and December 25, at 11 A.M., 1 P.M., 3 P.M., and 5 P.M. There is no 5 P.M. tour on Sunday. Tours take one hour and cost $12 for adults and $10 for seniors and children six to twelve.

The new Art & Observation tour adds a stop at the seventy-story Top of the Rock Observation Deck for a panoramic view of New York City. These tours depart every two hours, from 10 A.M. to 4 P.M., and take one hour and thirty minutes. Cost is $20 per person.

The NBC Studio tour costs $18.75, or $15.50 for seniors and children six to twelve. Tours leave every thirty minutes, from 8:30 A.M. to 4:30 P.M., Monday to Thursday; every fifteen minutes Friday and Saturday from 9:30 A.M. to 5:30 P.M.; and Sundays until 4:30 P.M. These are very popular and reservations are strongly recommended.

You can take a combination Rockefeller Center/NBC tour package for $23.45; tickets are available only through their call center at 212-664-7174. Children under six are not permitted, and there are no bathroom facilities available on the tours. Call for more tour information and scheduling changes for all tours at 212-664-3700.

Times Square

🚇 Times Square-West 42nd Street station (N, Q, R, S, W, 1, 2, 3, or 7 train) or West 42nd Street-Port Authority Bus Terminal (A, C, or E train)

🖰 www.timessquarenyc.org

Once the seediest part of Manhattan, Times Square has been completely revitalized. Now it is a fun New York day and/or night spot that is a family favorite. Everyone loves just walking through the bustling streets and looking at the glowing billboards while street vendors offer their wares, from pastel portraits to your name in hand-painted decorative letters. Every year, twenty-six million people visit Times Square.

New Yorkers call the intersection of Broadway and Forty-second Street the Crossroads of the World, because it's said that if you stand at the corner long enough you'll meet everyone you've ever known.

≡FAST FACT

Times Square celebrated its 100th anniversary under its current name in 2004. In 1904, when the new New York Times building opened (once the second-tallest structure in New York City), the square around it was renamed after the famous newspaper. To inaugurate this change, the Times dropped the first ball on New Year's Eve. Today more than a million people watch the ball drop on New Year's Eve from Times Square.

The Times Square neighborhood is located between West Forty-second and West Forty-fourth streets from Sixth to Eighth avenues. The four-block stretch has something for everyone (see page 85). Kids love the flagship Toys Я Us store (with its famous indoor Ferris wheel), Madame Tussauds Wax Museum, a Hello Kitty store, as well as the ESPN Zone restaurant and arcade and nearby Hershey's chocolate store and Lazer Park. Favorites of teens are the MTV studio and store, as well as the Hard Rock Cafe, Quicksilver (for skateboarders), and the Virgin Megastore, where celebrities are often on hand to sign CDs. It's also great fun to stand outside looking into the street-level ABC Studios when a show is being aired.

At night, the stars of the show are the spectacular advertisements. In fact, that's their name: "Spectaculars." Parents might go after-hours to the legendary B.B. King's. There are also many good family, chain, and fast-food restaurants in the area, as well as multiplex theaters for the latest in high-admission cinema. You can get all sorts of information, in addition to theater ticket and MetroCard sales, at the Times Square Visitors Center, 1560 Broadway. Call 212-869-1890. Free walking tours are offered on Fridays at noon.

World Trade Center Site

West Street (between Liberty and Vesey streets)

World Trade Center station (E train)

www.wtc.com

In the aftermath of the terrorist attacks of September 11, many visitors to New York City feel compelled to visit the site of the tragedy. Eight buildings were destroyed or had to be subsequently demolished, and nearly 3,000 lives were taken when hijackers flew two jet planes into the 110-story Twin Towers.

Visitors to the site can view its rebirth. Already completed is 7 World Trade Center, and work has begun on the tallest building, Freedom Tower. It is expected to be completed in early 2011. The building is full of symbolism. It will be 1,776 feet tall, its base is the same dimensions as the towers it replaces, and it will have glass parapets at the heights of the two fallen towers. You can view a massive WTC timeline made up of large panels that run along Church Street.

In January 2004, the Lower Manhattan Development Corporation announced the winners of an international competition for the World Trade Center Memorial that drew more than 5,000 entrants from sixty-three countries. *Reflecting Absence*, designed by Michael Arad and Peter Walker, is composed of two large reflecting pools amid a large open space of trees. The names of those who died in the attacks are to be distributed, in no particular order, around one of the reflecting pools. On a lower level there will be an underground space for exhibits, a research library, and lecture halls. The unidentified remains of those killed will be housed in a room at this level as well.

CHAPTER 7

New York City Landmarks

AS THE SONG says, New Yorkers want to be king of the hill, top of the heap, A-number-1. This drive, the famous New York drive (some call it pushiness or edginess), has made the city the phenomenon it is. New York has long been a pioneer in the world of architecture, and the city includes some of the most recognizable landmarks in the country. New Yorkers may sometimes be smug in their belief that their city is the center of the universe, the arbiter of taste, the starter of trends, but these landmarks were the biggest and the best when they were built and are still enduring symbols of vision and accomplishment today.

Chrysler Building

⬚ East 42nd Street and Lexington Avenue
🚊 Grand Central-East 42nd Street station (S, 4, 5, 6, or 7 train)

When the Chrysler Building was finished, it overtook the Eiffel Tower to become the tallest in the world. It was in a three-way race for the title (Forty Wall Street, now the Trump Building, also briefly held the top spot) and secured the honor—for only a year—after the builders erected a secretly built and delivered spire tower. The Empire State Building ultimately claimed the title of tallest building when it was completed in 1931.

The Chrysler Building is still the tallest brick building in the world and the second tallest building in New York. With seventy-seven floors, standing 1,046 feet high (319 meters), the Chrysler Building is an art deco masterpiece that continues to inspire New Yorkers every night with its illuminated crown of steel. Noted for its creative and clever use of automotive ornamental detail, such as the radiator-cap gargoyles and hood-ornament eagles on the eight corners of the sixty-first floor, the building has been a favorite of architecture buffs for more than seventy-five years.

≡FAST FACT

In the 1930s, during Prohibition, the Chrysler Building housed an ultra-swanky speakeasy known as the Cloud Club on its sixty-sixth through sixty-eighth floors. It was said to have lavish pink-marble bathrooms and a bar featuring Bavarian wood, and members had their own private lockers. The spectacular floors have since been dismantled.

The building is known for its elegant lobby, which features African red marble and a majestic mural depicting the construction of the building itself, with portraits of some of the actual workers. The lobby was once a showroom for Chrysler-Plymouth cars. Each of the twenty-one elevators has a different design.

Grand Central Terminal

⌨ East 42nd Street and Park Avenue (Lexington and Vanderbilt Avenues)

🚊 Grand Central-East 42nd Street station (S, 4, 5, 6, or 7 train)

✆ 212-340-2210

✎ www.grandcentralterminal.com

First of all, it's the Grand Central Terminal, not station. Sticklers will point out that train lines begin and end here, not pass through. Before you go in, look at the clock above the entrance. The sculptural group was the largest in the world when crafted. It surrounds a clock thirteen feet in diameter—the largest example of Tiffany glass ever made.

A Visual Tour

Inside, start by the information desk and look up at the clock. Countless liaisons have begun here through the years. The four clock faces are solid opal and worth between $10 million and $20 million. You can't see it, but there's a secret staircase inside the booth that leads down to an information desk on the lower level. If you look up, you will see a beautifully painted astronomical mural, its colors radiant after a recent restoration.

If you're sharp-eyed, you'll notice something weird—the zodiac is backwards. After decades of debate on the cause, the official reason (possibly politically motivated) is that the artist, Paul Helleu, wanted to show the celestial sphere from the outside. Keep looking up and you'll see the glint of real gold on the chandeliers. This was a surprise to the restorers since it was always assumed the light fixtures (a real innovation when they were made) were brass.

 TRAVEL TIP

The kids will love the whispering gallery in the terminal. Go down the Oyster Bar ramps and station one person on either side of the entrance arch. Face the corner and whisper. A quirk in the acoustics makes the whisper audible to the person on the other side of the arch.

Notice the grand staircases. Years ago, there was only one, but restoration uncovered evidence that the original architect wanted a pair to balance out the huge room. The second one was constructed almost ninety years later. The original is the one by the steakhouse. Near the original staircase, look up and you'll see a dark patch. This was left by the restorers to show what the ceiling looked like before cleaning. Lab tests showed that the dirt is really tar and nicotine from tobacco smoke.

Before you leave the main level, look around at the stone carvings, and you'll see many acorns and oak leaves. These were taken by "Commodore" Cornelius Vanderbilt, the railroad magnate who built the terminal, as his family crest symbols.

The terminal is a veritable cornucopia of consumption and a festival of foods. There are retail shops in this one building that would rival any shopping mall or busy retail street. Gifts, necessities, and indulgences are around every corner and in every concourse. There are clothes for the entire family, toys, electronics, health and beauty, jewelry, books—and don't forget the New York Transit Museum Gallery and Store (see page 182). There are also services such as a pharmacy, optician, bank, watch repair, shoeshine, and currency exchange.

≡ FAST FACT

The long-running radio program "Grand Central Station" started with the words, "As a bullet train seeks its target, shining rails in every part of our great country are aimed at Grand Central Station, heart of the nation's greatest city: Grand Central Station! Crossroads of a million lives! Gigantic stage on which are played a thousand dramas daily."

Eating Facilities

Grand Central is an epicenter for enormous eating. The world-famous Oyster Bar & Restaurant ($$–$$$) on the lower level has been dishing out an immense selection of fresh seafood since the day the terminal opened in 1913. It boasts thirty types of fish and thirty types of oysters! Even more astounding is the wine list, which offers seventy selections by the glass. Nonseafood-eaters can try the sirloin or chicken.

Check out the Dining Concourse. Its more than twenty eateries serve every cuisine you'd care to sample. The kids will love the choices and will relish eating in the dining car seating areas that emulate trains of long ago. This is also the home of three sit-down restaurants: Brooklyn's famous Junior's (see page 300); Two Boots, a kid-friendly, fast, New Orleans-style pizza place; and Zócalo, for Mexican delights.

JUST FOR PARENTS

Although the kids can't go, try to visit the Campbell Apartment, an elegant lounge set inside what was the office of 1920s financier and railroad executive John W. Campbell. He decorated it as the hall of a thirteenth-century Florentine palace. Proper attire is required.

Upstairs, the east end of Grand Central yields another secret surprise: a European-style food hall called the Grand Central Market, where you can buy the highest-quality meats, cheese, vegetables, breads, salads, ready meals, and sweets to take back to the hotel, eat on a picnic, or even have shipped back home.

Up in the balcony reside the upscale restaurants and lounges. Here are Capriani Dolci ($$$) (Northern Italian), Charlie Palmer's Métrazur ($$$) (progressive American cuisine), and kid-fave Michael Jordan's The Steak House N.Y.C. ($$$), modeled after the famous luxury Twentieth Century Limited dining cars.

Hours and Tours

Grand Central is open from 5:30 A.M. to 1:30 A.M. seven days a week. You have a choice of tour options, free or paid. Tours are given Wednesdays by the Municipal Arts Society and a donation is suggested; there is an entirely free (read guilt-free) tour given Fridays that also includes the surrounding neighborhood. Both tours start at 12:30 P.M. Grand Central Tours runs an hour-long walk-through, but you must give them two weeks notice. There is a $5 per-person charge, with a $50 minimum per group. Call 212-340-2345.

New York Public Library

- 5th Avenue and West 42nd Street
- West 42nd Street-Bryant Park station (B, D, F, or V train)
- 212-930-0800
- *www.nypl.org/services/visitors.html*

The Humanities and Social Sciences branch of the New York Public Library is a historic landmark, a masterpiece of Beaux Arts architecture. Built in 1911, it is a two-block literary oasis, housing around six million books (apparently nobody really knows the exact number) plus millions of other documents. The library is a research facility, which means you can't check the books out, but anyone can use it to do research in one of the eleven reading rooms.

📋 TRAVEL TIP

The library hosts a constant stream of traveling exhibitions. Check the library's Web site for a current schedule; if you're lucky you may be able to see a Gutenberg Bible or a copy of the Declaration of Independence, but all of the exhibitions feature insightful commentary on art and literature.

The library's well-trained staff can locate a book for you in anything from a few minutes to nearly an hour, depending on how busy the library is and how far they need to travel to find the book. The stacks extend underground from Fifth to Sixth avenues. Cardholders can borrow books from any of the city's more traditional libraries, including the Mid-Manhattan Library, on Fortieth Street and Fifth Avenue, across the street.

This historic building, however, is indeed worth visiting, even if it's just for a brief look around. Built for $9 million on a $20 million plot—a sum originally raised to fund two libraries—this magnificent structure is guarded in the front by the two world-famous stone lions, *Patience* and *Fortitude*, which have been adopted as the library's mascots and logo. Replicas of the beloved duo are for sale in the library gift shop, book-end sized. (The shop, incidentally, is full of interesting and unusual items.) The interior is brilliantly decorated with marble hallways and staircases leading to the recently renovated main reading room with its original chandeliers and oak tables. The library also houses a magnificent art collection.

≡FAST FACT

The New York Public Library system has eighty-nine locations throughout the five boroughs. In total, it houses more than fifty million items. There are more than two million cardholders; library cards are free for New York City residents, but nonresidents can apply for a card for a $100 fee.

There are numerous divisions within the building, including the Arts and Architecture Division, the Map Division, the Jewish Division, the Oriental Division, the Current Periodical Division, and so on. Special collections include rare books, photography, and prints. Free tours are offered and recommended; they will provide you with a frame of reference—the enormity and grandeur of the building can be intimidating!

Lectures, special exhibits, and presentations are offered in the library. You may also stroll behind the building and visit Bryant Park, which is home to fashion shows and other events and where you can relax with a cappuccino or pastry. In the winter you can even ice skate!

RAINY DAY FUN

Even most New Yorkers don't know that the original stuffed bear that A.A. Milne immortalized in Winnie the Pooh—which belonged to his son, Christopher Robin—can be seen "in the fluff" in the children's section of the Donnell Library, at West Fifty-third Street between Fifth and Sixth avenues (nearest subway stop: Fifth Avenue-Fifty-third Street station; E or V train).

Location, Hours, and Tours

The library can be found on Fifth Avenue between West Fortieth and West Forty-second streets. Building tours are available Tuesday through Saturday at 11 A.M. and 2 P.M., Sunday at 3:30 P.M. Exhibition tours are at 12:30 P.M. and 2:30 P.M. Tuesday to Saturday, and 3:30 P.M. on Sunday. Please call for meeting locations and library hours of operation. The library is closed on most federal holidays.

Intrepid Sea, Air & Space Museum

🖃 Pier 86 (12th Avenue and West 46th Street)
🚇 West 42nd Street-Port Authority Bus Terminal (A, C, or E train)
✆ 212-245-0072
✉ www.intrepidmuseum.com

The USS *Intrepid* is an unusual museum experience the whole family will enjoy. The decommissioned aircraft carrier sits beside the Concorde SST, the submarine USS *Growler,* and the destroyer *Edson* on New York's Hudson River. Together, the air and sea craft provide an education in American flight and warfare technology from World War II to the present.

The Intrepid

The USS *Intrepid* was used by the U.S. Navy from 1942 until the early 1970s and saw action in World War II, the Korean War, and the Vietnam War. At its peak, the great ship housed more than 3,000 sailors and carried more than 100 airplanes and helicopters on its massive deck. The ship, weighing in at nearly 42,000 tons when loaded, is virtually a full military installation at sea, and fighter planes are still perched on the deck for viewing.

Most of the planes featured on the *Intrepid* were never actually carried by the ship, such as the A-12 Blackbird, one of the fastest, highest-flying planes ever built. The CIA had this titanium aircraft designed to photograph activities on the other side of the Berlin Wall during the Cold War. A reproduction of a World War I biplane, complete with propeller, can be found on the lower deck.

TRAVEL TIP

The entire USS *Intrepid* complex closed for renovation and repairs in 2006 and is scheduled to reopen on November 11, 2008. The museum areas will be enhanced and expanded, and many of the military aircraft will be restored. In addition, Pier 86 will be rebuilt. If you visit after the reopening, this listing should give you some idea of what to expect.

Museum Features

The unique seaside museum explores the undersea world, both on the *Growler* and through special exhibitions about submarines and underwater study. Within the museum you'll also find Pioneer's Hall, which looks back at the airplanes of the twentieth century, and the Technologies Hall, which highlights modern technology, including weaponry.

Onboard the ships of the Intrepid Sea, Air & Space Museum, you'll climb narrow staircases and squeeze through tight corridors.

A tribute to the space program features a space capsule retrieved from the sea in the days before the space shuttle made a smooth landing on solid ground. You can also visit a Concorde jet that once flew from London to Paris at supersonic speed.

There is a gift shop on the premises where you can buy the very popular *Intrepid* baseball cap. There is a mess hall inside, and the food is considerably better than that once offered to sailors, with a good selection of sandwiches and hot items.

 RAINY DAY FUN

The Intrepid Sea, Air & Space Museum is actually a good place to go during a rainy or cold day. There's a lot to do below deck, such as pilot a G-force flight simulator or explore the cockpit of a navy A-6 jet fighter. You can also watch a twenty-minute film on the museum and listen to real war stories from the volunteer crew members. There's also a station to send e-mail messages to current troops.

Hours and Fees

Before it closed, the USS *Intrepid* was open 10 A.M. to 5 P.M. weekdays, 6 P.M. on weekends, from April through September, but closed on Mondays October through March. Admission was $14 for adults; $10.50 for students over twelve, seniors, and veterans; and $9.50 for children five through eleven. Self-guided tours of the USS *Intrepid*, USS *Edson*, and USS *Growler* were free with admission. At the time of this writing, no decision was made as to any changes.

Metropolitan Museum of Art

    ⊡ 1000 5th Avenue (at 82nd Street)

    🚇 East 86th Street station (4, 5, or 6 train)

    📞 212-535-7710

    ✎ *www.metmuseum.org*

The Metropolitan (affectionately known as the Met) is one of the top four art museums in the world. It ranks right up there with the Louvre in Paris, the Prado in Madrid, and the Vatican Museum in Vatican City. Even if the kids insist they hate art, the kids' gift shop is entrancing and offers lots of good stuff for less than $10. Besides, few boys have been known to be able to resist the lure of the incredible armor and sword collections or the Egyptian mummies. And what young girl could turn down a tour of the Costume Institute?

There are more than two million pieces in the museum collection, and the Met is so large it will take more than a day to see it all. Your best bet is to target the wings that interest you and your family the most. Check the special exhibits as you wait in line to make your suggested contribution. You can pick up a family guide at the information kiosk or download one online.

☰ FAST FACT

The Costume Institute has a collection of more than 30,000 articles of clothing. The institute puts together exhibits to showcase its vast collection. Items include courtly fashions from the eighteenth century to cutting-edge twenty-first century style.

Let the Tour Begin

As you enter and head to the ticket area in the great hall, you will notice the marble stairway leading up to the famed European collection of nineteenth-century classics. To your left will be Greek and Roman art, and to your right is the Egyptian Wing (where, if you go down the stairs, you will find the gift shop's sale merchandise, often at 50 percent off).

The Egyptian wing features some 36,000 objects, many of which are from the original installation of 1906. You can find ancient jewelry, mummies, sculpture, hieroglyphics, and the famed Temple of Dendur.

≡FAST FACT

The Temple of Dendur is an authentic, full-size Egyptian installation from the early Roman period (about 15 B.C.E.). In 1965, the Met accepted it as a gift from the Egyptian government in recognition of the American contribution to the international campaign to save the ancient Nubian monuments from flooding after the construction of the Aswan High Dam.

The famous collection of weaponry includes armor, firearms, and swords from European, Middle Eastern, and Asian collections, and it even features armor for horses.

The American Wing

The vast American Wing provides a look at 15,000 paintings, sculptures, and decorative arts acquired by the museum since it was established in 1879. Here you'll find a restored Frank Lloyd Wright living room from 1915 and Louis Comfort Tiffany's exquisite fountain. There's a formidable array of American furniture, as well as glass, textiles, quilts, and silver.

African, Oceanic, and American Art

The Met's first floor houses the arts of Africa, Oceania, and the Americas, featuring 11,000 objects spanning 4,000 years in the Michael C. Rockefeller Wing. Works from New Guinea, Melanesia, and Polynesia and stone objects from pre-Columbian cultures of Mexico and Central and South America highlight this vast and very rare collection.

European Art

The first floor is also home to the European sculpture and decorative arts, some medieval art, and twentieth-century art (the famous Van Goghs, Monets, Cézannes, Jackson Pollocks, and Picassos).

On the second floor, along with the European paintings (Renaissance through nineteenth century) and the American Wing, you'll find musical instruments, Asian and Islamic art, and the collection of drawings and prints and photographs.

The Met was named by *Child* magazine as the second most family-friendly art museum in the United States. It has an active schedule for families: gallery tours, projects, workshops, and special family audio and printed guides. The Web site has further details at *www.metmuseum.org/events/ev_family.asp*.

≡ FAST FACT

The Met's extensive collection of European art includes more than 2,000 works. This includes thirty-seven paintings by Monet and twenty-one by Cezanne, making it one of the world's largest collections of Impressionist art.

Eating Facilities

The Met offers a range of dining choices, from the lightest snack to a full sit-down feast. There is a completely redesigned cafeteria ($) on the lower level where you can get hot meals, pasta, salads, soups, and kids' meals. This is the best place to eat with children.

The Petrie Court Café ($$) on the ground floor serves sit-down meals with European-style waiter service. It also offers a self-serve continental breakfast, Sunday brunch, and afternoon tea. If you plan to visit Petrie Court Café, reservations are suggested; call 212-570-3964.

💼 TRAVEL TIP

The Roof Garden Café is located near the European Sculpture Court. Sculptures include works by Bernini and Rodin's *The Burghers of Calais*. Both the café and the sculptures are located on the fifth floor of the museum and afford wonderful views of Central Park.

The American Wing Café is temporarily relocated and is being called the Balcony Café ($). Wherever it is when you visit, it serves wonderful appetizers and drinks to the strains of live classical music. It is not recommended for the kids. A second bar, the Roof Garden Café ($), is located in the spectacular open-air space called The Iris B. and Gerald Cantor Roof Garden. It overlooks Central Park and the Manhattan skyline and is a delightful, even romantic, place to stroll during the summer. Sandwiches and drinks are self-serve. The youngsters are welcome. Cocktails are served between 4 P.M. and 8 P.M. on the roof garden Friday and Saturday only and in the balcony bar.

 JUST FOR PARENTS

The Metropolitan's museum gift shop is superb. You'll find replicas of the jewelry from famous paintings as well as scarves, Christmas ornaments, mouse pads, tea sets, posters, and signed limited editions of contemporary prints. This is a great place to pick up something for the folks back home, and there's always at least one item that screams "New York."

Hours and Fees

The museum is open Tuesday through Sunday from 9:30 A.M. until 5:15 P.M., and until 8:45 P.M. on Fridays and Saturdays. It is closed on January 1, Thanksgiving Day, December 25, and Mondays except on some holidays. Recommended admission is $20 for adults, $15 for seniors sixty-five and older, and $10 for students. Children under twelve are free when accompanied by an adult. Free tours are offered—check the information desk for schedules. Audio tours of the collection are available for rent but are offered free to visitors with sight or hearing problems. Free podcasts are available. There is validated fee parking, but it is limited.

Radio City Music Hall

🖳 1260 6th Avenue (between West 50th and 51st streets)

🚇 West 47th–50th Street-Rockefeller Center station (D, B, F, or V train)

📞 212-247-4777

✐ www.radiocity.com

Billed as the show palace of the nation, Radio City Music Hall opened in December of 1932 as the largest indoor theater in the world. Some 300 million people have now enjoyed entertainment at the famed 6,000-seat theater. The art deco elegance, twenty-four-karat gold-leaf grand foyer ceiling, and newly restored 4,178-pipe Wurlitzer organ create a unique ambiance. It's a mixture of warmth and excitement that makes the theater a special stop for both tourists and New Yorkers. A sixty-by-thirty-foot mural called *The Fountain of Youth* adorns the grand staircase in the main lobby, while the world-famous marquee wraps around the front of the building and spans a city block.

The multitiered theater has housed concerts, awards shows, television productions, family attractions, and film premieres. Although the acoustics and sight lines have always been excellent, a recently completed $122 million renovation to the landmark property has enhanced the theater with state-of-the-art video and audio technology.

☂ RAINY DAY FUN

The Radio City Christmas Spectacular usually runs for nearly two months, from November into January, featuring the Parade of the Wooden Soldiers and Living Nativity shows. The Christmas Spectacular is ideal family fare, but you must call and order tickets well in advance. More than a million people fill Radio City to see the show each year.

Radio City is also known for the Rockettes, who were first formed in 1925 as the Missouri Rockets in St. Louis. By 1932, the precision dance team ended up in New York City on the stage of the brand new Radio City Music Hall. Nearly seventy years later, they are still going strong. The troupe of 150 dancers is famous for its high-kicking chorus line and is now seen both at Radio City and at other events and on television, including the Macy's Thanksgiving Day Parade, Super Bowl halftime, and the presidential inauguration ceremony.

Tours and Fees

If you can't see a show at Radio City Music Hall while you are in town, you might want to take the Stage Door Tour of the theater. Tours cover the premises from the Grand Stage to the backstage. The itinerary is subject to change because of rehearsals and preshow activities. You'll even get to meet a Rockette at the end of the tour.

≡FAST FACT

The sorority of Rockettes includes more than 3,000 women and dates to 1932. There are thirty-six Rockettes at a time, and they must all be trained in tap, jazz, ballet, and modern dance. There are eight costume changes in the ninety-minute Christmas Spectacular Show, and Rockettes have as little as eighty seconds to switch from one costume to the next.

The one-hour tours of Radio City are offered Monday to Sunday from 11 A.M. to 3 P.M. The cost is $17 for adults, $14 for seniors, and $10 for children under twelve. Same-day tour tickets are sold at the Radio City Avenue store. Advance tour and event tickets can be purchased at the Radio City box office or by telephone through Ticketmaster (212-307-7171; a surcharge applies). Radio City is accessible to people with disabilities; arrangements for wheelchairs can be made by calling 212-632-4039.

St. Patrick's Cathedral

🖹 5th Avenue (between 50th and 51st streets)

🚊 West 47th–50th Street-Rockefeller Center station (B, D, F, or V) or 5th Avenue-53rd Street station (E or V train)

📞 212-753-2261

✍ *www.saintpatrickscathedral.org*

Designed by renowned American architect James Renwick and completed in 1879, this magnificent church sits amid the busy Rockefeller Center area and remains the seat of the New York archdiocese. While holiday masses draw crowds and television cameras, numerous tourists visit the ornate Gothic cathedral daily. They stop and look around, awed by the majesty and magnificence of this grand cathedral, and are free to participate in daily masses and confessions as well as the stations of the cross at 6 P.M.

The best-known cathedral in New York City, St. Patrick's is the largest Roman Catholic church in the United States, seating some 2,200 people. With its statues, Rose Window, Tiffany altar, award-winning stations of the cross (from the 1893 Chicago World's Fair), ornate white spires, and sheer size and splendor, the cathedral is a very special stop for nearly three million tourists of all faiths who visit annually.

≡FAST FACT

Across the street from St. Patrick's Cathedral, Atlas bears the weight of the world on his shoulders in Lee Lawrie's 1936 sculpture. The sculpture is the largest in Rockefeller Center. Lawrie also contributed other sculptures and artistic works to New York City, but his depiction of Atlas is his most recognizable.

St. Patrick's Cathedral is but a few steps from Rockefeller Center and Radio City Music Hall, in the heart of midtown Manhattan. It is open to visitors from 6:30 A.M. to 8:45 P.M. It is a marvelous area to stroll through, enjoying the serenity and majesty of the sights and stores of the area, and the cathedral has a lovely crèche for the Christmas holidays. There is a gift shop in the cathedral open from 8:30 A.M. to 8 P.M., and another at 15 East Fifty-first Street (between Fifth and Madison avenues), which is open 10 A.M. to 6 P.M. most evenings. It features religious Belleek china and Lladro porcelain sculptures, as well as rosaries and postcards.

South Street Seaport

⌨ 19 Fulton Street (between Water and Front streets)

🚋 Fulton Street-Broadway-Nassau Street station (A, C, J, M, Z, 2, 3, 4, or 5 train)

✆ 212-732-8257

✎ www.southstreetseaport.com

Avast, ye hardies! Care to be a pirate and ship off to exotic shores? Arrr, this might just be the next best thing. Spanning eleven blocks, South Street Seaport is a combination historic site and shopping mall. Declared a historic landmark in 1967, the seaport was restored and remodeled over the next several years by the Rouse Corporation, the organization that also developed Quincy Market in Boston. The combination of historic ships and architecture, trendy stores, and spectacular views of the Brooklyn Bridge and the harbor make it a popular attraction.

The seaport's cobblestone streets are home to quaint shops, fine restaurants, minimalls, a maritime museum, piers, and, of course, the South Street Seaport Museum's fleet of ships—the country's largest fleet of privately maintained historic vessels.

Ships docked along Pier 16 include several sailing vessels from the nineteenth century, some of which still offer rides. The *Pioneer*, a 102-foot schooner from 1885, sets sail several times daily, starting at 1 P.M. The *W. O. Decker* can hold up to six people for a unique tugboat ride along the river. The *Lettie G. Howard* is a meticulously restored fishing schooner built in 1893 and used today as a training vessel and for occasional public sails. Call 212-748-8590 for information.

 **TRAVEL TIP**

Some sights may have rules and regulations regarding packages, strollers, cameras, and bringing food inside. Some may have other restrictions; for example, pregnant women and young children are not allowed on the Skyride at the Empire State Building.

Other old sailing vessels sit docked along Piers 15 and 16. These include the tall sailing ship *Peking*, one of the largest sailing ships ever built; the *Wavertree*, the largest extant wrought-iron sailing ship; and the *Ambrose*, a lightship once used to guide ships into New York. Walking tours and special exhibits are also available. The tug *Helen McAllister* was built in 1910 and is the only remaining tug of her generation. You may watch her being restored.

Pier 17 is a fantastic attraction in its own right, with more than 100 shops and eateries. The seaside mall will keep your family interested and well-fed for as long as you want to stay. From fast food to sit-down dining, everybody's taste is covered. *Bodies . . . The Exhibition*, a collection of more than twenty human bodies preserved in various poses, found a home here.

South Street Seaport Museum

⊡ 12 Fulton Street, Pier 16 (between Water and Front streets)

🚇 Fulton Street-Broadway-Nassau Street station (A, C, J, M, Z, 2, 3, 4, or 5 train)

📞 212-748-8600

✏ *www.southstseaport.org*

Just inland from the seaport you will find the wonderful South Street Seaport Museum, founded in 1967. Inside this tribute to the vessels of the sea you can view model ships, paintings, prints, and drawings, as well as crafts, sailing gear, shipboard tools, handicrafts, and artifacts from the sailors and fishermen of a bygone era. The museum is also home to thousands of photographs and two million excavation items, many of which are also on display. There are three exhibit areas in all, plus a nearby gallery, children's center, crafts center, and a huge maritime reference library. Not to be missed is the working nineteenth-century press, Bowne & Co. Stationers, where you can have personal items printed on an antique press or purchase unique items and books from the gift shop. Admission is free.

Planning Ahead

To get the most out of a visit to the seaport, it's best to plan for a clear day to enjoy strolling and even going for a boat ride. Unless it's a particularly warm day, it's advisable to have a sweater, jacket, or sweatshirt along, as the East River breezes kick up while you are sailing. You might schedule walking around the seaport to coincide with breakfast or lunch. Remember to give yourself a couple of hours for the museum! The best thing about the seaport is that it provides a little of everything—history, shopping, activities, entertainment, photo opportunities, and food. It also provides a great place to stroll or sit and relax and watch the people. Give yourself several hours.

≡FAST FACT

Quite the contrast to the skyscrapers that make up the New York skyline, Schermerhorn Row is a street of restored nineteenth-century warehouses and counting houses along the south side of Fulton Street (at the South Street Seaport). The row is home to museum galleries as well as shopping and restaurants. The stores themselves are from the modern era and include The Body Shop, Brookstone, and other popular retailers.

Location and Hours

The two-hour ride on the *Pioneer* begins at 1 P.M. and 9:30 P.M. and costs $25 for adults, $20 for seniors or students with an ID, and $15 for children twelve and under. The 4 P.M. and 7 P.M. sailings are $5 more. You can purchase tickets at the Pier 16 ticket booth. Call 212-748-8590 for information or to order tickets by phone from 9:30 A.M. to 5:30 P.M.

The Seaport Museum costs $8 for adults, $6 for students, and $4 for children five to twelve; on Mondays it's $5 for adults, $3 for students, and $1 for children five to twelve. From April through October the museum is open daily, except Monday, from 10 A.M. to 6 P.M. From November through March, gallery hours are 10 A.M. to 5 P.M., ships from noon. The museum is closed Tuesday to Thursday.

United Nations

📧 1st Avenue (between 42nd and 49th streets)

🚇 Grand Central-East 42nd Street station (S, 4, 5, 6, 7 train)

📞 212-963-8687 (tours)

✎ www.un.org/tours

The United Nations was established on October 24, 1945, in the aftermath of World War II. There were fifty-one countries in the initial formation, and their goal was to maintain peace and provide humanitarian assistance around the world. Over the years, the United Nations has grown to include some 192 member states.

Countries joining the United Nations agree to accept a charter that outlines the basic principles of international relations. While the U.N. has tried to help maintain world order and promote peace, it is not a lawmaking entity and has taken criticism for not being able to prevent international conflicts. Yet its policies and programs have helped to promote harmony between nations and respect for human rights.

The United Nations is affiliated with many other organizations that are involved in other activities, including international air travel, telecommunications, protecting the environment, and improving the quality of life for refugees and people living in poverty. UNICEF is one among many programs the United Nations has established over the years to help the international community.

The United Nations is made up of six branches, five of which occupy an eighteen-acre tract of land in New York City. David Rockefeller originally donated the land, which is designated as international territory. The five components of the New York headquarters include the General Assembly, the Security Council, the Economic and Social Council, the Trusteeship Council, and the Secretariat. The sixth body is the International Court of Justice, which is headquartered at The Hague in the Netherlands.

Touring the U.N.

The vast riverside promenade overlooking the East River is spectacular, with a rose garden, carefully landscaped lawns, and sculptures from nations worldwide. There are four main buildings on the site, including the General Assembly, the tall glass-enclosed Secretariat Building, the Conference Area (including Council Chambers), and the Dag Hammarskjöld Library. Flags from all member nations flank the buildings and landscape.

≡FAST FACT

The United Nations functions much like a country. The United Nations compound is considered international territory; it belongs not to the United States but to all of the members of the United Nations together. The United Nations has six official languages: Arabic, Chinese, English, French, Russian, and Spanish.

The United Nations is best visited on a clear day so that you can stroll through the promenade and enjoy the scenery and the view. Guided tours are available every day except January 1, Thanksgiving,

December 25, and weekends in January and February. The tours take you through all the main areas of the United Nations, including inside the General Assembly (unless it is in session) and the Security Council Chamber. The numerous exhibits, artwork from around the world, and décor of the buildings are all explained.

The United Nations Bookshop on the premises features a vast assortment of books and periodicals in many languages, plus marvelous children's books, posters, United Nations calendars, and more. At the Gift Centre, you can purchase unique handcrafted items plus gifts from around the world, as well as flags and the more typical souvenirs.

RAINY DAY FUN

You can learn all about the United Nations charter, its day-to-day activities, and the functions of the various branches and numerous associated agencies. Web sites include the U.N. home page at *www .un.org,* a Web site locator at *www.unsystem.org,* and UNICEF at *www .unicef.org.* There is also a Web page devoted to humanitarian relief for victims of disasters at *www.reliefweb.int.*

The United Nations Coffee Shop in the public concourse offers light fare Monday to Friday, 9 A.M. to 5 P.M., and is open a half hour later on weekends. Closed weekends in January and February, the Delegates Dining Room is available for lunch only, between 11:30 A.M. and 2 P.M., and reservations are a must! Make them as far ahead as possible by calling the maître d'hôtel at 212-963-7625. Proper attire is required—you may be sitting next to an important delegate from the other side of the world!

There is also a post office on the premises, so you can get those postcards out immediately—with U.N. stamps. Remember, you are not in United States territory here! Also lots of interesting philatelic items at face value for you stamp collectors, including personalized stamps.

Location and Hours

There are exhibits on various topics in the Visitor's Lobby, open from 9 A.M. to 5 P.M. seven days a week from March to December, weekdays only in January and February. Info at 212-963-TOUR (8687).

U.N. tours are given in some twenty languages; call ahead to check on specific availability 212-963-7539. The cost is $13 for adults, $9 for seniors, $8.50 for students under thirty with ID, $7 for children five to fourteen; children under five not admitted on tours. Each tour lasts forty-five minutes. Tours are available from 9:30 A.M. to 4:45 P.M. Monday to Friday, 10 A.M. to 4:30 P.M. Saturday and Sunday (no weekend tours in January and February). Tours leave the lobby of the General Assembly every thirty minutes.

The United Nations Bookshop is open Monday through Friday, 9 A.M. to 5 P.M., and opens a half hour later on weekends. Call 1-800-553-3210 for more information. The gift center is open from 9 A.M. to 5:15 P.M. (closed weekends in January and February).

The U.N. is wheelchair accessible, and wheelchairs are provided free of charge.

CHAPTER 8

Central Park

CENTRAL PARK IS an 843-acre oasis in the middle of the busiest city in the world. New Yorkers consider it a kind of communal backyard and performing arts center, where they bike, jog, walk their dogs, picnic, play Frisbee, watch shows, play instruments, meditate, write the next great American novel, and generally chill out. Visit *www.centralparknyc.org* to find everything you need to know about the park. For any information on the park, call the city information hotline, 311 in N.Y.C., or 212-NEW-YORK (639-9675) if you're calling from out of town.

How It All Began

The idea to set aside space for a public park in Manhattan came to William Cullen Bryant as early as 1884. A journalist, poet, and political activist (New York's Bryant Park is named after him), Bryant was inspired by the city parks of Paris and London. More than a decade later, Frederick Law Olmsted and Calvert Vaux began designing the rolling lawns and picturesque vistas that would become Central Park, the first landscaped park in the country.

🧳 TRAVEL TIP

There are at least eight free guided tours to familiarize you with Central Park and its fascinating history. Experienced tour guides fill you in on the nitty-gritty about the world's premier park. Most tours are given on the weekend, but there are some weekday tours. For tour information, call the Charles A. Dana Discovery Center at 212-860-1370.

Building the park was not an easy task; the land was primarily swamps, bluffs, and rocky outcroppings. Thousands of workers blasted rock and then planted trees and grass in its place. Some six bodies of water, three dozen bridges, and miles of irrigation pipes were part of the undertaking. Workers planted more than 400 varieties of trees and nearly 1,000 types of shrubs. A significant number of residents living on the site were displaced.

☂ RAINY DAY FUN

Central Park features prominently in countless television episodes and more than 240 movies, including *Ghostbusters,* where a gargoyle runs amok in Tavern on the Green, and *When Harry Met Sally,* where Harry and Sally have lunch at the Boathouse Cafe. Other films shot in or around Central Park include *An Affair to Remember, Annie Hall, Barefoot in the Park, The Fisher King, Hannah and her Sisters, Kramer vs. Kramer, Love Story, Tootsie, Wall Street, Zelig, Spiderman 3, Night at the Museum,* and *Borat.*

Slowly the park emerged, stretching from Fifty-ninth Street on the south end to 110th Street on the north. From Fifth Avenue across to

Central Park West, the equivalent of Eighth Avenue, the marvelous park became the crown jewel of the city, with fancy carriages and well-dressed New Yorkers parading along the paths. Since its completion, the park has become a refuge for New Yorkers and visitors looking for a respite from the busy city streets.

Central Park Today

Today, Central Park is a haven for a myriad of activities as varied as New Yorkers themselves—bicycling, rollerblading, meditating, jogging, boating, folk singing, ice skating, arguing politics, strolling, or taking a ride in a horse-drawn carriage. You'll find poets and peasants, kids and grannies, and people playing Frisbee, softball, football, guitars, tennis, chess, and checkers, as well as people flying kites. There are great rocks for climbing, horses for riding, and places to sit and listen to concerts under the stars. From sunbathing to folk dancing, Central Park is the ultimate resort, and except for a few sites and activities that charge an admission, it's all free.

≡FAST FACT

Nearly twenty-five million visitors enjoy the riches of the park annually; more than fifty groups or organizations, including running clubs and bird watching groups, hold their gatherings in the park. It is the most frequently used urban park in the country.

On a spring, summer, or warm fall or winter day, the park gives you the opportunity to step into another world within the city. The high-rise buildings flank the outskirts of the great park. As you venture deeper, the sounds of traffic and the fast pace that is New York City fade away. Everything in Central Park moves at a slower pace, except perhaps the rollerbladers (who, incidentally, are banned from certain areas). Strolling through, you'll find yourself stopping to enjoy street performers, including musicians, jugglers, mimes, dancers, and clowns. Buy a pretzel, climb the side of a giant rock formation, or simply toss down a blanket and lie on the grass. Designated quiet areas prohibit radios without earphones or musicians from disturbing your escape from the world.

Completely manmade, Central Park is full of sights, statues, lakes, ponds, bridges, and the second-most popular zoo in the city. Many of the best-known sights and landmarks within the park have been there since the nineteenth or early twentieth century.

The Central Park Wildlife Center

🖳 64th Street and 5th Avenue
🚃 Lexington Avenue-East 63rd Street station (F train)
📞 212-439-6500

Commonly known as the Central Park Zoo, the wildlife center is one of the best bargains you'll find in the city. The zoo is small, but it's the source of many a smile from the millions of children who visit every year. The country's oldest public zoo, it was remodeled in the early 1990s; the neighboring children's zoo reopened in 1997. Both are operated by the Wildlife Conservation Society.

The main zoo does not have large animals, such as lions and tigers, but it does have a large sea lion pool as the centerpiece. (Feeding time is fun to watch.) To cool off, you might want to stop in the Polar Circle, an indoor enclosed exhibit featuring more penguins than you can count (hint: there are more than sixty). The tuxedoed waddlers frolic in a re-created wintry arctic setting, complete with mini-glaciers and icy waters. Tufted puffins also live in the Polar Circle.

Venturing through the zoo, you will find a large land and water home for New York City's popular polar bear couple, Ida and Gus, who gambol happily a few yards from Fifth Avenue, along with a family of red pandas. They all have plenty of room to play and are fun to watch when they're not taking an extended nap. Nearby is Monkey Island, home to numerous Japanese snow monkeys and other simian species.

A large, indoor (and hot) tropical rain forest exhibit comes complete with tall trees, waterfalls, and other vegetation; it is home to numerous birds, Colobus monkeys, and insects. Following along the trail, you'll find yourself smack in the middle of the Amazon, right in the middle of New York City!

The beautifully landscaped zoo takes about an hour to visit at a leisurely pace. There is a café that serves primarily snack foods, hot dogs, and sandwiches. There's also a gift shop with all kinds of zoovineers.

≡ FAST FACT

The famous Delacorte clock is located just outside the zoo. It was constructed on top of an archway in 1965. It consists of six bronze animals on a small carousel that rotates on the hour, with the animals moving as the chimes peal.

Hours and Fees

The zoo is open year-round from 10 A.M. to 4:30, 5, or 5:30 P.M., depending on the time of year. The winter months may be a bit brisk for strolling. Admission is $8 for adults, $4 for seniors (sixty-five and older), $3 for children ages three to twelve, and free for children under three. The zoo is accessible to people with disabilities.

Buying a ticket also entitles you to visit the neighboring Tisch Children's Zoo, an imaginatively designed little world where children can visit and pet goats, pigs, sheep, and other child-friendly animals. Engaging shows and fun exhibits let children happily learn about the world around them. It is unusual in that it is just as much fun for the little ones as the older kids. Summer days can make for long lines on weekends, but the lines generally move quickly. The Children's Zoo is open Monday to Friday from 10 A.M. to 5 P.M. and on weekends from 10:30 A.M. to 5:30 P.M.

Central Park Playgrounds

New York mothers are convinced that without the park's fresh air their children would wither and die. Playgrounds are cherished and can be found all throughout the park in different configurations. Some twenty-one playgrounds offer different themes and styles centered on fun activities, including the largest sliding board in Manhattan at East Sixty-seventh Street's Billy Johnson Playground. Other playgrounds include the timber-style Diana Ross Playground at West Eighty-first Street, donated by the singer who played a concert in the park in 1983, and the Wild West Playground, at West Ninety-third Street, sporting a Western theme with a small stream running through it.

Playgrounds also can be found off the Great Lawn at East Seventy-second Street, East Seventy-sixth, East Seventy-ninth, East Eighty-fifth, two at West Eighty-fifth, and West Eighty-sixth streets. Playgrounds around the reservoir are at East Ninety-sixth Street, West Ninety-first, and West Ninety-third. North end playgrounds are at East 100th and 108th streets, and on the west side at Ninety-sixth, 100th, 110th streets, and West 110th and Lenox Avenue. Playgrounds in the south end of the park are located at West Sixty-first Street, two at West Sixty-seventh, East Sixty-seventh Street, and East Seventy-second.

The park's playgrounds are well maintained and fenced in. Remember to be attentive to your children and to keep the playgrounds clean.

The Carousel
⌨ 64th Street, in midpark
📞 212-879-0244

The carousel in Central Park is more than ninety years old, but it is not the park's original. The original carousel in the park was built in 1871 and turned by horsepower—and not the horsepower that runs your car! It was later destroyed in a fire and rebuilt only to be destroyed by fire for a second time. In 1951 the park rescued the derelict fifty-year-old carousel from Coney Island and refurbished it; this is the carousel in the park today. It is one of the largest in the country, with fifty-eight beautifully hand-carved horses and two chariots. Adults and children can sit atop one of the colorful horses and go for a spin on this antique treasure for only $1.25 per ride.

Sports and Activities

Central Park has a wealth of sports and outdoor activities all year round, from ice skating in the winter to boating in the summer.

Wollman Memorial Rink

🖬 Use the Central Park South (West 59th Street)-6th Avenue entrance

🚃 West 57th Street station (F train)

✆ 212-439-6900

✍ *www.wollmanskatingrink.com*

By winter, Wollman Rink is a midcity paradise for ice skaters; in the summer months, the ice gives way to the Victorian Gardens Amusement Park. For those who enjoy watching, the terrace above offers a lovely view of the skaters. Ice skating prevails from November to March. On weekdays, ice skating is $9.50 for adults and $4.75 for children and seniors. On weekends, fees go up to $12, $8.50, and $5, respectively. Skate rental is $5.

 TRAVEL TIP

You can also skate in the winter at Lasker Rink and Pool at 106th Street, midpark; it is the only public swimming facility in the park during the summer months. For more information, call 212-534-7639.

The Charles A. Dana Discovery Center
⌨ 36 West 110th Street (between 5th and Lenox avenues)
🚇 Central Park North (110th Street) station (2 or 3 train)
📞 212-860-1370

The Dana Discovery Center is one of the newest points of interest and education for children—and grownups too. The center, in a chateau at the northeast corner of the park, offers environmental studies on an eleven-acre section of the recently restored Harlem Meer. Various exhibits and workshops at the center focus on ecology, orienteering, and nature. Schedule time for the walking tours and performances; during the week it's a haven for class trips. It is open Tuesdays to Sundays from 11 A.M. to 5 P.M.

The Swedish Cottage Marionette Theater
⌨ 79th Street Transverse
🚇 West 81st Street-Museum of Natural History station (B or C train)
📞 212-988-9093

This is a fun-filled place to find entertainment for the little ones. The cottage is originally from the nineteenth century and has since been renovated. Puppet shows are performed Tuesday through Friday at 10:30 A.M. and noon, and on Saturdays at 1 P.M. Call to make reservations. Tickets are $6 for adults and $5 for children.

The Loeb Boathouse and the Lake
⌨ 72nd Street and Park Drive North (enter park at 72nd Street and 5th Avenue)
🚇 East 68th Street-Hunter College station (6 train)

The boathouse and lake are located on the east side of the park between Seventy-fourth and Seventy-fifth streets. The second biggest body of water in the park, the eighteen-acre lake offers plenty of boating activity and makes for a scenic, romantic place to stroll. From April through September, you can rent a rowboat at the Loeb

Boathouse seven days a week from 10 A.M. to 5:30 P.M. (last rental); the boat must be returned by 6:30 P.M. The cost is $10 for the first hour, $2.50 for each additional fifteen minutes, with a $30 cash deposit. A boat can hold up to five people. By law, kids under twelve must use a life jacket, and they are provided for free. Call 212-517-2233 for further information.

Maybe the most enchanting evening in all of New York are the gondola rides, offered in the summer on weekdays from 5 P.M. to 9 P.M., and on the weekends from 2 P.M. to 9 P.M. The cost is $30 per half hour.

Model Boat Rentals

Like the legendary Tuileries in Paris, you can rent miniature wooden boats and sail them along the Conservatory Water, pushing them back and forth with wooden sticks. On spring and summer weekends, this is often a very crowded area. Boat rentals are on a first-come, first-served basis and go for $10 per hour. This activity is seasonal. Conservatory Water is located on the east side from Seventy-second to Seventy-fifth Street.

Tennis, Anyone?

Tennis players can enjoy swinging away on some of the best-maintained public courts in the country at the Tennis Center, located between West Ninety-fourth and West Ninety-sixth streets near the West Drive. The twenty-six clay and four asphalt courts are open from April through November. If you'll be staying in the city for an extended period or visiting often, you can buy a season permit at the Arsenal in the park at Sixty-fourth Street and Fifth Avenue. For more information, call 212-360-8133. Seasonal permits cost $100 for adults, $20 for seniors, and $10 for children under seventeen. If you want to play once, you can purchase a single-day permit for $7 per person at the Tennis Center. There's an on-site pro shop, snack bar, and restrooms. Lessons are available too. For court reservations (a must), call 212-280-0205.

And There's More

Even though the historic Claremont Stables were recently closed, you can still go horseback riding in Central Park by booking a guided tour with the Riverdale Riding Center. For safety, riders must be at an advanced level, certified by an instructor at Riverdale. You must be able to walk, trot, and canter and control a horse in large—and sometimes busy—open spaces. The cost is $100. Info at 718-548-4848; *www.riverdaleriding.com.*

 JUST FOR PARENTS

Take a romantic carriage ride. The carriages line up along Central Park South between Fifth and Sixth avenues and Fifty-ninth Street at the southern end of Central Park across the street from the Plaza Hotel. Rides cost $34 for the first thirty minutes and $10 for each additional quarter hour. For more information call 212-736-0680 or visit *www.centralparkcarriages.com.* Like cab rides, these are cash only, and please remember to tip the driver.

Bicycle riding is also a very popular park activity. Designated bike paths are clearly marked. Rent a bike at the Loeb Boathouse seven days a week during the months of March through November from 10 A.M. to 6 P.M. The fee is $6 to $15 per hour, $21 for tandems. Children's trailers are $6. Helmets are included free with all rentals. You must leave a credit card, driver's license, or passport as security.

If you prefer more intellectual pursuits or if you want your kid to learn the ancient game of chess, visit the Chess and Checker House at West Sixty-fifth Street, just west of the Dairy. It has twenty-four outdoor chess and checkers tables protected from the sun. During the summer, chess experts teach six- to thirteen-year-olds how to play for free. You can even borrow chess or checker pieces at no charge ($20 returnable deposit plus ID required) from the Dairy. There are also numerous places throughout the park to sit and play these and other board games. Chess and Checker House is open Tuesday through Sunday, 10 A.M. to 5 P.M.

Sights and Landmarks

There is an awful lot to see and do in the park. You could spend an afternoon just looking for some of the famous landmarks, such as the statues and fountains.

Alice in Wonderland

The giant *Alice in Wonderland* statue, featuring huge bronze figures of Sir John Tenniel's classic illustrations of the Lewis Carroll tale, is one of the all-time kid favorites. It can be found north of the model boathouse on East Seventy-fourth Street. Most New Yorkers have at least one snapshot of themselves as kids crawling up the mushroom stalk. The philanthropist George Delacorte commissioned this statue from sculptor José de Creeft in memory of his first wife, Margarita. It was dedicated in 1959.

≡FAST FACT

New York City native George Delacorte was a publisher and philanthropist. The *Alice in Wonderland* statue was one of several he donated to Central Park. He also donated money to establish the Delacorte Theatre in Central Park, which hosts Shakespeare in the Park every year.

The Arsenal

The Arsenal was built in 1851, prior to the construction of the park. Today the historic structure, located on Fifth Avenue just inside the Sixty-fourth Street entrance, serves mostly as office space for the Parks and Recreation Department. It housed Civil War troops back in

1864 and 1865, and in 1869 it served briefly as the first home of the American Museum of Natural History. Visitors can view the original plans for Central Park, murals, and building design features. Open Mondays to Fridays, 9 A.M. to 5 P.M. Admission is free.

Balto, the Alaskan Sled Dog

The famous *Balto* statue commemorates the Alaskan sled dog that saved a town by bringing medicine through the tundra to its sick inhabitants. The story is told in the animated children's movie, *Balto*, which you should rent before visiting Central Park. The statue is east of the Mall on Sixty-seventh Street and is a great place to take a picture. The plaque on the statue reads: "Dedicated to the indomitable spirit of the sled dogs that relayed antitoxins 660 miles across rough ice, across treacherous waters, through Arctic blizzards from Nenana to the relief of stricken Nome in the Winter of 1925." See him on the main path leading toward the zoo.

Bethesda Terrace

Bethesda Terrace is home to the multilevel Bethesda Fountain, dedicated in 1873 and named for a pool in Jerusalem. It was designed to be the heart of the park. One of the most photographed fountains in the world, the *Angel of the Waters* sculpture sits high atop overlooking the European-style terrace. A stone staircase leads down to the three-tier fountain that sits near the Mall with a backdrop on the lake.

The view is spectacular from the top of the stairs, with rowboats in the background below lush trees with their branches and green leaves hanging over the waters. The boathouse can be seen to the right. The terrace surrounding the fountain is a busy stopping point for the numerous visitors who stroll by and stop to enjoy the beauty of the scene. Street performers, including jugglers, magicians, and musicians, delight the kids—and their parents too, for that matter. Bethesda Terrace is by Seventy-second Street, toward the east side (or Fifth Avenue side) of the park.

≡FAST FACT

There are numerous statues throughout the great park, including a number of famed monuments to leaders from nations around the world. Among the many famous statues in the park are the *107th Regiment Civil War Statue* (commemorating Union soldiers) and *Still Hunt* (a panther perched on a ledge watching over one of the many trails).

Belvedere Castle
Midpark at 79th Street
212-772-0210

This is the only castle on park grounds, and the massive stone structure was originally built in 1872. The highest point in the park, the castle is the place to go to get a great view of the acreage around it, including the Great Lawn and the Delacorte Theater, home to Shakespeare in the Park, a free first-come, first-serve season of Shakespearean plays performed during the summer months. Inside the castle you'll find the Henry Luce Nature Observatory (which encourages visitors to explore the natural world through microscopes and telescopes), various displays, programs for the kids, and workshops. The castle is also home to the instruments of the U.S. Weather Bureau. For more than eighty years, meteorological instruments here have provided New Yorkers with the temperature in Central Park. Open Tuesdays through Sundays, 10 A.M. to 5 P.M.

The Dairy
Midpark at 65th Street
212-794-6564

The Dairy was originally the park's first fast-food restaurant. Today the small Victorian building is a visitor center and gift shop, housing books and information about the park. You can also purchase souvenirs such as T-shirts, mugs, and framed photographs. Just north of the Woll-man Rink, the Dairy is a place to get maps, buy books about the park, and find out about park events and park history. The Dairy is open Tuesday through Sunday from 10 A.M. to 5 P.M., and admission is free.

Hans Christian Andersen Statue
▣ 75th Street, near 5th Avenue

This larger-than-life statue of the children's author of such classics as *The Little Mermaid* and *The Ugly Duckling* was made to be climbed on! Another great photo op for the little ones, it can be found west of Conservatory Water. The statue depicts Andersen reading from *The Ugly Duckling* as a bronze duck approaches.

The Harlem Meer
✆ 212-860-1370
▣ East side from 106th to 110th streets
✎ www.centralparknyc.org

The Meer is an eleven-acre lake (or *meer*, in Dutch) that sits on the northeast corner of the park by Fifth Avenue at the foot of Harlem. It was restored and reopened in 1993 and features numerous plants, shrubs, trees, and winding paths around the lake. There are walking tours for those who want to look more closely at and learn about the plant life. You can also find a newly created island.

The Harlem Meer is one of the few places in Manhattan where you can actually go fishing. Bamboo poles and bait are available free of charge at the Charles A. Dana Discovery Center, adjacent to the Meer. Fish must be thrown back to maintain the careful ecological balance of life. Poles are available with a photo ID on a first-come basis Tuesday through Sunday from 10 A.M. to 4 P.M.; Sundays to 3 P.M. Groups of up to fifteen can reserve poles by calling 212-860-1370. An adult with photo ID must accompany the group. There is a $20 charge for the group, payable up front (in effect, the deposit). Go online at *www.centralparknyc.org* for more information.

 TRAVEL TIP

Woodlands, meadows, and even battlegrounds from the War of 1812 can be found within a short walk of the Meer. Although many people still don't know about the Meer, in nice weather you can find some hundred people a day fishing there.

The Reservoir

The Reservoir is a 106-acre body of water, built in 1862 smack in the middle of the northern part of the park above Eighty-sixth Street. It was renamed the Jacqueline Kennedy Onassis Reservoir in 1995. The path surrounding the reservoir, just more than 1.5 miles in length, is now the park's most popular jogging track, home to thousands of runners in training for races. Although the reservoir is no longer used for the city's drinking water, it still remains the largest body of water in the park. The view across the reservoir is stunning, and the trees, including cherry trees, and numerous birds make for great scenery. A reconstruction of the original fence has recently been erected.

Lawns, Gardens, and Wide-Open Spaces

Many New Yorkers, particularly those in Manhattan, live in modern apartments that are not as spacious as they would like. The park offers some elbow room—places to lie on the grass and enjoy the wide-open space. Of course, on a warm spring or summer day even those places can get crowded, but you can find the serenity of the park if you look carefully. Off-the-beaten-path locations are often just down the road or over a large rock from where you are.

A truly awe-inspiring experience is lying in Central Park and looking up and out at the tall buildings standing high and flanking the peaceful setting. The city is so close yet so far away; the park is a refuge unto itself. Two of the most notable wide-open spaces in the vast park are the Great Lawn and the Sheep Meadow.

The Great Lawn

A reservoir until the 1930s, this lawn was recently replanted and resodded and is lovingly maintained to serve as one of the prime locations for outdoor fun in the park. Frisbees fly by, as do softballs and hardballs from countless games played all spring and summer on the more than two dozen baseball diamonds in the park. The lawn has also seen massive crowds (with estimates of anywhere from 200,000 to nearly a million people) for concerts from the likes of Paul Simon, Elton John, and Diana Ross. Pope John Paul II spoke to throngs of people on the Great Lawn in 1995. The lawn spans some fourteen acres of open air and has been the central gathering point for the largest crowds in the city. It lies midpark from Seventy-ninth to Eighty-fifth Street.

≡FAST FACT

Central Park Conservancy offers many free and fascinating tours of various parts of the park starting in April and continuing through June. Their teen docent-led tours operate until the fall. For a full schedule, log onto *www.centralparknyc.org* and click on "Activities/ Programs" on the top menu, then click on "Walking Tours."

The Sheep Meadow

This really was a sheep meadow until the mid-1930s—it was a large piece of flat land, originally designed for military practice but used as a pasture for the park's flock of sheep. Today the sheep are long gone, and the fifteen-acre area on the west side of the park is a haven for sunbathers. There is less activity here than on the Great Lawn, with no ball playing or loud radios allowed. You may look up and see a kite overhead in the spring. Essentially, though, the Sheep Meadow is reserved for sedentary pleasures such as relaxing and picnicking. Just north of the Sheep Meadow, located at Mineral Springs at West Sixty-ninth Street, is the Lawn Sports Center, which is home to croquet players and lawn bowlers.

≡FAST FACT

Sheep Meadow is the first park location in New York to offer free high-speed Wi-Fi access. The New York City Department of Parks & Recreation, with help from WiFi Salon and Nokia, has established seventeen Wi-Fi hotspots in parks across New York City. Check *www .wifisalon.com* for more information.

Gardens Galore

Among the numerous gardens that highlight the park are the Shakespeare Garden, Strawberry Fields, Lilac Walk—with twenty-three varieties of lilacs from around the world—and the Conservatory Garden.

The Shakespeare Garden is tucked between the Swedish Cottage and the Belvedere Castle. Dedicated to the great writer, the little-known garden was dedicated in 1916, the 300th anniversary of Shakespeare's death, and restored in 1987. The nearby Delacorte Theater features free summer Shakespeare plays, produced by the Joseph Papp Public Theatre (call 212-539-8500 for more information). Plaques around the garden are inscribed with quotes from the works of Shakespeare, and the flowers within are those mentioned in his works, including thyme, sage, rosemary, and lavender plus several varieties of seasonal flowers.

Strawberry Fields (on the west side, between West Seventy-first and West Seventy-second streets) is dedicated to a writer, singer, and legend of a different era, John Lennon. The current landscaping and maintenance of the 2.5-acre garden is the result of a $1 million gift to the park by Yoko Ono. The couple visited the garden often when they lived across the street in the Dakota Apartments.

JUST FOR PARENTS

Every summer since 1954, New Yorkers have been treated to free stellar performances of classic plays (usually Shakespeare) at the Delacorte Theater. Recent actors include Natalie Portman, Patrick Stewart, Meryl Streep, Denzel Washington, Kevin Kline, and Christopher Walken. Although tickets are free, you have to wait in line on the day of the show at 1 P.M., and you can only get two tickets per person. Performances are at 8 P.M. and the theater seats 2,000. Call 212-539-8500 or go to *www.publictheater.org* for information.

A serene setting, the romantic garden is home to tree clusters, outcroppings, and plantings and is considered one of the most beautiful areas in Central Park. The 2.5-acre park features a reproduction of a marble mosaic from Pompeii with the word "Imagine" set in it, a gift from the city of Naples, Italy. Aside from the garden's name, taken from one of Lennon's songs, the mosaic is the only specific tribute to the former Beatle in the garden. Fans gather there each year on the anniversary of Lennon's tragic death, and it is common to find flowers, letters, and photos left in tribute.

The formal Conservatory Garden is actually three gardens representing French, Italian, and English landscaping styles on six acres near Fifth Avenue and 105th Street, just south of the Harlem Meer. Originally opened in 1937, the outdoor gardens replaced greenhouses that occupied the site beginning in 1898. A 1982 restoration and landscaping brought back the gardens that have been home to weddings and other festive occasions.

The North Garden is a French-style design surrounding a large bronze fountain known as *Three Dancing Maidens*. The flowerbeds around the centerpiece are lush with 20,000 tulips in the spring and 2,000 Korean chrysanthemums in the fall. The Central Garden features an Italian design with a big manicured lawn leading to a central fountain with huge surrounding hedges. Pink and white blossoms and trees surround the garden. The South Garden is English in style. A lily pond and large bronze fountain is dedicated to the children's book *The Secret Garden*. A new addition is a shady woodland slope that surrounds the outer ring of trees, shrubs, and flowers with plants, and it is especially beautiful in the spring when thousands of daffodils come into bloom.

You can download information and a map for a self-guided tour at *www.centralparknyc.org*. Click on "Activities/Programs" on the top menu, click on "Walking Tours," then look for the information under "Self-guided Tours." The downloadable self-guided tours are in PDF format. Custom tours, with a minimum of six people at $12 per person, are offered. Info at 212-360-2726.

≡FAST FACT

More than 270 species of birds have been spotted by bird enthusiasts in the park, primarily in an area known as the Ramble, a thirty-six-acre wooded area with wildly growing bushes, waterfalls, and even a brook. The area, near the East Seventy-ninth Street entrance, can be somewhat deserted, so it's best to explore it in a group.

Fine Dining

Although many think that fine dining in Central Park consists of whatever you pack for your picnic, there are several other options.

Tavern on the Green ($$$)

🖃 Central Park West (between West 66th and 67th streets)

🚇 West 66th Street-Lincoln Center station (1 train) or West 72nd Street station (B or C train)

📞 212-873-3200

✎ *www.tavernonthegreen.com*

A glittering jewel, Tavern on the Green is a wonderful place to have a leisurely lunch, a romantic dinner, or a terrific Sunday brunch. The structure, a classic example of mid-Victorian architecture, was originally built in the late nineteenth century (just off the entrance at West Sixty-seventh Street) as a sheepfold to hold the park's resident flock. Today thousands of tourists and New Yorkers flock to the upscale, sprawling, dazzling restaurant. From floor to ceiling and wall to wall, the restaurant's décor is stunning. Stained glass, exquisite chandeliers, ornate gold trim, flowers, statues, outdoor dining—it's all part of the experience.

With its expansive glass-enclosed Crystal Room looking out over the park and sparkling lights lining the trees around the structure, Tavern on the Green provides a wonderful dining experience. During the holiday season, the lights and seasonal display are spectacular. Tavern on the Green has revived live music in the Chestnut Room and dining outdoors (in the warmer weather) in its outdoor garden. It is also the only place in the park where you can legally buy alcoholic beverages; with that in mind, the restaurant offers an extensive wine list. The Easter Sunday meal at Tavern on the Green, with a petting zoo for kids, is legendary. Special events are held during the year, some especially for kids. There is also a delightful gift shop on the premises.

═FAST FACT

Central Park SummerStage presents free performances of music, dance, film, and the spoken word all summer. Famed and emerging artists perform at Rumsey Playfield, midpark between Sixty-ninth and Seventy-second streets. Go to the East Sixty-eighth Street-Hunter College station (6 train) or West Seventy-second Street station (B or C train) and walk through the park. Information and schedules at 212-360-2777 or *www.summerstage.org*. Performances are accessible to mobility– and hearing–impaired persons.

As for the food, the lobster bisque and crab cakes are favorites, as are the sirloin and shrimp brochette. There's a limited children's menu, but portions are large, so you could share with a child. The staff is very child-friendly. Dessert is always delicious, especially the surprisingly light chocolate banana mousse cake. Reservations are a good idea, and they must be backed up by a credit card. There is a twenty-four-hour cancellation policy. If you don't cancel in time, you will be charged $25 per person.

The Boathouse ($$)

🖃 East 72nd Street and Park Drive North (enter park at East 72nd Street and 5th Avenue)

🚇 East 68th Street-Hunter College station (6 train)

📞 212-517-2233

✎ *www.thecentralparkboathouse.com*

Located in the Loeb Boathouse at East Drive between Terrace Drive and the Seventy-ninth Street Transverse, this is the only lakeside dining in the city. The three restaurants run from very casual to elegant, and hours vary with the season. Call before you go. You can dine indoors or outside on the terrace overlooking the lake. If you can't find the Boathouse, a trolley will pick you up at Seventy-second Street and Fifth Avenue or at the Metropolitan Museum of Art's garage at Eightieth and Fifth and take you there. The service runs about every fifteen minutes on Monday to Friday nights and for brunch and dinner on weekends.

Sheep Meadow Café ($$–$$$)

🖃 Central Park West at West 69th Street

🚇 West 72nd Street station (B or C train)

📞 212-396-4100

Lunch and snack bar by day, great grill at night. This is a seasonal place, and such places sometimes fall with the leaves. Check to see if they are still blooming before you go.

Other Options

There are many outdoor concession stands with outdoor seating to grab a bite, including the Ballplayers House (next to the carousel, midpark at Sixty-fifth Street), Kerbs' Ice Cream Café (Conservatory Water, East Seventy-fourth Street, near the Perimeter), Wollman Rink (midpark at East Sixty-third Street), Ferrara Italian Café (Merchant's Gate, West Sixty-first Street and Central Park West), and the Leaping Frog Café (in the zoo, Sixty-fourth Street and Fifth Avenue). All are easily accessible and busy during the summer months.

You can also stop at one of a wide range of licensed vendors or do as many New Yorkers do and bring your own bag or picnic lunch. Pick up a sub/hero/grinder or whatever you like at one of the gazillion sandwich shops/delis around town and settle down for a meal under the trees.

CHAPTER 9

Manhattan Museums

NO CITY OFFERS as much cultural diversity as New York, and no city in this country can boast of such a vast array of museums. Nearly 150 museums grace the five boroughs, ranging from broad themes such as natural history and art to specific cultural, ethnic, and historical collections, including modern art, Jewish culture, and the city's own transit system.

The city's museums take you on an eye-opening educational foray into the past, the present, and, in some cases, the future. Unlike those boring class museum trips of years ago, today's museum fuses the knowledge of well-trained guides with the excitement of modern technology to best present everything from dinosaur bones to air force fighter jets.

Children's Museum of the Arts

    ▥ 182 Lafayette Street (between Grand and Broome streets)
    🚇 Spring Street station (6 train), Canal Street station (N train), or Prince Street station (R or W train)
    📞 212-274-0986
    ✎ *www.cmany.org*

This is one of the oldest museums of the visual and performing arts, and it's designed for children twelve and under and their families.

There are numerous activities designed for kids from ten months and up. Children can paint, sculpt, and do collage in the Open Art Studio. The museum offers both self-guided and docent-guided workshops where an artist-in-residence works with kids and their families.

Hours and Fees

Open Wednesday to Sunday, noon to 5 P.M.; Thursdays to 6 P.M. Admission is $9 per person; children under one year are free. Pay as you wish Thursdays from 4–6 P.M. Admission covers all materials. Wheelchair and stroller accessible. There is no eating facility in the museum, but the staff will direct you to many good family restaurants in the neighborhood.

Children's Museum of Manhattan

- 212 West 83rd Street (Tisch Building, between Broadway and Amsterdam Avenue)
- West 86th Street station (1 train)
- 212-721-1234 (information)
- 212-721-1223 (staff)
- *www.cmom.org*

The Children's Museum of Manhattan (CMOM) has hands-on exhibits providing fun for kids ages birth to ten. The museum is designed to enhance learning in five key areas: literacy, the arts, media and communication, the environment, and early childhood education.

A quarter of a million children visit annually to take part in the various interactive exhibits. The museum hosts a series of traveling children's exhibits on the main floor and in the basement. An urban tree house (open May through September) teaches children about their environment.

On the higher floors you'll find various activity rooms featuring arts and crafts, climbing, and a small theater where puppet shows, storytelling, and other performances are given. A new wing features

"Playworks for Early Learning," an exhibit for kids from birth to four, which the *New York Times* said "has taken innovation to the next level and incorporated research and child-development into every level."

TRAVEL TIP

You may not be able to resist the temptation to browse the great works in New York's museums, but the works that delight you may make your kids miserable. To avoid a lifelong hatred of these "stuffy places," use the same trick museum docents do to hook kids on their tours—use the interrogative method. Pick a work and ask your children what they see. How does it make them feel? Why? What story is being told? For older kids, what is the artist trying to tell you?

One of the nicest aspects of the museum is that it avoids video and computer-generated activities, allowing children to see, hear, and discover the real sights and sounds around them as they play. This is a museum for children—not about them—designed to pique their interest. You will enjoy seeing it all through their eyes. Pick up a schedule when you enter, and you'll know what shows, workshops, or story readings are taking place that day. When you're done, be sure to wash your children's hands, since hundreds of eager youngsters enjoy the hands-on museum every day.

There is a small gift shop with children's items. There is no restaurant on the premises. Strollers and food are not allowed.

Hours and Fees

The museum is open Tuesday through Sunday and on public school holidays from 10 A.M. to 5 P.M. Admission is $9 for children and adults, $6 for seniors, and free for children under one year.

The Cloisters

- 191st Street in Manhattan, in Fort Tryon Park
- West 190th Street station (A train)
- 212-923-3700
- *www.metmuseum.org*

Perched high above the Hudson River and tucked away in Fort Tryon Park is the Cloisters, a marvelous museum dedicated to medieval art and architecture. The Cloisters has one of the world's most extensive collections of art and artifacts from the period between the twelfth and sixteenth centuries. Byzantine, early Christian, Romanesque, and Gothic works are all represented in this site, run by the Metropolitan Museum of Art.

Silver, enamels, stained glass, metalwork, ivories, jewelry, and fifteenth-century manuscripts are all on exhibit. Among the many highlights are the renowned fifteenth- and sixteenth-century Unicorn Tapestries. From the galleries, you can stroll out into the lavish gardens with their rich and varied plant life. The building, which opened in 1938, is unusual in that it was built to include cloisters (courtyards from places devoted to religious seclusion) from real French monasteries. Special programs, gallery talks, and other free presentations are held on Saturdays. After your journey to the past, you will want to explore the grounds surrounding the sprawling structure, Fort Tryon Park.

═FAST FACT

Every fall, Fort Tryon Park transforms into a medieval town for the annual medieval festival. It features music and dance, magic and minstrels, jugglers and jesters, free jousts, and vendors demonstrating and selling handicrafts and medieval wear. Info at 212-795-1600 or *www.whidc.org/home.html.*

The Cloisters is upper Manhattan's foremost sight and worth the trip. There is a wonderful gift shop on the premises that is always well stocked with knight and princess paraphernalia for kids, and it's all quite affordable.

Hours and Fees

The museum is open Tuesday through Sunday from 9:30 A.M. to 5:15 P.M. from March through October, and until 4:45 P.M. from November through February. The museum is closed on Mondays, January 1, Thanksgiving Day, and December 25. Tours are free and are held Tuesdays through Sundays at 3 P.M. and Sundays at noon. Garden tours are held in May, June, September, and October, Tuesdays through Sundays at 1 P.M. Suggested admission is $20 for adults, $15 for seniors sixty-five and older, and $10 for students. Children under twelve are free. It's suggested you call to confirm in advance.

Cooper-Hewitt National Design Museum

⊡ 2 East 91st Street (at 5th Avenue)

🚇 East 86th Street station (4, 5, or 6 train) or East 96th Street station (6 train)

☎ 212-849-8400

✉ www.cooperhewitt.org

The former estate of Andrew Carnegie, the Cooper-Hewitt National Design Museum is the last branch of the Smithsonian Institution remaining in New York. Exhibits include an extensive collection of arts and crafts by designers of outstanding decorative objects in the form of textiles, jewelry, drawings, prints, woodwork, and even wallpaper. In short, if you can think of anything that has been designed, you'll probably find it here.

Exhibits from the massive collection change every few months, as the Cooper-Hewitt facility is not as large as some of the city's other museums. It owns the Beatles's psychedelic Rolls Royce and has an incredible collection of wallpaper. Hands-on exhibits and activities guide kids through the design process.

There is a gift shop on the premises that sells designed objects, books, and gift items. A recent multimillion-dollar renovation has given the Cooper-Hewitt National Design Museum a new look. Nothing stuffy about it, its Web site has a blog and several podcasts.

Hours and Fees

Parking in the area is not easy to find, so public transportation is your best bet. The design museum is open Monday through Thursday from 10 A.M. to 5 P.M., Friday from 10 A.M. to 9 P.M., Saturday from 10 A.M. to 6 P.M., and Sunday noon to 6 P.M. Closed January 1, Thanksgiving Day, and December 25. There is no restaurant on the premises. Admission is $12 for adults, $9 for seniors and students with ID, and free for members and children under twelve.

The Frick Collection

　⊞ 1 East 70th Street
　🚇 East 68th Street station (6 train)
　✆ 212-288-0700
　✍ *www.frick.org*

Paintings by the old masters are appropriately housed in a 1913 mansion that was transformed into a museum in 1935. Henry Clay Frick, former Pittsburgh steel giant, built the Manhattan mansion to house his family and art collection.

Upon entering the Frick, you'll feel as if you are entering an elegant private mansion. Here you'll find great works by American, British, French, Italian, Spanish, and Dutch artists. There are Rembrandt's *Self-Portrait* and *The Polish Rider* and Manet's *The Bullfight*, along with works by El Greco, Piero della Francesca, Vermeer, Whistler, Goya, Renoir, and other legendary painters. Other artistic pieces include clocks, fabulous eighteenth-century furniture, oriental carpets, and Limoges enamels. The Frick sells a guide to its paintings and offers prerecorded self-guided tours with lively, fascinating commentary about each work.

The Frick Library, in an adjacent building, contains hundreds of thousands of photos of the artwork and a quarter of a million publications. The Seventieth Street garden, designed by landscape architect Russell Page, provides a sanctuary from the rest of the city and the rest of the world.

A gift shop sells posters, books, and reproductions of the great works. There is no restaurant. Gallery talks are frequently offered. The famed Frick chamber music concerts are held regularly in the Music Room. Tickets are $25, but the concert can be heard in the Garden Court where no tickets are required.

Hours and Fees

Parking in the area is very difficult. The museum can be covered in a couple of hours, and you may want to enjoy a leisurely stroll through the garden. The museum is wheelchair accessible.

The Frick is open Tuesday through Saturday from 10 A.M. to 6 P.M. and Sundays from 11 A.M. to 6 P.M. It is closed on Mondays and major holidays. Admission (which includes audio guide) is $15 for adults, $10 for seniors (sixty-two and older), and $5 for students with valid ID. Children under sixteen must be accompanied by an adult, and children under ten are not admitted to the museum. Pay what you wish Sundays 11 A.M. to 1 P.M.

The Guggenheim Museum

⬛ 1071 5th Avenue (between 88th and 89th streets)
🚊 86th Street station (4, 5, or 6 train)
✆ 212-423-3500
✑ www.guggenheim.org
✑ www.ticketweb.com

New Yorkers seem to have that same architectural contrariness as the French, who have come to love the blatantly ugly Eiffel Tower, Pompidou Center, and that pyramid at the Louvre. Likewise, Gothamites look upon the giant spiral shape of the Guggenheim with affection and even appreciation. Not that anyone has a choice—it's hard to miss. The distinctive architecture, the work of Frank Lloyd Wright, has just come out of a two-year exterior renovation in time for its fiftieth anniversary.

TRAVEL TIP

For $65 for adults and $49 for youths ages twelve to seventeen, City-Pass allows you to experience six of the city's most popular attractions: the Empire State Building Observatory, the American Museum of Natural History, the Guggenheim Museum, the Museum of Modern Art, the Metropolitan Museum of Art, and a two-hour Circle Line Harbor Cruise. It's a $131 value and is good for nine days. It also includes discount coupons for shopping and dining, attraction information, a map, and insider tips. You can buy the CityPass at any of the above sites, call 707-256-0490, or go online at *www.citypass.com.*

Built in the late 1950s, the Guggy (as it is known to New Yorkers) was designed to display the vast collection of modern works of Solomon R. Guggenheim. Frank Lloyd Wright died before the building was complete, making this his final masterpiece. Patrons wind their way down the six stories of the sprawling circular structure while viewing great works of art in both permanent and special exhibits. An additional tower gallery was opened in 1992 with the intention of housing the growing collection of permanent works, and it's a particular favorite with kids who visit. Picasso, Chagall, Klee, Kandinsky, Degas, Manet, Toulouse-Lautrec, and van Gogh are all represented in a collection of breathless quality.

The museum occasionally has a program of special events for families. Go online before you come and buy the tickets to these events ahead of time.

On the premises you will find a museum store. The Museum Café is a casual place to grab a snack.

Hours and Fees

The museum hosts Family Sundays on the second Sunday of each month. Admission is $18 for families with children under eighteen and up to two adult companions. There are also free family highlight tours on these days. Other days, admission to the Guggenheim (which includes an audio tour) is $18 for adults, $15 for students with valid ID and senior citizens, and free for children under twelve. Hours for the Guggenheim are Saturday through Wednesday from 10 A.M. to 5:45 P.M. and Friday from 10 A.M. to 7:45 P.M. On Fridays from 5:45 P.M., the museum has a pay-what-you-wish policy. The museum is closed on Thursdays.

Jewish Museum

⌨ 1109 5th Avenue (at 92nd Street)
🚊 East 96th Street station (4, 5, or 6 train)
✆ 212-423-3200
✎ www.jewishmuseum.org

The Jewish Museum is a very family-friendly place with much to interest all family members of any faith. Housed in a mansion that was built at the start of the twentieth century, the history presented within these walls dates back thousands of years and recounts the story of the Jewish people. The lower two floors of the four-story structure are set up for ongoing special exhibitions; the top two floors house a permanent exhibit, Culture and Continuity: The Jewish Journey. There is also an exhibition aimed expressly at children.

The breadth of the collection is impressive and includes painting, sculpture, photography, numismatics, film and video, and antiquities. In fact, with the expansion in the early 1990s, this is now the largest Jewish museum devoted to culture and history outside of Israel. The National Jewish Archive of Broadcasting is the largest repository of broadcast materials on twentieth-century Jewish culture in the United States.

From the Exodus out of Egypt to the festival of Hanukkah, the drama and significance of the events are effectively conveyed. There is a section dedicated to rituals and Jewish tradition featuring ancient prayer shawls, menorahs, and wedding cups, plus a film explaining some of the longtime traditions. Another section is devoted to the Holocaust. The roots and expression of anti-Semitism are also explored.

Second Sundays are family fun days at the museum. There are special programs, events, and activities for the whole family for the whole day. Tours, storytelling, arts and crafts, and performances are all free with admission.

The exhibitions, films, and interactive computers can take several hours to experience fully. There is often a wait to get in, so plan early and, as with most of the city's museums, try for a weekday. A gift shop offers books and other items relating to Jewish culture. You'll also find a very reasonable glatt kosher café on the premises.

Hours and Fees

The museum is open Saturdays to Wednesdays from 11 A.M. to 5:45 P.M. and on Thursdays from 11 A.M. to 8 P.M. It is closed on Fridays, all major Jewish holidays, January 1, Martin Luther King Jr. Day, and Thanksgiving Day. Admission is $12 for adults, $10 for seniors (sixty-five and older), $7.50 for students, and free for members and children under twelve. There is no admission charge on Saturdays, but the café, gift shop, and interactive exhibits are closed. There is a reciprocal discount with the Museum of Jewish Heritage.

Lower East Side Tenement Museum

⌦ 108 Orchard Street (Visitor's Center)

🚆 Delancy Street station (F train), Essex Street station (J, M, or Z train), or Grand Street station (B or D train)

✆ 212-431-0233

✐ *www.tenement.org*

Housed in an actual tenement that was home to a total of more than 7,000 immigrants in the years from 1863 to 1935, the museum offers several guided tours through furnished rooms stocked with photos and artifacts. Together these tell the story of the immigrants who lived throughout the Lower East Side.

The museum, chartered in 1988, is comparatively small and exemplifies urban dwelling and the immigrant experience. Several first-rate tour guides recount the stories of different families who lived in the tenement and describe the possessions that were donated to the museum.

Across the street at the visitors' center, visitors can view a film featuring interviews with historians and former residents of the old tenement. A slide show, called "Urban Pioneers," describes the history of the tenement. The museum has free outdoor exhibits and a gift shop.

For an in-depth experience, check out one of the walking tours, which highlight aspects of the surrounding neighborhood. The Confino Living History Tour, a costumed, interactive experience even five-year-olds will enjoy, runs on the weekends.

Parking, Hours, and Fees

You can find free parking in the lot on Broome Street, between Norfolk and Suffolk, for up to four hours. The museum is accessible by various guided tours only, which take about an hour. The Getting By Tour costs $17 for adults, $13 for students and seniors, and is suitable for children ages eight and older. Tours begin in the visitor center Tuesday through Friday every forty minutes from 1:20 to 5 P.M. and on Saturdays and Sundays on the half hour from 11:15 A.M. to 4:45 P.M., depending on the season. Check the Web site for updated times and holiday hours.

The Confino Living History Tour, suitable for children five and older, operates Saturdays and Sundays at noon, 1, 2, and 3 P.M. Cost is $17 for adults and $13 for students and seniors. It is strongly recommended that you make a reservation or buy tickets ahead of time.

Mount Vernon Hotel Museum and Garden

(formerly the Abigail Adams Smith House Museum)

- 421 East 61st Street (between 1st and York avenues)
- 59th Street station (4, 5, or 6 train)
- Lexington Avenue-East 59th Street station (N, R, or W train), East 59th Street station (4, 5, or 6 train), or Lexington Avenue-East 63rd Street station (F train)
- 212-838-6878
- *www.mvhm.org*

Surrounded by the high-rise apartment buildings that comprise much of the Upper East Side, this quaint house and garden was made into a museum for visitors coming to the 1939 World's Fair in Queens. Once part of a much larger property owned by Abigail Adams (daughter of President John Adams) and her husband, Colonel William Smith, the museum you see today was originally a carriage house built in 1799. The neighboring mansion became a hotel in the early nineteenth century. However, when the hotel burned down, this carriage house then became a (much smaller) hotel. It later served as a private residence before becoming a museum.

The stone structure has been refurbished over the years and houses eight rooms of furnishings from the federal period. In one, the Gentlemen's Tavern Room, take a seat and read the latest newspaper (from 1828). Afterward, stroll through the gardens around the small museum. The Colonial Dames of America are responsible for the restoration and upkeep of this city landmark.

Friendly and informed tour guides will fill you in on the background and history of this delightful little museum. Frequent events center around the historic period. Families with young children can get a family pack of interactive activities. A gift shop sells books, handmade products, and reproductions of period items (like toys).

The museum may not merit a separate trip, but if you are shopping at Bloomingdale's or simply visiting the Upper East Side, it's a nice little place to drop by for an hour or so. Mount Vernon Hotel Museum and Garden is a bit of a secret, so it doesn't get too crowded.

Parking, Hours, and Fees

Don't even think about parking around here unless you want to find a meter on First Avenue and feed it every hour until 4 P.M. (when you have to move your car or lose it to a tow truck).

The museum is open Tuesday through Sunday from 11 A.M. to 4 P.M. In June and July it is open Tuesdays from 6 P.M. to 9 P.M. for Summer Garden Evenings. The museum is closed in August and on major holidays. Admission is $8 for adults, $7 for seniors and students, and free for children under twelve.

Museum of the City of New York

- 1220 5th Avenue (at 103rd Street)
- East 103rd Street station (6 train)
- 212-534-1672
- www.mcny.org

Why not learn firsthand about the city's history while you visit New York? This is one of two museums (along with the museum of the New-York Historical Society) devoted to the history of the city it calls home. With an enormous wealth of materials of all types, this is perhaps the more fun of the two galleries paying homage to New York City.

Set in a massive mansion looking out on the northern portion of Central Park, the Museum of the City of New York offers provocative special exhibitions along with a wide range of permanent exhibits celebrating different aspects of the city. It's a good idea to choose your favorites, as you'll never get to all of it in one day.

Major exhibits found in the vast museum include the prints and photography collection. The thousands of photographs, plus the largest known collection of Currier & Ives lithographs, trace the history of New York City. An ongoing multimedia presentation, *Timescapes,* traces the growth of New York from a tiny settlement to a great city.

You don't have to be a theater aficionado to appreciate the stunning collection celebrating the Great White Way, Broadway, and American theater. Costumes and memorabilia, set designs, posters, paintings, and photographs recount the legends of the Broadway stage as well as Yiddish theater, which thrived in New York in the early twentieth century.

 TRAVEL TIP

To save money, take advantage of the many free, suggested donation, and pay-what-you-wish deals offered by museums. Some are open-ended, and some are only for a few hours at some point during the week. This is wonderful if you have kids who can't handle more than that. Access a long list of deals at *http://gonyc.about.com/ cs/museums/a/museumdeals.htm.*

A decorative arts collection includes precious metals and other rare items. The highlight is a look at New York's domestic interiors with furniture from 1790 through 1890.

The New York Toy Stories exhibit is a tribute to toys of the children of the city, dating back to the 1800s. Cast-iron toys, wooden soldiers, mechanical toys, rare dolls, boats, and renowned dollhouses are on display in this unique exhibit that all ages can enjoy.

The museum shop sells items relating to the exhibits and to the city of New York, including books, videos, and toys (not the ones on display, but some good reproductions). You can buy New York City photo reproductions or reproductions of Currier & Ives prints that provide a nice reminder of your trip (even better than postcards). There is no restaurant in the museum and few choices in the surrounding blocks, so eat before or after your visit.

Hours and Fees

The museum is open Tuesday through Sunday (and holiday Mondays) from 10 A.M. to 5 P.M. Suggested admission to the museum is $9 for adults, $5 for seniors and students, and children under twelve are free. Families are $20 (two adults maximum).

Museum of Comic and Cartoon Art

▦ 594 Broadway (between Prince and Houston streets), Suite 401

🚇 Prince Street station (N, R, or W train) or Broadway-Lafayette Street station (B, D, F, or V train)

✆ 212-254-3511

✎ *www.moccany.org*

Founded in 2001 as a tribute to comic and cartoon art, the museum features exhibits on comics, cartoons, anime, film, political illustration, and computer art. Small children will delight in the amusing cartoons, and older children and adults will appreciate the museum's focus on the art form's creation and its place in social commentary. A vast range of subject matter is covered, from the most beautiful artistic renderings of graphic novels to the slapstick of early comic strips to intensely creative computer animation to Saturday morning toons.

Every Monday features a great free event. Doors open at 6:15 P.M., but get there early. Open Friday to Monday, noon to 5 P.M.; Tuesday to Thursday by appointment.

Admission is $5, kids under twelve are free.

Museum of Modern Art

▦ 11 West 53rd Street (between 5th and 6th avenues)

🚇 53rd Street-5th Avenue station (E or V train)

✆ 212-708-9400

✎ *www.moma.org*

The Museum of Modern Art (MoMA) recently emerged from an incredible $858 million renovation that doubled the size of this important institution and gave it a new life on its seventy-fifth anniversary. The new museum is 630,000 square feet and still incorporates some of the original architectural elements of Philip Johnson's classic 1953 design in the new concept by Yoshio Taniguchi.

⬛ TRAVEL TIP

Although most museums are closed on Mondays, some New York museums are closed on different days. The Museum of Modern Art is closed on Wednesdays, the Guggenheim is closed on Thursdays, the Jewish Museum is closed on Fridays, and the New York City Police Museum is closed Sundays.

MoMA is an international force, its influence felt in all parts of the art world. It is a chief arbiter in determining important, emerging, or enduring works in modern art. Important exhibitions generate buzz for decades, forming watersheds in art history.

The collection is massive. To paraphrase from the museum's own literature, the collection contains more than 150,000 paintings, drawings, sculpture, photographs, prints, architectural models and drawings, and design objects. There are 22,000 films, video, and related materials, and 300,000 books and periodicals. The archives hold historical documentation that need about a half mile of shelf space. Special exhibits and film exhibitions change regularly; check the Web site for the latest offerings.

There are three restaurants in the building, all of which are comfortable for families. Café 2, on the second floor, serves rustic Italian food. Terrace 5 is a sleek and sophisticated café overlooking the sculpture garden. The Modern is an Alsatian restaurant with a separate bar area. It also overlooks the sculpture garden and is the only museum restaurant that allows you to linger past museum hours and leave through a separate exit.

The museum's new Design and Book Store came out of renovation as a striking backdrop to a unique collection of merchandise. There are two other MoMA shops. The Design Store is located across the street at 44 West Fifty-third Street (call for info at 212-767-1050). A second shop at 81 Spring Street at Crosby Street (information at 646-613-1367) is also open (see page 235). Items sold at MoMA stores represent the best of modern industrial and fashion design.

Hours and Fees

Open Saturday, Sunday, Monday, Wednesday, and Thursday from 10:30 A.M. to 5:30 P.M., Friday to 8 P.M. Closed Tuesdays, Thanksgiving Day, and December 25. Admission: adults $20, seniors (sixty-five and older with ID) $16, students (full time with current ID) $12, members and kids under sixteen are free. Friday nights from 4 to 8 P.M are free. A Top of the Rock ticket combines museum and Rockefeller Center Observatory admission for $30. Film showings are free to ticket holders, but there is a charge to nonadmission viewers.

JUST FOR PARENTS

The museum is sensitive to the needs of families. Before you go, log onto *www.moma.org/visit_moma/family.html* for valuable tips and preparation for visiting this (or, indeed, any) museum with your children.

The New York City Fire Museum

🖼 278 Spring Street (between Hudson and Varick streets)
🚇 Spring Street station (C or E train)
📞 212-691-1303
✉ *www.nycfiremuseum.org*

Set in a 1904 firehouse, the museum provides a walk through the history of firefighting, from eighteenth-century horse-drawn carriages to modern jaws of life rescue equipment. Its two floors hold the largest collection of fire-related artifacts in the country, and real firefighters lead tours. Exhibits range from toy fire trucks to very real shields, uniforms, and fireboat equipment.

For those who want to learn a bit more about New York's bravest, there is information about firefighting skills and equipment. You'll even learn about animals that have helped fight fires, including the Dalmatian, which has become the mascot of firefighters everywhere.

In contrast to other museums, you might find this one less crowded on the weekends, when the class trips aren't visiting. Although they probably won't appreciate the historical aspects, it's a great place to stop by with the kids for a couple of hours, particularly if you are planning a day at other lower Manhattan sights, such as the stock exchange, which may be less interesting to a six-year-old.

The museum gift shop sells authentic FDNY merchandise such as patches, hats, toys, books, T-shirts, and unique collectibles. The museum has no restaurant, but there are plenty of places to eat in the area.

JUST FOR PARENTS

A memorial exhibit features photos, paintings, children's artwork, and found objects from the site of the September 11 terrorist attacks, where 343 New York firefighters lost their lives.

Parking, Hours, and Fees

Some parking is available in front, and a parking lot is next door.

The museum is open Tuesday through Saturday from 10 A.M. to 5 P.M.; Sunday to 4 P.M. Closed major holidays. Suggested admission is $5 for adults, $2 for students or seniors, and $1 for children under twelve.

The New York City Police Museum

- 100 Old Slip (between Water and South streets)
- Wall Street station (2 or 3 train), Whitehall Street station (R or W train), or Broad Street station (J, M, or Z train)
- 212-480-3100
- www.nycpolicemuseum.org

This museum highlights the history of the police in New York City. It features exhibits on tracking down criminals, fingerprinting, and forensics. There is a Hall of Heroes for the officers who were killed in the line of duty and a special memorial to commemorate the police and Port Authority officers killed in the terrorist attacks of September 11.

A wide variety of police equipment is on display. Children will love the police motorcycles, police weapons, mug shots, and the mock jail cell. There is also an exhibit on women in policing. Some of the variously scheduled interactive programs may turn you and the kids into crime scene detectives or use your help in solving crimes. You may also opt to have your children photographed and fingerprinted (they'll love it) as part of the national Operation SAFE Child program. The museum and gift shop are wheelchair accessible.

Parking, Hours, and Fees

Hourly parking is available directly across from the museum. Open Monday through Saturday, 10 A.M. to 5 P.M. Suggested admission is $5 for adults, $3 for seniors, and $2 for children six to eighteen. Kids under six are free.

The New-York Historical Society

⌗ 170 Central Park West (between West 76th and West 77th streets)
🚇 West 81st Street station (B or C train)
📞 212-873-3400
✍ *www.nyhistory.org*

Founded in 1804, when "New-York" was still hyphenated, "New York's First Museum" houses millions of examples of Americana, including books, newspapers, maps, manuscripts, photographs, silverware, antique toys, posters, political cartoons, architectural drawings, carriages, furniture, and much, much more. The society also houses one of the most extensive American history research libraries you'll ever encounter.

The second oldest historical society in the country, the society's goal is to preserve all kinds of materials related to the city of New York. You can find everything from George Washington's inaugural chair to the world's largest collection of Tiffany lamps. Furniture is displayed chronologically so you can take notice of the changes in design and style through the centuries. Two must-see artistic highlights are the gallery of 1830s paintings from the collection of Luman Reed and the watercolors by John James Audubon—432 of them!—for his book *Birds of America*.

The historical society has a gift shop. The Café, catered by Eli Zabar, is open for lunch, snacks, and beverages 11 A.M. to 5 P.M. Tuesday to Sunday.

Parking, Hours, and Fees

Parking is difficult, so unless you want to pay for a neighborhood garage (if they have room), take public transportation.

The museum is open Tuesday through Sunday from 10 A.M. to 6 P.M. and selected holiday Mondays. On Friday the museum is free after 6 P.M. and closes at 8 P.M. The library is open Tuesday to Saturday from 10 A.M. to 5 P.M. An adult must accompany any children. You can cover the museum in half a day at a leisurely pace. Admission is $10 for adults, $7 for seniors (sixty-five and older) and educators, $6 for students, and free for children under twelve. Guided tours are held several times a day. Tours generally focus on certain sections of the museum, so ask beforehand if a tour covers the area(s) of interest to you. The museum is wheelchair and stroller accessible, and aids for the visually and/or hearing impaired are available.

The Paley Center for Media

🖳 25 West 52nd Street (between 5th and 6th avenues)

🚇 53rd Street-5th Avenue station (E and V train)

📞 212-621-6800 (recorded information)

📞 212-621-6600

🖎 *www.mtr.org*

Formerly known as the Museum of Television & Radio, the museum was established in 1965 by William Paley. The museum features a wealth of exhibits—for example, special tributes and galleries highlight the early years of television. Old television shows on display include the Beatles's first appearance on *The Ed Sullivan Show*, the most watched program at the museum. Vintage commercials provide a fascinating, whimsical glimpse of the past six decades and illustrate how society has changed. Search for your favorite multimedia broadcasts in an interactive computer catalog and access them in an individual or family viewing area. The Paley Center has an unrivaled collection of more than 140,000 clips spanning nearly a century of television and radio.

Two theaters and a screening room are used for interesting seminars and special evenings dedicated to television luminaries. There's a small gift shop in the lobby. No eating facilities are available, but there are plenty of restaurants and fast-food places in the neighborhood. The museum is wheelchair accessible, and listening devices and closed-caption decoders are provided on request.

 RAINY DAY FUN

Every Saturday from 10 A.M. until noon, the museum offers a special radio re-enactment where up to twenty kids (over the age of nine) get to re-enact an old radio play from the original script with sound effects. It's $10 per person, and you have to make a reservation, but your child will be mailed a CD of the visit!

Hours and Fees

The Paley Center is open Tuesday through Sunday from noon to 6 P.M., except Thursdays when the museum is open until 8 P.M. Admission is $10 for adults, $8 for students and seniors, and $5 for children under fourteen. Guided tours are offered; go to the front desk for information. The museum is closed January 1, July 4, Thanksgiving, and December 25.

The Skyscraper Museum

⌨ 39 Battery Place (near West Street, in the Ritz-Carlton Hotel)

🚇 Bowling Green station (4 or 5 train)

📞 212-968-1961

✎ www.skyscraper.org

Nothing says New York like skyscrapers, so where else should the only museum dedicated to the subject be located? Sharing a building with the Ritz-Carlton Hotel, the Skyscraper Museum is located in the historic tip of Manhattan, where it all began. It is located within walking distance of the World Trade Center site and is the repository of information on the World Trade Center, from its original design model to what the future site will look like.

Through exhibits, various programs, and publications, the museum explores every aspect of the skyscraper. It runs family programs on various Saturdays, with workshops appropriate for kids four to nine. Check its Web site under "Education" for a schedule, and check out the "Cool Stuff for Kids" section for "cool swag, merch, and high fashion" that will interest them. The museum itself will interest every member of the family with its always fascinating exhibits, displays, and models.

Hours and Fees

The museum is open from noon to 6 P.M., Wednesday to Sunday. Admission is $5 for adults and $2.50 for seniors and students.

Sony Wonder Technology Lab

⌨ 550 Madison Avenue (between East 56th Street and Madison Avenue)

🚇 East 59th Street station (4, 5, or 6 train), Lexington Avenue-East 59th Street station (N, R, or W train), East 57th Street station (F train), or 5th Avenue-East 53rd Street station (E or V train)

📞 212-833-8100

📞 212-833-5414 (tickets)

✎ www.sonywondertechlab.com

This might be the closest thing to heaven for today's kids. The four floors of interactive electronic gadgetry will satisfy every member of the family. Interactive is the byword as you explore, witness, use, and wonder at the latest in technology and digital entertainment. You can create your own movie, jam with musicians, or design a video game. There's an HDTV theater. This place has it all—Tech in the Plaza demonstrations, animated films, arcade events, Saturday children's screenings, family workshops, and kid workshops.

Hours and Fees

The museum flips the on switch Tuesday through Saturday 10 A.M. to 5 P.M. and Sunday noon to 5 P.M. Last admission is thirty minutes before closing. Closed Monday and major holidays. Admission is free, but this is a popular museum and requires dated and timed tickets. Tickets are distributed on a same-day basis, but get there early. Get advance registration (still free) one week to three months before your trip. Call 212-833-5414 between 9 A.M. and 2 P.M. weekdays or visit the Web site for further information.

The Sports Museum of America

⌨ 26 Broadway (at Morris Street)
🚊 Bowling Green (4 or 5 train)
✆ 212-837-7951
✎ *www.thesportsmuseum.com*

This unique attraction pays homage to all sports in a brand new 35,000-square-foot complex in lower Manhattan. It uses state-of-the-art exhibits and interactive displays to highlight the American fascination with sports. The museum has partnered with dozens of other sports museums across the country for resources and memorabilia.

The Sports Museum is the new home of the Heisman Trophy and the site of its annual presentation. It also houses the Billie Jean King International Women's Sports Center, the first museum dedicated to women's contributions to sports.

Sports-themed food is available at the museum, which also boasts 4,000 square feet of retail space. Visit the museum's Web site for current hours of operation and admission fees.

The Studio Museum in Harlem

- ▦ 144 West 125th Street (between Lenox Avenue and Adam Clayton Powell Jr. Blvd.)
- 🚇 West 125th Street station (2 or 3 train)
- 📞 212-864-4500
- 🖋 *www.studiomuseum.org*

The Studio Museum opened in 1968 as an exhibition space. It has grown over the past forty years into a full-fledged museum with galleries, workshops, and even a sculpture garden.

Some 100,000 visitors yearly browse the galleries that make up Harlem's premier museum. New permanent galleries have opened recently to add another 72,000 square feet of exhibit space to the current galleries. The collection includes nineteenth- and twentieth-century African American paintings and sculptures, twentieth-century Caribbean art, and traditional and contemporary art and artifacts from Africa.

The museum conducts many programs and events. There are also family programs that encourage families to spend time together. There is free admission to families on the first Saturday of each month when free tours and sketching opportunities are offered. The museum holds monthly family discussions and workshops, and family tours and passes are given for each new exhibition.

Parking, Hours, and Fees

Public transportation is the best way to get there, but there is parking in a municipal lot on 126th Street and Lenox Avenue.

The museum is open Wednesday through Friday and Sundays from noon to 6 P.M. and on Saturdays from 10 A.M. to 6 P.M. It is closed Mondays, Tuesdays, and major holidays. Suggested donation is $7 for adults and $3 for seniors and students with valid IDs; free to children under twelve. The first Saturday of the month is free to families. A museum shop in the lobby sells books, posters, prints, and gift items.

Whitney Museum of American Art

- 945 Madison Avenue (at 75th Street)
- East 77th Street station (4, 5, or 6 train)
- 120 Park Avenue (at 42nd Street across from Grand Central Terminal)
- Grand Central-East 42nd Street station (S, 4, 5, 6, or 7 train)
- 1-877-WHITNEY (944-8639)
- *www.whitney.org*

Founded in 1930, the Whitney now houses more then 12,000 works by nearly 2,000 artists. The museum features twentieth-century and contemporary American art, including paintings, sculpture, photography, and more. Most famous for its awesome collection of New York impressionist painters of the Ashcan school, it has an extensive collection of works from the estate of Edward Hopper. Also included in the Whitney's collection are examples of Alexander Calder's circus figures and mobiles. The museum also has significant holdings of works by Reginald Marsh, Marsden Hartley, Georgia O'Keeffe, and Louise Nevelson.

≡FAST FACT

For more than half a century, the Whitney Biennial has been the place where emerging artists launch their careers. If you are lucky enough to be visiting during a biennial year, try to make this event. Any material that is inappropriate for children will be marked as such outside the room.

The original 1966 building, designed by German Bauhaus architect Marcel Breuer (of Breuer chair fame), has been expanded to help accommodate the nearly half a million visitors who come to admire the art each year. It is actually the third structure to house this famous collection started by Gertrude Vanderbilt Whitney. The oddly shaped building, a work of art itself, is surrounded by a sculpture garden and walls.

Sarabeth's Restaurant (212-570-3670) is open for lunch and brunch within the museum. The Whitney Museum Store and Museum Bookstore offer gift ideas and books primarily about American art.

The museum has an extensive program of family and children's art activities. Go online before exploring and see if there is a half-day program when you are visiting.

Parking, Hours, and Fees

Take public transportation; this is a very busy area not known for its street parking.

The museum is open Wednesday through Sunday from 11 A.M. to 6 P.M. except Friday, when hours shift to 1 to 9 P.M. (From 6 P.M., it's pay-what-you-wish admission.) The Whitney is closed on Monday and Tuesday. Admission is $15 for adults, $10 for seniors (sixty-two and older) and students with a valid ID, and free for children under twelve. The museum is wheelchair accessible; strollers are allowed but may be restricted in certain exhibitions.

CHAPTER 10

Brooklyn and Queens

RUNNERS IN THE New York City Marathon make their way through all five boroughs, beginning in the morning in Staten Island and ending in the afternoon at the finish line in Manhattan's Central Park. For most visitors, however, it's more enjoyable to explore the boroughs on separate trips. You can get almost anywhere in the boroughs from midtown Manhattan in about forty-five minutes by train.

Visiting Brooklyn

The onetime home of Woody Allen, Mae West, Neil Diamond, Mel Brooks, Barbra Streisand, and numerous other celebrities, Brooklyn is the composite of numerous distinctively ethnic neighborhoods, including Brighton Beach with its large Ukrainian and Russian population, the Italian community of Bensonhurst, and the Orthodox Jews that make up Borough Park.

There's no doubt as you drive or walk through different sections of Brooklyn that the neighborhoods take on their own identities. Park Slope, for example, is a trendy outgrowth of Manhattan, with fashionable shops and cafés. Sheepshead Bay is home to seafood fresh from the fishing boats that dock at the marina. Brooklyn Heights, sitting high on a hill overlooking Manhattan, is a posh neighborhood founded in the early nineteenth century as a suburban alternative to city life. Bensonhurst is an older Italian-American neighborhood, rich with tradition. Row houses and red brick buildings characterize the various residential neighborhoods, stores line the bustling streets, and municipal buildings make up the downtown section of the busy borough.

TRAVEL TIP

The city has privately run express bus service to and from many prime locations in the boroughs. Call the city's information line at 311 (or 212-NEW-YORK [639-9675]) from outside the city) to find out which express buses service your desired destination.

While Brooklyn is home to a lot of small, tightly knit neighborhoods, the overall borough is one in which residents take great pride. Brooklyn is as big as many of our country's largest cities (only Los Angeles, Chicago, and New York itself are larger).

Brooklyn Museums and Attractions

Brooklyn is connected to Manhattan by one of the most iconic bridges in the United States, a tourist destination in its own right.

The New York City Transit Museum
🖃 Boerum Place and Schermerhorn Street
🚇 Borough Hall station (2, 3, 4, or 5 train)
📞 718-694-1600
✑ *www.mta.info/mta/museum/general.htm*
✑ *www.transitmuseumeducation.org/trc*
✑ *www.mta.info*

Gallery Annex & Store
🖃 Shuttle Passage, Main Concourse
🚇 Grand Central Terminal
📞 212-878-1016

Housed in a historic 1936 IND subway station in Brooklyn Heights, and easily accessible by subway, the New York Transit Museum is the largest museum in the United States devoted to urban public transportation history, and one of the premier institutions of its kind in the world. The museum explores the development of the greater New York metropolitan region through the presentation of exhibitions, tours, educational programs, and workshops dealing with the cultural, social, and technological history of public transportation. Go to *www.mta.info* for details of current exhibits and programs or to shop the museum's online store.

≡FAST FACT

DUMBO (Down Under the Brooklyn Bridge Overpass) was Brooklyn's answer to Manhattan's SoHo. It became the location for a number of art galleries. Go the first Thursday of the month from 5:30 P.M. for gallery and studio open houses.

The Gallery Annex, in Grand Central Terminal (in Manhattan), presents changing exhibits and has an adjoining retail store with interesting items relating to the transit system, including subway token watches, strap-hanger ties, and more. Admission to the Annex is free. Open Monday through Friday from 8 A.M. to 8 P.M., Saturday and Sunday from 10 A.M. to 6 P.M. Information at 212-878-0106.

Hours and Fees

The New York City Transit Museum in Brooklyn is open Tuesday through Friday from 10 A.M. to 4 P.M., Saturday and Sunday from noon to 5 P.M. Admission is $5 for adults and $3 for seniors (sixty-two and older, free on Wednesdays) and children (three to seventeen). Wheelchair accessible.

☂ RAINY DAY FUN

The newly expanded Brooklyn Children's Museum at 145 Brooklyn Avenue in Crown Heights (on the Web at *www.brooklynkids.org*) was the first children's museum in the world, and kids can explore a variety of age-appropriate interactive experiences. Open seven days a week and most school holidays.

Coney Island

🖺 Along Surf Avenue between 37th Street and Ocean Parkway

🚇 Coney Island-Stillwell Avenue station (D, F, N, or Q train)

"Coney" is the English spelling for the Dutch word *konijn*, meaning rabbit. Coney Island was named for the many rabbits that were once found in the area, which originally was an island, or close to it.

Coney Island was once the hotspot of the borough, billed as the World's Largest Playground. In its heyday, the early 1900s, attractions like an elephant-shaped hotel, a replica of Baghdad called Luna Park, and a popular nightspot called Dreamland drew large crowds.

Today a stroll on the boardwalk is the perfect way to take in the sea air, and the beach is the place for sun and relaxation in the summer heat. Nathan's has been serving its world-famous hot dogs since 1916, and you can still, uh, relish the experience.

The screams from thrill rides still echo through the park all summer long, and the Ferris wheel will give you a view of all of Coney Island and much of Brooklyn. The amusement park, Astroland, the last relic of what Coney Island once was, has been sold and was set for demolition at press time. The developer's plans call for a mix of amusements and attractions, along with a hotel to accommodate the anticipated tourists. The expected date of completion is 2011.

The former owners of Astroland have retained some of the rides and announced they hope to relocate. The newly invigorated Coney

Island, along with Rye Playland, just north of the Bronx in Westchester County, are among the few amusement parks around New York City.

Experience the nostalgia many people associate with Coney Island by looking at the old parachute jump ride, now simply "the tower," which hasn't been operative for more than thirty years. You can also see the history of Coney Island at a small Coney Island museum. The Sideshows by the Seashore (at West Twelfth Street and Surf Avenue; call 718-372-5159 for information) is home to an old-fashioned circus sideshow with a fire eater, sword swallower, snake charmer, and other entertainers. Note that the show will be too intense for preteens. The adjoining Coney Island Museum is full of fascinating memorabilia from the neighborhood's illustrious past. The boardwalk outside also leads to the New York Aquarium.

═══FAST FACT

In the movie *Annie Hall,* Woody Allen claimed he grew up in a house under the roller coaster in Coney Island. The house, once the Kensingon Hotel, was real. It was under the old Thunderbolt roller coaster, which was demolished in 2000.

In the off-season, October through April, the neighborhood is relatively deserted, save for the annual visit from the Polar Bear Club. This bunch of zanies make the news every January by putting on their bathing suits and heading into the ocean for a truly chilling experience.

If you're heading to Coney Island, prepare to spend the day—a warm late spring or summer day is ideal. Bring your blanket, sunscreen, and some patience; parking is not easy. The subway ride from Manhattan will take about an hour. Coney Island can still provide, after all these years, some good outdoor family fun in an old-time landmark neighborhood that is a staple of Brooklyn's historic past.

 **TRAVEL TIP**

The Coney Island season kicks off in May with the Mermaid Parade, a twenty-year tradition in which a parade of women—and some men—dress up in their mermaid best to parade along the boardwalk.

The New York Aquarium

⊡ Surf Avenue and West 8th Street

🚊 West 8th Street-NY Aquarium station (F or Q train)

📞 718-265-FISH (3474)

✉ www.nyaquarium.com

The city's only full-scale aquarium dates back to 1896 and has been in Coney Island since the mid-1950s, attracting thousands of visitors annually. On fourteen acres off the boardwalk, the New York Aquarium has operated longer than any other similar facility in the country. There are temporary exhibits and special events on occasion, but the permanent attractions are the major crowd pleasers. Such popular exhibits include the Sea Cliffs exhibit, with walruses, penguins, otters, and seals in a re-creation of their native habitat; the new Alien Stingers exhibit of mysterious sea jellies; and the Aquatheater, where sea lions and dolphins perform year round.

With 350 species and more than 8,000 aquatic animals in a host of massive tanks, the aquarium is packed with delights of the underwater world. A new 165,000-gallon exhibition, Glover's Reef, will put you eye-to-eye with jawfish, eels, sharks, and more than thirty-five other species in a coral reef ecosystem. Recently added is the Deep Sea 3D ride ($4 with your ticket, $6 alone), which will carry you down to the deepest depths of the ocean to meet some of nature's oddest creatures. Computer enhanced over the years, the aquarium also offers a wealth of information for learning more about the creatures of the sea.

The aquarium is fun and educational for both children and parents. It's an enjoyable place to spend a few hours after a stroll on the boardwalk. On summer weekends it can get overly crowded with long lines for everything, so it's best to arrive early on a weekday if possible. The aquarium offers dining at the new SeaSide Café and an outdoor snack bar with tables in the plaza.

Hours and Fees

The aquarium is open every day of the year and can be visited Monday through Friday between Memorial Day and Labor Day from 10 A.M. to 6 P.M. and on weekends from 10 A.M. to 7 P.M. The aquarium closes at 5 P.M. on weekdays and 5:30 P.M. on weekends from September to October and April to May. It closes at 4:30 P.M. between October and April.

Admission is $12 for adults, $8 for seniors (sixty-five and older) and children ages two through twelve, and free for children under two. Children under sixteen must be accompanied by an adult. Parking is available for $10, but lots fill up quickly on weekends so get there early.

The Brooklyn Botanic Garden

⌨ 1000 Washington Avenue

🚆 Eastern Parkway-Brooklyn Museum station (2 or 3 train)

✆ 718-623-7263

✎ *www.bbg.org*

Smack in the middle of Brooklyn are fifty-two of the most lavishly beautiful acres New York City has to offer. More than 750,000 people visit this spectacular tribute to Mother Nature annually. The Brooklyn Botanic Garden is located among the red brick buildings, row houses, storefronts, and municipal buildings that characterize much of the borough.

Consisting of gardens, greenhouses, and exhibits, the garden offers a visual mirage of colors and a host of pleasing fragrances all year round. The following are just some of the attractions offered by the garden:

- The Shakespeare Garden, like its Central Park counterpart, features flowers mentioned in the works of William Shakespeare in a setting modeled after an English cottage garden.
- The Cranford Rose Garden has tens of thousands of rose bushes. They grow in formal beds, up over arches, and onto the accompanying pavilion. The Rose Garden opened in 1928 and comprises one acre of a massive outdoor flower gallery.
- The Japanese Hill-and-Pond Garden is brilliantly landscaped with bridges, waterfalls, a koi pond, a viewing pavilion, a waiting house, and shrubs carefully designed and shaped. Established in 1915, it is one of the oldest and most popular Japanese-inspired gardens outside Japan.
- The Fragrance Garden, built in the 1950s, is designed for people who are visually impaired. It features flowers in raised beds, various aromas, and textured foliage. Braille plaques help guide visitors. Enjoyed by the sighted as well, it was the first garden of its kind in the country.
- The Children's Garden, first opened in 1914, is a place where children can learn about plants by enjoying the hands-on experience of planting and gardening. Instructors teach children of all ages about plants, insects, and animals. A thirty-minute tour covers activities and displays and gives children a chance to care for and harvest flowers and vegetables. Some 25,000 youngsters have tended this garden over the years.

═FAST FACT

The Brooklyn Botanic Garden features its own Celebrity Path in homage to a surprisingly long list of famous Brooklynites. Among those included are Mel Brooks, Mary Tyler Moore, and Maurice Sendak; their names are inscribed on stepping stones that meander through trees and plants just south of the Japanese Garden.

- Osbourne Garden is a formal setting, complete with fountain, seating, and columns found in traditional Italian gardens. Within the three-acre garden is a 30,000-square-foot center lawn surrounded by flowering trees and shrubs.
- The Steinhart Conservatory, built in the late 1980s, is a modern $25 million complex. Its greenhouses display the thousands of indoor plants that are part of the Botanic Garden. A new attraction is an extremely rare Wollemi pine. Touted as a major botanical find of the century, the Wollemi pine was believed to be extinct for two million years, but a small grove of trees was discovered in Australia's Blue Mountains, setting off worldwide excitement for a majestic plant that managed to survive seventeen ice ages over the past millennia.
- The Terrace Café offers gourmet lunches and beverages with outdoor dining in the warmer months.

Location, Hours, and Fees

The Brooklyn Botanic Garden is located on Washington Avenue, on the south side of the Brooklyn Museum.

From April through October, the garden is open Tuesday through Friday from 8 A.M. to 6 P.M. (weekends from 10 A.M. to 6 P.M.). From November through March, the garden closes at 4:30 P.M. The garden is closed on Thanksgiving Day, December 25, and New Year's Day.

Admission is free to the public on various days off-season and Saturday mornings until noon; otherwise, it is $5 for adults over sixteen, $3 for seniors (sixty-five and older, free on Fridays) and students with IDs, and free for children sixteen and under. A discounted Brooklyn Art and Garden Ticket includes both the Garden and Brooklyn Museum.

Guided tours are free and feature seasonal highlights. They are offered at 1 P.M. on all weekends except major holiday weekends. Thirty-minute Children's Garden family tours are offered on Tuesday afternoons at 2 P.M. in June, July, and August.

TRAVEL TIP

It's easy to get around Brooklyn's cultural sites with a free shuttle. The Heart of Brooklyn Trolley leaves from Prospect Park's Wollman Center and Rink on the hour and makes stops throughout Prospect Park, as well as near the Brooklyn Public Library, Brooklyn Museum, Prospect Park Zoo, and Brooklyn Botanic Garden. It operates Saturdays, Sundays, and holidays from noon to 6 P.M. throughout the year. You can get information and a map at *www.heartofbrooklyn .org,* or call 718- 638-7700.

Brooklyn Museum

200 Eastern Parkway (at Washington Avenue)
Eastern Parkway-Brooklyn Museum station (2 or 3 train)
718-638-5000
www.brooklynmuseum.org

Of New York City's museums, the Brooklyn Museum is second in size and importance of its collection only to the Met. Founded in 1823 as the Brooklyn Apprentices Library Association (with Walt Whitman as one of its first librarians), the museum now resides inside a massive 1893 Beaux-Arts structure designed by McKim, Mead, and White (who also designed the West Wing of the White House). It houses more than one million paintings, artifacts, drawings, and photographs and even has its own newly renovated subway station.

One of the world's most renowned collections of Egyptian art— Brooklyn Museum curators go to Egypt every year for digs—covers the third floor. Jewelry, ivory, gold, and even a wrapped 2,600-year-old human mummy can be found in the installation that was ten years in the making.

The building houses masks and shields from Central Africa and art of the Pacific from Polynesia, Malaysia, and Indonesia. There is a large collection of pan-American art, including a fifteenth-century

Aztec stone jaguar, textiles, ceramics, and gold objects. An extensive collection of Asian art includes works from Cambodia, China, India, Iran, Korea, Japan, Thailand, Tibet, and Turkey.

There are eleven period rooms, ranging from a seventeenth-century Brooklyn Dutch farmhouse to a magnificent smoking room from the Rockefeller house. Paintings and sculptures from American and European artists span some seven centuries, with masterpieces from Frans Hals, Monet, Degas, and Picasso.

In 2007, the Elizabeth A. Sackler Center for Feminist Art opened on the fourth floor. The 8,300-square-foot space encompasses a gallery that contains Judy Chicago's seminal work *The Dinner Party.*

RAINY DAY FUN

The Brooklyn Museum hosts a series of programs of art, music, and dance called Target First Saturdays, from 5 P.M. to 11 P.M. Admission to the museum and its events are free, and sandwiches, salads, and beverages are served all evening. There's also a cash bar with wine and beer. It is one of the museum's most successful programs and is widely attended, especially in the summer. Line up for tickets thirty minutes early.

There's plenty here to interest the younger set, and it provides a great cultural history for visitors from around the world. A sculpture garden boasts a recently restored thirty-foot replica of the Statue of Liberty.

Hours and Fees

The museum is open Wednesday through Friday from 10 A.M. to 5 P.M.; Saturdays and Sundays from 11 A.M. to 6 P.M.; and the first Saturday of the month from 11 A.M. to 11 P.M. Suggested contribution is $8 for adults, $4 for seniors (sixty-two and older) and students with a valid

ID, and free for children under twelve. Limited on-site parking is available at the rear of the museum. Parking fee is $3 for the first hour, $2 each additional hour, $12 maximum. On Target First Saturdays there is a flat $4 fee beginning at 5 P.M.

Destination Queens

The largest of the five boroughs, Queens has hosted two World's Fairs and is home to the city's two major airports, the Mets, and Queens College (whose heralded alumni include Jerry Seinfeld, Paul Simon, and Marvin Hamlisch). Queens is a far-reaching borough in the center of it all. It connects to Manhattan and the Bronx by bridge and to Brooklyn and Long Island by land.

Named for Queen Catherine, the wife of King Charles II of England, and colonized in 1683, the sprawling borough combines a taste of the suburbs with urban flair.

Numerous architectural styles typify the various neighborhoods, including old red brick buildings, row houses, and attached houses of the 1950s and 1960s. There are large estates in the aptly named area of Jamaica Estates, and a quaint old-fashioned, wall-enclosed residential community called Forest Hills Gardens. You will also find some modern office buildings springing up—along with movie studios—in Long Island City.

▐ TRAVEL TIP

Driving in Queens can take some getting used to. Avenues and streets can have the same name so you might find yourself on a crossroad between Twentieth Drive and Twentieth Avenue.

Not unlike Brooklyn, Queens has its share of ethnically diverse neighborhoods. The borough is most famous for its wonderful Greek restaurants in Astoria, Little India in Jackson Heights, and its own Chinatown in Flushing.

Places to Visit in Queens

Queens, once the sleepy bedroom community of Manhattan, is awakening with new vitality. With creative types and an energetic immigrant community, the borough is changing. It has become a growing art center and a destination for great ethnic food, so you can have an unusual day touring its one-of-a-kind sights.

Hall of Science

47-01 111th Street
Flushing Meadows-Corona Park

111th Street station (7 train)

718-699-0005

www.nyscience.org

Part of the 1964 World's Fair, this museum has recently undergone an expansion and renovation. An interactive hands-on museum, the Hall of Science features more than 400 exhibits for youngsters and parents to explore, play with, and learn from, including a high-powered telescope. Microbiology, quantum physics, geology, audio technology, and other subjects are covered in a fun way.

A 30,000-square-foot outdoor science playground adjacent to the museum features an oversized seesaw, a light-activated kinetic sculpture, and other activities to climb in, climb on, run through, and explore. Designed to show the principles of physics while providing a good time, the playground/science park is open for children six and over. There is a $3 per-person charge above the admission.

The museum has a gift shop with a wide range of science-related items, from inexpensive gadgets to microscopes and telescopes. A newly refurbished café is run by Dream Street.

Location, Hours, and Fees

The Hall of Science is located in Flushing Meadows-Corona Park. Parking is available in the Hall's private lot for a $10 fee on weekends, holidays, and weekdays in the summer.

September to May: open Tuesday to Thursday 9:30 A.M. to 2 P.M., Friday 9:30 A.M. to 5 P.M., and weekends 10 A.M. to 5 P.M. Closed Mondays except holidays. June: Monday to Thursday 9:30 A.M. to 2 P.M., Friday 9:30 A.M. to 5 P.M.; weekends 10 A.M. to 6 P.M. July and August: Monday to Friday 9:30 A.M. to 5 P.M., weekends 10 A.M. to 6 P.M.

Admission is $11 for adults and $8 for seniors (sixty-two and older) and children (two to seventeen). There is free admission from Memorial Day to Labor Day on Fridays from 2 P.M. to 5 P.M. and Sundays from 10 A.M. to 11 A.M. Closed January 1, Labor Day, Thanksgiving Day, and December 25.

TRAVEL TIP

If you make a day of art in Queens, you might want to try some of the restaurants along the way. There's a good Greek restaurant, S'Agapo Taverna, at 34–31 Thirty-fourth Avenue; a lovely restaurant with a view, the Water's Edge, at 44 Drive and the East River; and what has been called the perfect diner, Court House Square, at 45–30 Twenty-third Street, Long Island City.

Museum of the Moving Image

⌨ 35th Avenue (at 36th Street)

🚇 Steinway Avenue station (G, R, or V train)

📞 718-784-0077

📞 718-784-4520 (Administrative Office)

✎ www.movingimage.us

Although you can't tour the studios, you can get a great glimpse at movie-making history at the Museum of the Moving Image. Queens was the center of the New York film industry in the early days, and the museum's location just over the bridge from Manhattan in close proximity to Silvercup Studios (home to *Sex and the City* and *The Sopranos*) and Kaufman Astoria Studios is perfect for paying tribute to motion pictures and television.

The original 50,000-square-foot museum, opened in 1988, is housed in part of the historic old studio built by Paramount in 1920. A massive renovation and expansion will nearly double the museum's size and triple the exhibition area. The museum will remain open and functioning during the work, which is scheduled to be completed in 2009.

The latest in electronic technology will provide visitors with a mind-blowing experience as new and historic works are brought to life. Three floors of exhibit space feature attractions such as Behind the Screen, a look at the history of the cinema, complete with movie memorabilia. A digital play computer space exhibit of classic video arcade games and new home-computer games brings the museum into the twenty-first century.

The museum features fourteen interactive exhibits. Visitors learn sound and music editing, and they can make their own animated cartoon or a video flip book. You can even dub your own voice over a movie scene. The charming, whimsical Tut's Fever Movie Palace is a minitheater built like the movie palaces of the 1930s, showing classic images and serials like *Flash Gordon, Buck Rogers,* and *The Lone Ranger.* The regular ongoing film programs will be held off-site during the renovation.

The museum store sells movie books, toys, posters, jewelry, postcards, and other objects with movie and television themes. There is also a café for light dining and snacks. Because these are located in the work area, operation may be affected. More of an actual hands-on experience for the family than its video library counterpart, the Radio and Television Museum in Manhattan, Moving Image is off the beaten path but worth the short ride. If you plan a visit to this wonderful museum, make sure to call first and check on programs, exhibits, and hours, which may or may not be affected by the renovation work.

Location, Hours, and Fees

The Museum of the Moving Image is located one mile from the Queensboro Bridge. You can take the subway or drive and park without much trouble on the weekend.

Moving Image's hours are a complicated affair and may change during the renovation, so go to the Web site or call ahead. Closed Monday and Tuesday, open all other days at 11 A.M. Closes Wednesday and Thursday at 5 P.M., Saturday and Sunday at 6:30 P.M., and Friday at 8 P.M. Admission is $10 for adults, $7.50 for seniors and college students with a valid ID, and $5 for children. The museum is free on Fridays after 4 P.M. Closed on Memorial Day, Thanksgiving Day, and December 25.

Queens Museum of Art

🖾 Flushing Meadows-Corona Park
🚊 Willets Point-Shea Stadium or 111th Street stations (7 train)
📞 718-592-9700
✑ *www.queensmuseum.org*

This distinctive museum features the history of the two major World's Fairs held in Flushing Meadows Park, complete with memorabilia. Once a garbage dump, the park was transformed into the fairgrounds to host the 1939 and later the 1964 World's Fairs. The 1939 building was known as the New York City exhibit in the 1939 and 1964 World's Fairs and housed the General Assembly of the new United Nations from 1946 to 1950. The unmistakable Unisphere was the 1964 fair's symbol and is the largest globe in the world.

A stunning 9,000-square-foot miniature replica of New York City represents all five boroughs block by block, house by house, with changes made from time to time as new buildings replace older ones. The scale is one inch per 100 feet, and the detail is awesome. Much safer than a helicopter ride over the city, you could stand and look at the buildings, the bridges, and the neighborhoods for hours.

Also in the museum you'll find an extensive Tiffany lamp exhibition, special events, changing exhibits, weekend tours (with Spanish tours on Sundays), and an exhibit about the building itself. There is also an adjoining ice-skating rink if you want to take a spin on the ice during the winter months.

There are free drop-in family workshops every Sunday for children five and up and their adult companions. There is also an open art studio for kids with special needs. In addition, the museum's ArtZone is a family-friendly, interactive art space with changing programs.

Note: An extensive renovation and expansion to double the museum's size is planned to begin sometime in 2008. If you plan to visit, call ahead for information.

A gift shop sells World's Fair mementos. There is no dining facility, but the Web site lists many interesting restaurants around the two subway stops that service the museum.

Hours and Fees

The Queens Museum of Art is open Wednesday through Friday from 10 A.M. to 5 P.M. and Saturday and Sunday from noon to 5 P.M. The suggested admission is $5 for adults and $2.50 for seniors and students.

Isamu Noguchi Garden Museum

⌨ 9-01 33rd Road (at Vernon Boulevard), Long Island City

🚇 Broadway station (N or W train)

📞 718-204-7088

✎ www.noguchi.org

This beautiful garden museum is dedicated to the life and work of talented Japanese-American artist, architect, and sculptor Isamu Noguchi (1904–1988). The site is the home of a former engraving plant purchased in 1975 by the artist as a place to display his work. More than 250 of his works in wood, clay, stone, and metal, as well as models, furniture, stage sets, and much more can be seen throughout the thirteen galleries and in the open air garden. Noguchi designed one of the most popular coffee tables in America—a smoked teardrop over a curved black wood base, which is available in the store, along with a wide variety of furniture, tableware, lamps, clocks, books, prints, and sculpture tools and supplies.

Hours and Fees

The Isamu Noguchi Garden Museum is open Wednesday to Friday from 10 A.M. to 5 P.M. and on weekends from 11 A.M. to 6 P.M. Admission is $10 for adults, $5 for seniors and students with ID, and free to children under twelve. Pay what you wish on the first Friday of the month. Closed January 1, Thanksgiving, and December 25.

P.S. 1 Contemporary Art Center

⊡ 22-25 Jackson Avenue (at 46th Street), Long Island City

🚆 45 Road-Courthouse Square station (7 train)

✆ 718-784-2084

✐ www.ps1.org

P.S. 1 was one of the first contemporary art exhibition spaces outside Manhattan to draw the mainstream art world off the island. Once an abandoned 100-year-old school building, it is now a partner with the Museum of Modern Art. P.S. 1 exhibitions often feature local and emerging artists.

Hours and Fees

The center is open Thursday through Monday, noon to 6 P.M. Suggested donation is $5.

CHAPTER 11

The Bronx and Staten Island

THE BRONX AND Staten Island offer some of New York's major attractions. Yankee Stadium, the famed Bronx Zoo, and the spectacular New York Botanical Garden are world-class attractions. The Bronx also boasts Edgar Allan Poe's house, one of the oldest golf courses in the country, and a small island of fishermen and fabulous seafood restaurants. The view of the Manhattan skyline and the Statue of Liberty are just incredible from that twenty-minute ride on the Staten Island Ferry, so venture beyond the shores of Manhattan.

The Bronx

The borough was named after Jonas Bronck, a Swedish sailor who built a farm on the land in the seventeenth century. By the nineteenth century, fashionable estates, parks, the Botanical Garden, and other marvelously landscaped areas set the tone. Homes were spread out, and life along the Grand Concourse, the major thoroughfare of the borough, was grand. It wasn't until the twentieth century and after World War II in particular that the Bronx started to reflect the poverty and despair that has plagued much of the borough over the past twenty-five years.

JUST FOR PARENTS

Who would believe that one of the most romantic sites in all of New York is in the Bronx? In the middle of City Island there is a tiny inn and restaurant called Le Refuge Inn (at 718-885-2478, *www.lerefuge inn.com*). Run by two French immigrants, it is the perfect spot for a city getaway (it has wonderful accommodations) or just a very romantic dinner for two.

The Bronx has undergone a renaissance during the last few years and is a burgeoning center for the performing arts, the result of an influx of creative Latin American and African immigrants. Hip-hop started in the Bronx. Like most of the city, the Bronx has a wonderful diversity of ethnic neighborhoods, including the Caribbean section of Williamsbridge and Woodlawn and the Italian-based Belmont, with its local shops, bakeries, and old-time New York flavor.

Things to Do in the Bronx

It used to be that the mere mention of the words "the Bronx" brought shivers to one's spine. No more. A day in the Bronx can be quite a fun family affair, with a visit to the Bronx Zoo, Yankee Stadium, the New York Botanical Garden, and dinner in one of the fabulous Italian restaurants along Arthur Avenue.

The New York Botanical Garden
🖃 200th Street and Southern Blvd.
🚆 Bedford Park Blvd. station (train B or D)
✆ 718-817-8700
✐ *www.nybg.org*

The most beautiful 250 acres you'll find in the Bronx, and possibly in all of New York City, are in the New York Botanical Garden. A serene refuge from the big city, the garden is worth the trip to the northern borough, especially if you also visit the neighboring Bronx Zoo.

The site was selected back in 1891 and developed as a place for the public to enjoy the beautifully landscaped outdoors. Today the facility incorporates dramatic rock outcroppings, wetlands, ponds, a waterfall, and a forty-acre forest, along with sixteen specialty gardens including a rose garden and a rock garden. A Victorian-era glass-house has been home to indoor plants since 1902 (the orchids are world-renowned), and there is a museum building and stone cottage. The garden is also in the scientific research game; its new Plant Studies Center and a new plant studies library is one of the biggest in the country with more than 1.26 million print and nonprint items.

 TRAVEL TIP

Plan ahead. Schedule shopping for later in the day. Major sights have gift shops, and your purchases can add up (in weight and in cost). If you plan to take photos, check your camera batteries and bring an extra memory card or roll of film. The big chain pharmacies are a good place to buy inexpensive cameras, supplies, and water.

Included among the gardens you'll find the Peggy Rockefeller Rose Garden, with a central iron gazebo and thousands of varieties of roses. Along with a 2.5-acre rock garden, you'll enjoy a native plant garden with nine different habitats displaying plants indigenous to the northeastern United States. More than 150 herbs are found in the Nancy Bryan Luce Herb Garden, and the Demonstration Gardens offer a variety of gardens that visitors can re-create in their back-yards, including fragrance, country, and cutting gardens. In the Everett Children's Adventure Garden, youngsters can learn about tending to plants while engrossed in larger-than-life interactive games.

From bulbs to daffodils to daylilies to chrysanthemums, if it's a plant or part of a garden, it's most likely found in the New York Botanical

Garden. There is even a forest with birds and wildlife in one of the oldest tracts of uncut nature remaining in the city. The outdoor children's garden is a delight, and kids can build a bird's nest, look at pond life with a magnifying glass, and wander through mazes and topiary gardens. There is a wonderful botanical research center with workshops.

The garden shop is a great place for buying anything you need for a garden, from seeds to watering cans; it also has a great selection of gardening books and unusual gift items. You'll find a children's shop in the Everett Children's Adventure Garden, and on the weekends there are wonderful workshops for kids.

There are special events and several tours are offered, including a tram tour (a small extra fee), a golf cart tour (no putting allowed), and walking tours of the gardens or the forest. The Garden Café is a good place to grab a bite to eat, and picnic tables are available. A visitors' center provides maps as you enter—you will need one to find your way around.

Hours and Fees

The New York Botanical Garden is open Tuesday through Sunday from 10 A.M. to 6 P.M. from April through October, and from 10 A.M. to 5 P.M. from November through March. Grounds-only admission is $6 for adults, $3 for seniors, $2 for students with valid ID, and $1 for children two through twelve. There are extra fees for the Conservatory, Adventure Garden, Rock and Native Plant gardens, and the tram tour. These and more are included for free in the general admission ticket, which runs $13 for adults, $11 for seniors and students, and $5 for children. Admission is free all day Wednesday and Saturday from 10 A.M. to noon. Parking is available for $10.

The Bronx Zoo

⌨ Fordham Road and Bronx River Parkway

🚇 West Farms Square-East Tremont Avenue station (2 or 5 train)

✆ 718-367-1010

✎ *www.bronxzoo.com*

The Bronx Zoo has for more than a century been a marvelous adventure for children and adults alike. The zoo, now officially known as the International Wildlife Conservation Center, is home to more than 4,000 animals in a variety of settings designed to simulate their natural habitats. Encompassing 265 acres, it is the largest urban wildlife conservation facility in America.

The zoo provides a full day of activities for families, with numerous exhibits including the Congo Gorilla Forest, which covers more than 6.5 acres and re-creates an African rain forest with more than 400 animals from fifty-five species.

Other exhibits include JungleWorld, an indoor tropical rain forest exhibit, complete with Asian gibbons and numerous other fascinating creatures. The zoo also features the Wild Asia Monorail, a ride through the re-created forests and meadows of Asia. It's populated with all the creatures of those nature documentaries on public television, including elephants, rhinos, and Indo-Chinese tigers. The Baboon Reserve is a simulated archeological dig tracing the evolution of the Gelada baboons, complete with numerous baboons playing on the side of the miniature mountain range.

Kids love the World of Darkness, which gives you a glimpse into the nocturnal creatures of the night, including various bats and rats. The Himalayan Highlands exhibit features red pandas, endangered snow leopards, and other animals of the Himalayas.

The Children's Zoo allows the kids to meet, greet, and feed a variety of animals and participate in various kid-friendly activities. Closed during winter months, the Children's Zoo costs $3 more for admission and includes a petting zoo. Still other exhibits include Mousehouse, Skyfari, World of Birds, and African Plains. Feedings and demonstrations are carried on throughout the day.

Nobody goes hungry at the zoo. There are numerous food stands and mobile carts, plus a wealth of restaurants: the Dancing Crane Café, the Terrace Café near the Children's Zoo, Asia Restaurant, and the African Market. There is also an unusual gift shop with some unique choices for friends and family.

Tickets are sold up until an hour before the zoo closes, but you should allow yourself at least three hours to see everything. Check the weather before you plan a day at the zoo to avoid getting caught in any inclement weather.

Hours and Fees

The Bronx Zoo is open 365 days a year, although several exhibits close down during the winter months. The hours are 10 A.M. to 5 P.M. (4:30 P.M. during the winter). Admission is $14 for adults, $12 for seniors, and $10 for children two through twelve. Wednesdays are by donation. Zoo rides cost extra, including the Skyfari ($3), camel rides ($5), and the Zoo Shuttle ($3). The Wild Asia Monorail tour is open from May to November and costs $3 extra per person. A Pay-At-One-Price ticket that covers most attractions at a savings is available May to October. Strollers and wheelchairs are available for rent. Parking is $10.

Wave Hill

🖃 West 249th Street and Independence Avenue

🚆 231st Street station (1 train), then the Bx7 or Bx10 bus to 252nd Street

🚆 Riverdale station (Metro-North)

📞 718-549-3200

✍ *www.wavehill.org*

This is one of those beautiful, quiet spots in the big city. It's the site of a former mansion overlooking the Hudson River with undisturbed vistas of the New Jersey Palisades. Artists, writers, and readers come here just to sit and think. This twenty-eight-acre public garden houses a greenhouse and a conservatory as well as herb, wildflower, and aquatic gardens. There are wonderful art workshops for kids every Saturday and a delightful café with deliciously creative sandwiches and soups (which may be a bit outré for your kids, so check the menu on Wave Hill's Web site). There is also a terrific gift shop. Celebrity weddings are often held here.

Hours and Fees

Wave Hill is closed Mondays except for certain holidays. From April 15 through October 15, the estate is open Tuesday through Saturday, 9 A.M. to 5:30 P.M.; closing time is an hour earlier during the winter. In July and August, Wave Hill stays open until 9 P.M. for the sunsets. Admission is $6 for adults, $3 for seniors (sixty-five and older) and students, $2 for children six and older, and free for children under six. Admission is free all day Tuesday and on Saturday from 9 A.M. to noon. Parking is available. Closed January 1, Thanksgiving Day, and December 25.

≡FAST FACT

Take your kids to Poe's Cottage at Kingsbridge Road and the Grand Concourse Kingsbridge Road station (B, D, or 4 train). This is where Edgar Allan Poe and his wife lived between 1846 and 1849, and it is believed that he wrote "The Bells," about the church bells of St. John's College (now Fordham University), while living there. Open Saturday 10 A.M. to 4 P.M., Sunday 1 P.M. to 5 P.M. Admission is $3 for adults, $2 for seniors and children twelve and under. Get more information at *www.bronxhistoricalsociety.org* or 781-881-8900.

City Island

A small bridge connects this 230-acre, four-block-wide island in Long Island Sound with the northeast section of Bronx. Less than an hour from Manhattan by car, City Island is a worthwhile excursion that even some longtime New Yorkers don't know about. It's quaint, it's fun, and if you love seafood, bring your appetite. The best way to get there is by car. If you prefer public transportation, take the 6 train to Pelham Bay Parkway, and then the Bx29 bus. April through October are the months to visit.

Fishing, sailing, and boat-building have been more than just pastimes on the island since its founding days in the eighteenth century. The soul of this little island is contained in a charming little museum run by the City Island Historical Society. The City Island Historical Museum (190 Fordham Street) contains displays, models, memorabilia, tools, photographs, maps, and writings about the sea in general and City Island in particular. There is no admission fee, but donations are welcome. Open Sundays from 1 P.M. to 5 P.M. or by appointment. For information, call 718-885-0008.

An attractively laid out miniature golf course, Turtle Cove, is located next to a full-sized driving range, where you can stop to play along the way as you head to City Island Bridge. Once over the bridge, the smell of fresh seafood will entice you. City Island has all the great seafood that can be found on the shores of Maine or Massachusetts. The tiny island is also chock full of boats, and you can rent one and take a ride.

As you drive along the one main road on the island, you'll encounter a slew of restaurants. With names like Crab Shanty, The Harbor, Lobster Box, Lobster House, Sammy's Fish Box, and Sea Shore, you'll immediately get the message that it's time to don a bib and prepare for some great seafood. Portions in most of these eateries are large, the food is fresh, and the dining experience at most of the twenty-plus restaurants is first rate.

Yankee Stadium

  ▣ East 161st Street and River Avenue

  🚃 East 161st Street-Yankee Stadium station (B, D, or 4 train)

  📞 718-293-6000 (box office)

  📞 718-579-4531 (stadium tours)

  ✎ *www.yankees.com*

If you want to experience a bit of sports history, act fast. Built in 1923, the year the Babe hit his first home run, and home to the winningest baseball franchise in major league history, this venerable structure will soon be rubble. A new Yankee Stadium will rise in its place. Pains have been taken to design a state-of-the-art facility with the flavor and feel of the old stadium. It will have the same dimensions and a similar look but fewer seats to accommodate sixty luxury suites. The new Yankee Stadium will be ready opening day 2009.

Meanwhile, the headquarters of Yankees fans nationwide and worldwide remains, holding the spirits of Hall of Famers matched by no other team—Babe Ruth, Lou Gehrig, Joe DiMaggio, Mickey Mantle, Whitey Ford, and Yogi Berra, among many others.

The stadium itself sits on 11.6 acres and is actually the third home of the Yankees, who played in the Polo Grounds in upper Manhattan (1913 to 1922) and before that in Hilltop Park (1903 to 1912), also in upper Manhattan. The present Yankee Stadium underwent a major renovation in 1976.

With very little foul territory, seats are as close to the field as you'll find anywhere. The ambiance is still that of real baseball, without artificial turf, skyboxes, waterfalls, or massive electronic scoreboards overshadowing the game itself. If you arrive early, you can visit Monument Park, just over the centerfield fence. The park features monuments and plaques for great Yankees, including the aforementioned Hall of Famers plus Bill Dickey, Phil Rizzuto, Roger Maris, Thurman Munson, Elston Howard, Casey Stengel, and others. These will be moved to the new stadium.

TRAVEL TIP

Yankee Stadium holds 57,545 visitors, but getting a ticket is never easy when the Yankees are playing well. With fewer seats, it will be that much harder to get tickets in the new stadium. If you plan on being in town to watch a game, act early. Tickets can be purchased at Ticketmaster (call 212-307-1212) locations throughout the city, at the Yankee Stadium box office, or on the Yankees' Web site, where you can print your own ticket.

Parking

For day games, the subway is quick and gets you right to the stadium. If you'd prefer not to travel the subways at night, you can park in any of several lots around the ballpark. Avoid those that say valet parking; they cost more and you're kept waiting in line to get your car after the game. Self park in a lot and walk with the crowds. This is not a neighborhood for seeking out street parking or wandering away from the stadium area. Stadium tours are offered at noon during the week.

Staten Island

The Rodney Dangerfield of the boroughs, Staten Island gets no respect. To a New Yorker, the island was something like Australia—hard to get to, left to its own devices, and populated by people who were similar but, well, different in some way. Staten Island's inclusion as part of the city came as a prize in a sailing contest in 1687, when the Duke of York gave the island to Manhattan. Residents of the borough today, in response to being the fifth wheel, sometimes talk of separating from the rest of New York City. In fact, in 1993 they voted to do so, but it never happened.

RAINY DAY FUN

Even native New Yorkers don't know that Staten Island has an exceptionally child-friendly zoo. It's small, but that's what makes it so charming. You'll find a South American rain forest, a reptile house with one of the world's finest collections, an aquarium, and a children's center. For more information, call the zoo at 718-442-3100 or visit its Web site at *www.statenislandzoo.org*.

While it remains part of New York City, Staten Island is a suburban, sprawling setting, rich with its own ethnic and cultural diversity. The island is an enjoyable twenty-five-minute ferry ride from Manhattan. Less densely settled than the other boroughs, it has several large open spaces, including the Greenbelt, La Tourette Park, Willowbrook Park, and the William T. Davis Wildlife Refuge.

Take the Ferry to Staten Island

Staten Island is one of the best-kept secrets of New York City. It is rich in history, and its main attractions place you in a different time. For the kids, it is the past made alive, for you, a fascinating and unique experience.

The Staten Island Ferry

🖃 1 Whitehall Street, Manhattan

🚊 Whitehall Street station (R or W train) or South Ferry station (1 train)

📞 718-876-8441

✍ *www.nyc.gov/dot*

✍ *www.siferry.com*

Separated by distance and water, for most of its history the only way to get to Staten Island was by ferry—a short sail from Brooklyn, a longer one from Manhattan. Staten Island was connected to Brooklyn by the Verrazano-Narrows Bridge, which opened November 21, 1964, at a cost of $320.1 million, but it still left the New York Ferry a necessity for those who relied on public transportation. The ferry ride is wonderful, made even better because it's free!—and you get a great view of lower Manhattan and the Statue of Liberty. Let your imagination roam free as the salt air and sound of waves against the hull transport you to a pirate ship, a cruise liner, or an immigrant steamer. Once you make landfall, there's another world to discover! The 5.2-mile trip takes twenty-five minutes, and service operates 24/7. There is no charge.

≡FAST FACT

The stunning mural of Staten Island that greets visitors at the St. George Terminal on Staten Island was created by Michael Falco. A Staten Island native, Falco used thousands of photos of Staten Island to create the image of a peaceful shore with the Verrazano-Narrows Bridge and the Bayonne Bridge in the background.

Historic Richmond Town

🖃 441 Clarke Avenue (at Arthur Kill Road)

📞 718-351-1611

✐ www.historicrichmondtown.org

The twenty-seven buildings of Historic Richmond Town survived the American Revolution and the modernization of the city.

Included in the historic town you'll find the oldest surviving elementary school, the Voorlezer House, which dates from 1695; a stately Greek Revival courthouse from 1837 (transformed into a visitors' center); a 1740s farmhouse; and an 1860s general store furnished as a nineteenth-century print shop. Located in the former county clerk's office, the museum's exhibits feature items made in Staten Island and a "Toys!" exhibit with hands-on activities.

💼 TRAVEL TIP

Richmond Village often has special events on the weekends. From pumpkin picking in October to holiday-themed events in November and December, these experiences contribute to the season and show the family how colonial people celebrated. But the village isn't stuck in the past. It hosts events like the Multiple Sclerosis Walk in the spring.

Other exhibits within the quaint setting include early American crafts. Attractions feature demonstrations of quilting, carpentry, spinning, and weaving, fireplace cooking, and other aspects of colonial life. Along with guided tours of the buildings, the unique historical setting hosts a fair every Labor Day weekend. Throughout the year you'll find other events, like flea markets, an annual summer re-enactment of Civil War battles, a nineteenth-century outdoor dinner (complete with plates and utensils of a bygone era), Saturday night concerts, an autumn celebration, and Christmas festivities.

Tours are given Wednesday to Friday at 2:30 P.M., on weekends at 2 P.M. and 3:30 P.M., September to June. The village is open to self-guided tours July and August.

The museum store sells reproductions, items made by the village craftspeople, and books on Staten Island history. A Victorian-style full-service restaurant offers casual dining.

 ## JUST FOR PARENTS

Early residents brewed their own beer, and modern visitors can get a taste as well. Ironically, the area is near Prohibition Park, which was a strictly alcohol-free neighborhood in the 1880s.

Location and Hours

Historic Richmond Town is located at La Tourette Park, on Clarke Avenue. Once you take the ferry over to Staten Island, you can take an S74 city bus (thirty-minute ride) or drive—there's plenty of free parking! Admission is $5 for adults, $4 for seniors, and $3.50 for children ages five through seventeen. Historic Richmond Town is open Wednesday through Sunday from 1 P.M. to 5 P.M. from September to June, Wednesday to Friday from 10 A.M. to 5 P.M. and Saturday and Sunday 1 P.M. to 5 P.M. in July and August. Closed on major holidays.

Fort Wadsworth

⊞ Wadsworth Avenue and Bay Street

☎ 718-354-4500

✐ *www.nps.gov/*

From 1795 through 1995, various military branches ran this strategically located fort that protected New York Harbor—it was the longest continually manned military installation in the United States. Today the 226-acre site is run by the National Park Service and is home to U.S. Coast Guard personnel. Fourteen historic defense structures still stand, overlooking the harbor and the neighboring Verrazano-Narrows Bridge. Views are outstanding!

≡FAST FACT

Led by one determined volunteer, the lighthouse at Fort Wadsworth has undergone a complete renovation. Staten Island resident Joe Esposito, a lighthouse buff, worked with the National Park Service to conduct a $27,000 renovation. The new solar-powered Fort Wadsworth lighthouse reopened in 2005 after being dark for forty years.

The center has a short film on the history of the fort, plus other exhibits. Ranger-led tours are also available Wednesday to Sunday at 2:30 P.M.; a 10:30 A.M. tour is added summer weekends. New to the tour is an 1890s officer's quarters. Within the park itself you can fish, hike, or follow a trail by foot or by bike. Special events include lantern-tour nights, living history re-enactments of rifle or musket demonstrations, special hikes, and more.

There is a gift shop where books and other unusual items are on sale. A picnic area is available (except during the summer months when it is reserved for staff; call for details) where you can enjoy a day of history and fun in the great outdoors. Bring a camera for shots of New York Harbor.

Hours and Fees

Admission is free, and the park is open from dawn to dusk. The visitors' center is open Wednesday through Sunday from 10 A.M. to 5 P.M.

 TRAVEL TIP

Getting to Staten Island is a fun adventure in itself. In addition to the ferry, the island is connected to the rest of the Big Apple by several express buses from Manhattan and Brooklyn. In Staten Island, the Staten Island Railway, part of the Metropolitan Transit Authority, like the subways, operates from the ferry terminal through the entire borough to Tottenville along the east coast. Get a Staten Island bus and rail map free from the MTA at 212-330-1234 or *www.mta.info* (select "FAQS/Contact Us").

Snug Harbor Cultural Center

⊞ 1000 Richmond Terrace

🚍 S40 bus from the ferry terminal

✆ 718-448-2500

✍ *www.snug-harbor.org*

A small historical city within a city, Snug Harbor houses some twenty-six historical structures and acres of public parkland, with meadows, wetlands, and gardens. Greek Revival and Victorian architecture characterize many of the buildings, which include a music hall built in the late nineteenth century and a main hall dating back to 1833. Five Victorian artists' cottages and a Veterans Memorial Hall from 1856 are also among the classic structures you'll find here. While Historic Richmond Town has a greater focus on history, Snug Harbor is a home for culture and the arts.

Just a ten-minute bus ride from the Staten Island Ferry, Snug Harbor has a variety of attractions for varying interests. The New-house Center for Contemporary Art collection features cutting-edge contemporary art creatively displayed in vivid contrast to the nine-teenth-century main exhibit hall. All in all, the structures house some 15,000 square feet of exhibit space and thirty artist studios.

The Noble Maritime Collection is a fascinating and beautiful museum within Snug Harbor. Its main mission is to preserve, display, and interpret the works and artifacts of famed marine artist John A. Noble, but it mounts a variety of marine exhibits and programs throughout the year. The kids will love the model ships and Noble's Houseboat Studio, meticulously restored and moved frame by frame to its present location. The museum store has a wide variety of interest-ing nautical merchandise, with a particularly good children's collec-tion of books, toys, and ship models. Call ahead if you want a tour.

The Staten Island Botanical Garden is also part of Snug Harbor. The complex is home to several smaller gardens, including the Secret Garden (with a castle, a favorite for kids), the White Garden with white flowers, a bird and butterfly observatory, a fragrance garden, a rose garden, an herb garden, and a greenhouse. The Chinese Schol-ar's Garden, a sister to the Suzhou Garden in China and built by visit-ing Chinese artisans, is also on the premises. The garden serves as a living, working, growing scientific and educational center.

💼 TRAVEL TIP

Check Snug Harbor's Web site before you go for upcoming events. The center makes a real effort to put together innovative and inter-active programs for visitors. All programs tie into the cultural center's mission of preserving Snug Harbor's maritime history and making it accessible to visitors.

The Staten Island Children's Museum, also found in the Snug Har-bor Cultural Center, offers kids under twelve a variety of hands-on exhi-bitions in five interactive galleries, along with storytelling, workshops, and performances. There is a gift shop with books and souvenirs.

Open from dawn to dusk, 362 days a year, Snug Harbor hosts numerous outdoor events, including classical, pop, and jazz concerts in the south meadow and in the music hall. There is also an art lab with classes, workshops, and minicamps at the Children's Museum. The Snug Harbor gift shop sells jewelry, original art, posters, and books. Melville's Café serves sandwiches, entrées, and desserts.

While touring the site is fun, seeing one of the numerous performances will enhance your visit. Visiting Snug Harbor is a great way to sightsee, enjoy a concert, and have a picnic. It's not very expensive and is great for the whole family.

Directions, Hours, and Fees

Take the S40 bus from the ferry terminal for a short ride to Snug Harbor Cultural Center. The site is open free to the public from dawn to dusk. The Newhouse Center for Contemporary Art is open Tuesday through Sunday from noon to 5 P.M. Admission is $3 for adults, $2 for seniors and children under twelve.

Admission to the Staten Island Botanical Garden grounds is free. Admission to the Scholar's Garden is $5 for adults; $4 for seniors, children, and students with ID. Admission to the Secret Garden is an additional $1, or if you don't want a Scholar's Garden ticket, $2. Call 718-362-1019 for hours and information.

Admission to the Staten Island Children's Museum is $5 per person (free for children under one); on Wednesdays grandparents are free. It is open Tuesday through Sunday and most school holidays, noon to 5 P.M. when schools are open and from 10 A.M. when schools are closed. Call 718-273-2060 for information. The Noble Maritime Collection is open Thursday to Sunday, 1 P.M. to 5 P.M. Admission is $5 for adults; $3 for seniors, children, and educators; free to children under ten. Call for information at 718-447-6490 or go online at *www .noblemaritime.org*.

CHAPTER 12

Shopping in New York

NEW YORK EQUALS shopping. Designer shops along Madison and Fifth avenues, outdoor flea markets in Greenwich Village, incredible department stores, creative museum shops, and hundreds of fabulous, unique little stores make shopping in New York a one-of-a-kind experience. New York City boasts amazing food stores, ethnic stores, and markets where you can buy imported foods from anywhere you can imagine. And don't forget the street vendors and souvenir shops either. To some they may be tacky, but nothing says New York better than a $3 "I ❤ New York" T-shirt!

Department Stores

No city in the world has more department stores than New York.

Barneys New York
- 660 Madison Avenue (between East 60th and East 61st streets)
- East 59th Street station (4, 5, or 6 train)
- 212-826-8900

Co-op Upper West Side
- 2151 Broadway (between West 75th and West 76th streets)
- West 72nd Street station (1, 2, or 3 train)
- 646-335-0978

Co-op Chelsea
⊞ 236 West 18th Street (between 7th and 8th avenues)
🚃 West 18th Street station (1 train)
✆ 212-593-7800

Co-op SoHo
⊞ 116 Wooster Street (between Spring and Prince streets)
🚃 Prince Street station (N, R, or W train)
✆ 212-593-7800
✎ *www.barneys.com*

The flagship Madison Avenue Barneys store is full of top-of-the-line men's and women's clothing; the co-op stores sell casual sportswear. The best of the hottest designer lines can be found at Barneys, and prices can be quite high. But the chain also holds sales twice a year that are worth waiting for. The window displays are fabulous. They change frequently and are an attraction unto themselves. Fred's, in the Madison Avenue store, is one of the best in-house restaurants in the city. Barneys is open seven days a week.

TRAVEL TIP

You can take it with you, well, almost. Many New York restaurants and delicatessens have online catalogs and will ship you their wares (Junior's Cheesecake and H&H Bagels, for instance). The food sections of department stores such as Macy's also offer a similar service.

Bergdorf Goodman
⊞ 754 5th Avenue (between East 57th and East 58th streets)
🚃 5th Avenue-59th Street station (N, R, or W train)
✆ 1-800-558-1855
✎ *www.bergdorfgoodman.com*

Bergdorf is a boutique department store where each designer's shop has its own look and feel. Elegant and trendy, Bergdorf is a very New York experience. The Susan Ciminelli Day Spa on the ninth floor offers facials and treatments that will make you forget you are in a department store in one of the largest cities in the world. The John Barrett Salon in the penthouse, with its international staff of stylists and breathtaking view, is the *ne plus ultra* of self-pampering (with prices to match). The men's store is located across Fifth Avenue.

There are several excellent in-house restaurants to choose from. Bar III is located in the men's store, and Goodman's and BG are located in the women's store, the latter of which overlooks Central Park and serves an elegant afternoon tea Monday to Friday from 3 P.M. to 5 P.M.

Bloomingdale's

⌨ 1000 3rd Avenue (between East 59th and East 60th streets)

🚇 59th Street station (4, 5, or 6 train) or Lexington Avenue-East 59th Street station (N, R, or W train)

✆ 212-705-2000

✎ *www.bloomingdales.com*

"Bloomie's" is one of the last remaining New York City department stores to occupy an entire city block. If you can see past the glitz and glitter, Bloomingdale's has a tremendous selection of designer clothing for men, women, and children, and sales are run regularly. Personal shoppers are available.

The store has no fewer than five restaurants, including the wonderful Le Train Blu, serving French fare in an authentic small railroad car. The food is good, and the atmosphere is to die for.

Macy's Department Store

⌨ West 34th Street (at Herald Square)

🚇 West 34th Street-Herald Square station (B, D, F, N, Q, R, V, or W train)

✆ 212-736-5151

✎ *www.macys.com*

Macy's in New York calls itself the world's largest department store. Expect to get lost at least twice while navigating your way around this huge place. The main floor is designed in a beautiful marble art deco style, a perfect setting for the fine jewelry and extensive leather departments located on this level. Macy's caters to the mainstream shopper and carries a variety of reasonably priced clothing, though all the top designers can also be found here.

Macy's Cellar houses what might be the city's finest collection of cookware, housewares, and gourmet delicacies. Macy's also has three restaurants, including the family friendly Macy's Cellar Bar & Grill (see page 282), a hair salon, a branch of the Metropolitan Museum of Art's gift shop, a post office, and an American Express travel office. The store is open seven days a week.

RAINY DAY FUN

Macy's goes all out for major holidays. For the Spring Flower Show, more than two million flowers and topiary from all over the world are arranged in a spectacular display. The Fourth of July, Thanksgiving, and the year-end season are times for fireworks, parades, puppet shows, and family events. The world-famous window displays are not to be missed.

Henri Bendel
▢ 712 5th Avenue (between West 55th and West 56th streets)

🚇 5th Avenue-59th Street station (N, R, or W train), 5th Avenue-53rd Street station (E or V train), or 59th Street station (4, 5, or 6 train)

✆ 212-247-1100

✆ 1-800-HBENDEL (423-6335)

✑ www.henribendel.com

At Henri Bendel, you will encounter the cutting edge of fashion, with quite a few brand new and only-in-New York designers. Henri Bendel features its own in-house lines of clothing as well as some of the more exclusive designer brands. The prices are very high, as is the quality of the offerings. Henri Bendel is open Monday to Friday 10 A.M. to 8 P.M.; Sunday noon to 7 P.M.

Lord & Taylor

🖥 424 5th Avenue (between West 38th and West 39th streets)

🚆 East 33rd Street station (6 train)

☎ 212-391-3344

✍ *www.lordandtaylor.com*

Probably your mother's favorite store in New York City, this is the department store that has always catered to classic tastes. But it is trying hard to appeal to all people, and its look is becoming more contemporary (good gracious, it's showing men with over-sized shorts!) without losing that feel for quality. Its kid's selection has all the famous names you've come to know and love. You cannot go wrong purchasing Lord & Taylor's signature merchandise, from sleep-wear to French-milled soaps to sweaters. It's packed during sales. Of the two in-house restaurants, the Larry Forgione Signature Café (212-391-3015) on the sixth floor is the best bet for kids.

Saks Fifth Avenue

🖥 611 5th Avenue (between West 49th and West 50th streets)

🚆 West 47th–50th Street-Rockefeller Center station (B, D, F, or V train)

☎ 212-753-4000

✍ *www.saksfifthavenue.com*

Saks Fifth Avenue, one of New York City's most prestigious and famous department stores, is located across the street from St. Patrick's Cathedral and just east of Rockefeller Center.

≡ FAST FACT

You may think New York has a lot of department stores now, but there used to be a lot more. The legendary Gimbels, Alexander's, E. J. Korvette's, S. Klein, A&S, and May's catered to every budget. Bamberger's was a little higher up, and New Yorkers actually wept when B. Altman closed.

Saks is perhaps the most spacious store of its genre in New York City and takes pride in having a luxurious environment and elegant displays. The main floor offers numerous counters filled with accessories. Designer clothing for men, women, and children can be purchased. Saks' own house line, SFA Signature, features (slightly) more affordable prices. Saks also carries jewelry, cosmetics, and fragrances. In addition, there is a bridal salon, offering the latest in bridal fashion displayed in a gorgeous setting.

There are three eating place at Saks, and one is appropriately named Eat at Saks. There's also Snaks, and Café SFA, which serves gourmet lunch and light fare. Saks also delivers to any Manhattan hotel for $18. This is first-rate shopping at its finest. Even if you're not buying, you should at least browse.

Takashimaya New York

🔲 693 5th Avenue (between West 54th and West 55th streets)
🚇 Lexington Avenue-53rd Street station (E or V train)
📞 212-350-0100

Takashimaya is a unique, cross-cultural, six-story gift and souvenir boutique that offers a cross between designs of the east and west. Once you pass into this lovely atmosphere, you will be immediately enchanted by the beautiful aroma of fresh-cut flowers.

Takashimaya offers a rare and distinctive selection of merchandise—clothes, jewelry, home furnishings, accessories, and much more. The displays are equally unusual, expressing the sensitivity of

Japanese craftsmanship. It's very pricey but definitely worth a stroll down Fifth Avenue to visit and wander around this relaxing setting. The Tea Box serves many kinds of tea, soups, finger sandwiches, salads, and bento box lunches. It's open from 10 A.M. to 7 P.M. Monday to Saturday; noon to 5 P.M. Sunday.

Discount Stores

How do New Yorkers manage to survive in the capital of high prices? Because they know where the good, inexpensive restaurants are, how to get cheap tickets to shows, and where to shop for outstanding bargains. New York is the place where you can buy this week's hottest designer clothes at just a few dollars above wholesale and last week's for a fraction of the original ticket. Every hardworking New Yorker knows where to shop, and now you will too!

Century 21

⌨ 22 Cortlandt Street (between Church and Broadway streets)

🚇 Cortlandt Street Station (R or W train) or Fulton Street/
Broadway-Nassau Street station (A, C, J, M, Z, 2, 3, 4, or 5 train)

✎ 212-227-9092

✐ *www.c21stores.com*

The Century 21 Department Store is one of the best places to get top designer clothes for both men and women at a fraction of the regular retail price. Suits, handbags, and shoes are always worth shopping for. It also has lingerie, cosmetics, luggage, and housewares. Open Monday to Wednesday from 7:45 A.M. to 8 P.M.; Thursday and Friday to 9 P.M.; Saturday 10 A.M. to 8 P.M.; Sunday 11 A.M. to 7 P.M.

 TRAVEL TIP

T.J. Maxx (four stores in the city), Syms (two stores), Filene's Basement (four stores), and H&M (ten stores) are all here too.

Daffy's

📺 50 Broadway (at Morris Street)
📞 212-422-4477

📺 462 Broadway (at Grand Street)
🚇 Canal Street station (J, M, Q, R, W, Z, or 6 train)
📞 212-334-7444

📺 1311 Broadway (at West 34th Street)
🚇 West 34th Street-Herald Square station (B, D, F, N, Q, R, V, or W train)
📞 212-736-4477

📺 1775 Broadway (at West 57th Street)
🚇 West 59th Street-Columbus Circle station (A, B, C, D, or 1 train)
📞 212-292-4477

📺 125 East 57th Street
🚇 East 59th Street station (4, 5, or 6 train)
📞 212-376-4477

📺 355 Madison Avenue (East 44th Street)
🚇 Grand Central-East 42nd Street station (S, 4, 5, 6, or 7 train)
📞 212-557-4422

✍ www.daffys.com

Daffy's is a hardcore designer/bargain-shopper's delight with men's, women's, and children's clothes always on sale. It's the kind of place where you can shop for hours and buy $1,000 worth of designer clothes and accessories for $200, maybe less if you work hard at it. You'll find shoes, bags, and lingerie here too. Daffy's is open seven days a week, with several branches in New York.

Loehmann's

- 101 7th Avenue (at West 16th Street)
- West 14th Street station (1, 2, or 3 train)
- 212-352-0856

- 5740 Broadway (between West 234th Street and Tim Hendrix Place, Riverdale)
- West 238th Street station (1 train)
- 718-543-6420

- 2807 East 21st Street (at Emmons Avenue)
  Loehmann's Seaport Plaza
  Sheepshead Bay, Brooklyn
- Sheepshead Bay station (B or Q train)
- 718-368-1256

www.loehmanns.com

Loehmann's is a bargain-shopper's paradise for women's sportswear and designer clothes, as well as shoes, handbags, jewelry, fragrances, intimate apparel, and even swimwear. You can also find some men's clothing. Loehmann's Insider Club offers shoppers many money-saving benefits like a 15 percent birthday discount. It's free, it's good all over the country, and you can join on the Internet. On some seasonal items that are already discounted by up to 70 percent, that can mean an 85 percent total discount. If you visit, ask about the Back Room Event. Loehmann's is open Monday to Saturday 9 A.M. to 9 P.M.; Sunday 11 A.M. to 7 P.M.

TRAVEL TIP

It is hard to find a bathroom in midtown New York, so most New Yorkers know where the bathrooms are in department stores and hotels. You can always visit a Starbucks or McDonald's; they are everywhere and the bathrooms are usually quite clean.

Fortunoff
- 681 5th Avenue (between West 53rd and West 54th streets)
- 5th Avenue-53rd Street station (E or V train)
- 212-758-6660
- *www.fortunoff.com*

This is one of the premier affordable jewelry and china stores in the city, and you can also shop for kitchen, bathroom, home décor, outdoor, and baby merchandise. This multilevel store has an entire floor dedicated to silver, and Fortunoff also carries a fine display of crystal: Waterford, Lenox, Lalique, and other brands. It's one of the best places for wedding gifts.

These Shops Are Gems

Just for fun, go window shopping at the upscale jewelry shops along Fifth Avenue. You know the names, now live the fantasy.

Cartier
- 653 5th Avenue (at 52nd Street)
- 5th Avenue-53rd Street station (E or V train)
- 212-472-6400
- *www.cartier.com*

Pierre Cartier acquired this mansion on Fifth Avenue in exchange for $100 and a pearl necklace worth a million dollars. There are necklaces and jewelry here for models and royalty, but there are also some surprisingly affordable items for the rest of us.

Harry Winston
- 718 5th Avenue (at West 56th Street)
- 57th Street station (B train)
- 212-245-2000
- *www.harrywinston.com*

Harry Winston's gems are known worldwide. (The Smithsonian's Hope diamond was once owned by Mrs. Harry Winston.) The jeweler was immortalized by Marilyn Monroe in the song, "Diamonds Are a Girl's Best Friend."

Tiffany & Company

⌨ 727 5th Avenue (between West 56th and West 57th streets)

🚆 5th Avenue-59th Street station (N, R, or W train)

✆ 212-755-8000

✎ *www.tiffany.com*

One of the city's most prestigious stores, Tiffany's was founded in 1837 as Tiffany & Young. It is considered America's leading house of design and the world's premier jewelry retailer. The main and second floors are where Tiffany's finest jewelry can be bought for a hefty price. On the third floor you will find the silver collection, offering some beautiful pieces at more reasonable prices. On the fourth floor you can purchase crystal and fine china.

Tiffany's offers other classically designed products, such as watches and clocks, flatware, scarves and ties, stationery, pens and pencils, leather goods, and fragrances. Any purchase you make will entitle you to the instantly recognizable Tiffany blue box. A major tourist stop, visitors from around the world enjoy strolling through this famous store. You can buy a key chain as a $125 memento.

Flea Markets

New York City also offers a multitude of opportunities for flea-market bargain hunting. Annex/Hell's Kitchen Flea Market has brought two popular venues together. Go to West Thirty-ninth Street, between Ninth and Tenth avenues. A ton of vendors and happy browsers show up every weekend from 10 A.M. to 6 P.M. While you're here, you can grab a shuttle ($1 per person) to The Garage and the West Twenty-fifth Street Market. The Garage, at 112 West Twenty-fifth Street (between

Sixth and Seventh avenues) is a fantasy for browsers—two floors of eclectic goodies from furniture to handbags to art. Open weekends 6:30 A.M. to 5 P.M.

RAINY DAY FUN

Visit the Manhattan Mall, the only mall in Manhattan. The mall is accessible via the West Thirty-fourth Street-Herald Square station (B, D, F, N, Q, R, V, or W train) or the West Thirty-fourth Street-Penn Station (1, 2, or 3 train). The mall is open Monday to Saturday 9 A.M. to 9 P.M., Sunday 10 A.M. to 7 P.M. Get more information at 212-465-0500 or *www.manhattanmallny.com.*

Then walk over to West Twenty-fifth Street Market at 29 West Twenty-fifth Street (between Fifth and Sixth avenues) for yet more flea market wanderings. Open weekends dawn to dusk. Information at 212-243-5343; *www.hellskitchenfleamarket.com.*

The Green Flea Market is a wonderfully quirky New York flea market, with clothing, jewelry, trash and treasures, and even fresh fruits and homemade food. It's held on Saturdays, 11 A.M. to 7 P.M., in the West Village at Greenwich Avenue and Charles Street (between West Tenth and West Eleventh streets); West Fourteenth Street station (1, 2, or 3 train).

On Sundays, the flea market moves to the Upper West Side's Intermediate School 44 at Columbus Avenue (between West Seventy-sixth and West Seventy-seventh streets); West Seventy-ninth Street station (1 train) or Eighty-first Street-Museum of Natural History station (B or C train). It's open 10 A.M. to 6 P.M., April through October, and closes a half hour earlier November to March. For further information, contact 212-239-3025; *www.greenfleamarkets.com.*

Secondhand Bargains

New York has some of the best thrift and secondhand shops in this country.

Cheap Jacks

⌑ 303 5th Avenue (at 31st Street)

🚇 East 33rd Street station (6 train)

📞 212-777-9564

✎ www.cheapjacks.com

Cheap Jacks sells the best in vintage clothing, mainly from the 1920s to the present, but the stock can go as far back as the War of 1812. A favorite of the performing arts industry, you can rub shoulders with your favorite star as you check out a 1920s flapper dress. The service is high-end, along with some of the prices (but that Civil War uniform is *real!*).

This is the place for the unique and the unusual, not necessarily the cheapest. From furs to Tees, from a World War II bomber jacket to fifty-year-old cuff links, if you have a yen for the unusual, here it is. Cheap Jack's will make alterations while you wait.

Love Saves the Day

⌑ 119 2nd Avenue (between East 7th Street and St. Marks Place)

🚇 Astor Place (6 train)

📞 212-228-3802

At Love Saves the Day, you'll find wacky clothes and all the vintage lunchboxes and highball glasses you could ever want. Open seven days a week from noon until 9 P.M.

St. Luke's Thrift Shop

⌑ The Church of St. Luke in the Fields, 487 Hudson Street (at Grove Street)

🚇 Christopher Street-Sheridan Square station (1 train)

📞 212-924-9364

This large thrift shop carries a wide range of clothing for men, women, and children from tots to teens. There is also a selection of toys and games, furniture, and even bridal gowns. Locals shop here for designer duds for peanuts. St Luke's accepts credit cards. Open Monday to Friday, 11 A.M. to 6 P.M.; opens Saturday at 10 A.M.; closed Sundays. The Parish House was once the childhood home of author Bret Harte.

JUST FOR PARENTS

You can sit in on one of the famous auctions at Sotheby's (1334 York Avenue, at East Seventy-second Street, East Seventy-seventh Street station (6 train), 212-606-7000, *www.sothebys.com* or Christie's (20 Rockefeller Plaza, at Forty-ninth Street between Fifth and Sixth avenues, Forty-seventh–Fiftieth streets-Rockefeller Plaza station (B, D, F, V train), 212-636-2000, *www.christies.com*.

Trash & Vaudeville

📧 4 St. Marks Place

🚇 East 8th Street-NYU station (N, R, or W train) or Astor Place station (6 train)

📞 212-982-3590

Legend has it that this shop was started in the late 1970s by one of the former New York Dolls. This spacious thrift shop (really two— Trash *and* Vaudeville) is almost like a costume collection. Here's where to find great vintage threads, from funk and punk to outrageous, cool, and fun. Trash & Vaudeville is open Monday to Thursday, noon to 8 P.M.; Friday from 11:30 A.M. to 8 P.M.; Saturday, 11:30 A.M. to 9 P.M.; Sunday, 1 P.M. to 7:30 P.M.

Books, Perfume, Food, and More

New York is book country and always has been.

Books of Wonder

⌨ 18 West 18th Street (between 5th and 6th avenues)

🚇 18th Street station (1 train)

📞 1-800-207-6968

📞 212-989-3270

✎ *www.booksofwonder.com*

The oldest and largest children's bookstore in New York City, this wonderful store has everything for your kids. It is world-famous for its amazing collection of *Wizard of Oz* books and paraphernalia. The brilliant staff is, of course, very child-friendly. Open Monday to Saturdays 10 A.M. to 7 P.M.; Sunday 11 A.M. to 6 P.M.

═══FAST FACT

The Ladies' Mile, from Ninth to Twenty-third streets and Sixth Avenue to Broadway, was once New York's most fashionable shopping district. Competing department stores sprung up in the area in the mid-nineteenth century. Today much of the space has been converted into residential properties, but some retail space remains. Many of the buildings along this stretch are historical landmarks, including the unmistakable Flatiron Building.

Forbidden Planet

⌨ 840 Broadway (at 13th Street)

🚇 14th Street-Union Square station (L, N, Q, R, W, 4, 5, or 6 train)

📞 212-473-1576

✎ *www.fpnyc.com*

You can find almost anything you could want in science fiction, fantasy, horror, comics, and graphic novels here. There's a great collection of models, as well as figurines from television shows and movies. No matter what time you go, the store is always filled with teens.

Midtown Comics

▢ 200 West 40th Street (at 7th Avenue)

🚇 Times Square-West 42nd Street station (N, Q, R, S, W, 1, 2, 3, or 7 train)

▢ 459 Lexington Avenue (at East 45th Street)

🚇 Grand Central-East 42nd Street station (S, 4, 5, 6, or 7 train)

✆ 800-411-3341

✆ 212-302-8192

The megastore of comics—old comics, new comics, graphic novels, and everything in between—are on sale here. You'll also find action figures, statues, movies, books, posters, and collectibles. Looking for something in particular? They have an unbelievable 500,000 back issues. Open Monday to Saturday, 11 A.M. to 9 P.M.; Sunday, noon to 7 P.M.

The Strand

▢ 828 Broadway (at East 12th Street)

🚇 14th Street-Union Square station (L, N, Q, R, W, 4, 5, or 6 train)

✆ 212-473-1452

Another New York phenomenon, this is one of the largest bookstores in the world. The Strand has 2.5 million books, more than eighteen miles worth. There are always books on sale outside for $1, but it's the rows and rows of new, used, and rare books inside that will amaze you. A sacred tradition, book reviewers have been selling their advance copies here for decades, so you can sometimes get a popular title before it's officially published and at a 25 percent discount.

Hours are Monday to Saturday 9:30 A.M. to 10:30 P.M.; Sunday from 11 A.M. to 10:30 P.M. The Strand has an annex downtown at 95 Fulton Street (Fulton Street/Broadway-Nassau Street station; A, C, J, M,Z, 2,

3, 4, or 5 train). The Strand's Central Park kiosk is located at Sixtieth Street and Fifth Avenue, 10 A.M. to dusk, April to December.

Lush

- ⊟ 1293 Broadway (between West 33rd and West 34th streets)
- 🚇 West 34th Street-Herald Square station (B, D, F, N, Q, R, V, or W train)
- ℅ 212-564-9120

- ⊟ 2165 Broadway (between West 76th and West 77th streets)
- 🚇 West 72nd Street station (1, 2, or 3 train)
- ℅ 212-787-5874

- ✐ www.lush.com

A fabulous British soap and beauty store, Lush sells the most divine and creatively designed chunks of soap, bath products, fragrances, and hair and skin care products at fairly affordable prices and in wacky colors and shapes. New stores have been added at 529 Broadway, and 7 East Fourteenth Street in Union Square.

TRAVEL TIP

New York is famous for its designer sample sales when overstock is sold at a fraction of cost. Sometimes you can find a sign announcing a sample sale outside a building while walking through the garment district in the west thirties, but the best way to find one of these sales is to go online and search using the keywords "sample sale New York."

Sephora

- ⊟ 2103 Broadway (at West 73rd Street)
- ⊟ 1149 Third Avenue (at East 67th Street)
- ⊟ 10 Columbus Circle (Eighth Avenue)
- ⊟ 711 Lexington Avenue (at East 57th Street)

- 1500 Broadway (at East 43rd Street)
- 597 Fifth Avenue (at East 48th Street)
- 130 West 34th Street (at Broadway)
- 300 Madison Avenue (at East 47th Street)
- 555 Broadway (at Spring Street)
- 45 East 17th Street (at Broadway)
- 150 Broadway (at Liberty Street)
- 119 Fifth Avenue (at East 19th Street)
- Staten Island Mall

www.sephora.com

The original store opened on the Champs Élysées in Paris, and the chain has expanded into the United States. This cosmetics department store offers the wares of almost every makeup manufacturer in the world. You'll find hundreds of alphabetically arranged perfumes and plenty of lipsticks, eye shadow, mascara, and eyeliners to choose from here. There are bath products as well, and Sephora has its own brand. Samples are always on hand to try on with plenty of cotton balls and swabs. There are thirteen Sephora stores in New York.

Citarella

- 2135 Broadway (at West 75th Street)
- West 72nd Street station (1, 2, or 3 train)

- 1313 3rd Avenue (between East 75th and East 76th streets)
- West 77th Street station (6 train)

- 424 6th Avenue (between West 9th and West 10th streets)
- West 4th Street-Washington Square station (A, B, C, D, E, F, or V train)

- 461 West 125th Street (near Amsterdam Avenue)
- West 125th Street station (A, B, C, or D train)
- 212-874-0383

www.citarella.com

Cheeses, foie gras, meat, seafood, caviar, homemade pastas—Citarella's has been a gourmet food-lover's paradise since 1912. Fill a shopping bag and carry it home on the plane with you. Citarella has four locations in Manhattan.

Zabar's
- 2245 Broadway (between West 80th and 81st streets)
- 79th Street station (1 train)
- 1-800-697-6301
- 212-496-1234
- *www.zabars.com*

Zabar's is the ultimate deli/gourmet/good eats emporium. It's 20,000 square feet—almost a full city block of cheeses, deli meats, fish, caviar, breads, cakes and pastries, homemade salads, nuts and fruits, desserts, housewares, gifts, and signature products. It's open 365 days a year, and there is always a Zabar family member in the store. Store hours are Monday to Friday 8 A.M. to 7:30 P.M.; Saturday 8 A.M. to 8 P.M.; Sunday, 9 A.M. to 6 P.M.

Museum Shops and Souvenir Stores

The city's museums have some of the best, most unusual souvenir shopping in the city. You can pick up great one-of-a-kind gifts for friends and family.

Museum of Modern Art Design Store
- 44 West 53rd Street (between 5th and 6th avenues)
- 53rd Street-5th Avenue station (E or V train)
- 212-767-1050

- 81 Spring Street (between Broadway and Crosby Street)
- Spring Street station (6 train) or Prince Street station (N, R, or W train)
- 646-613-1367

- *www.moma.com*

This store offers visitors a wonderful opportunity to sample the museum's wares. There's an extensive offering of interesting games and kid's items, jewelry, classic modern furniture (even miniature versions for doll houses at full-size prices), housewares, posters, prints, and books. This is a great museum store to browse for a wedding or housewarming gift. The West Fifty-third Street store is open Saturday through Thursday, 9:30 A.M. to 6:30 P.M., Friday until 9 P.M. The Spring Street store is open Monday to Saturday, 11 A.M. to 8 P.M., Sunday until 7 P.M.

JUST FOR PARENTS

Babysitting in New York is expensive. If you are staying with a reputable hotel chain like Hilton, Sheraton, or Marriott, you can call ahead of time and ask them to reserve a sitter, who will be bonded, at a cost of at least $20 an hour (from October to December, the minimum for Friday and Saturday nights is $25 an hour). There is usually a two- or three-hour minimum, and you do have to tip. If your hotel does not provide sitter services, you can also contact the Baby Sitters' Guild. Call 212-682-0227 or online at *www.babysittersguild.com* for information. Cash or travelers checks only.

New York City Transit Museum Shop

Vanderbilt Place and East 42nd Street, in Grand Central Terminal
Grand Central-East 42nd Street station (S, 4, 5, 6, or 7 train)
212-878-0106

Boerum Place and Schermerhorn Street, in the Transit Museum, Brooklyn Heights
Borough Hall station (2, 3, 4, or 5 train)
718-694-1600

www.mta.info/museum

The Transit Museum has the ultimate New York gift shop. You can get that distinctive transit map on just about everything from T-shirts and bags to ties, and the jewelry made out of old tokens is always a conversation starter. The Grand Central store is open Monday through Friday from 8 A.M. to 8 P.M., Saturday and Sunday from 10 A.M. to 6 P.M. The Brooklyn store is open Tuesday through Friday from 10 A.M. to 4 P.M., Saturday and Sunday from noon to 5 P.M.

CityStore

⊞ Manhattan Municipal Building
   1 Centre Street (at Chambers Street), North Plaza
🚇 Chambers Street station (A, C, 1, 2, or 3 train)
📞 212-669-8246
🖎 www.nyc.gov/citystore

CityStore is the official store of New York City, with more things than you could ever imagine connected somehow, someway to the Big Apple. All sorts of books, DVDs, maps, fire and police department merchandise, scarves, sports memorabilia, jewelry, and great stuff for kids are on sale here. You can also find serious things like regulation books and parking cards. Open Monday to Friday, 9 A.M. to 4:30 P.M. Goods are available through its Web site.

Firestore

⊞ 7 Greenwich Avenue (between Christopher and West 10th streets)
🚇 Spring Street station (Q or W train)
📞 1-800-229-9258
🖎 www.nyfirestore.com

After September 11, everyone was wearing FDNY hats. Here's the place to buy them and give the money back to the real heroes—a portion of the proceeds goes to the widows and orphans of New York City firefighters. The store is open Monday to Thursday, 11 A.M. to 7 P.M.; Friday and Saturday, 11 A.M. to 8 P.M.; Sunday, noon to 6 P.M.

Bargain Shopping

Because it is such a shopping center, New York City has some of the best bargains in the world.

Jack's 99 Cent Stores

⊞ 110 West 32nd Street (between 6th and 7th avenues)

🚆 West 34th Street-Herald Square station (B, D, F, N, Q, R, V, or W train)

☎ 212-268-9962

⊞ 16 West 40th Street (between 5th and 6th avenues)

🚆 West 42nd Street-Bryant Park station (B, D, F, or V train) or 5th Avenue station (7 train)

☎ 212-696-5767

The ultimate ninety-nine-cent store, Jack's on West Thirty-second Street is the flagship location with two stories—the second floor has slightly more expensive items, such as gifts, linens, toys, and furnishings. Anything you might have forgotten at home—batteries, stockings, gloves, toothpaste—can be picked up for a buck, instead of paying overpriced hotel lobby convenience store prices. But the bargains are amazing too. You might even be able to pick up New York souvenirs for a dollar. There's an entire wall of kids' toys, many of them last year's hot Disney property.

▐█▌ TRAVEL TIP

There's a great Web site for locating the cross streets and avenues and the nearest subway stop. Go to *www.manhattanaddress.com*.

National Wholesale Liquidators

⌨ 632 Broadway (between West Houston and Bleecker streets)

🚊 Bleecker Street station (6 train) or Broadway-Lafayette Street station (B, D, F, or V train)

✆ 212-979-2400

✎ *www.nationalwholesaleliquidators.com*

This store offers heavily discounted and wholesale prices on all types of gifts, toys, electronics, and housewares. It has everything for the home from toothpaste to television sets, linens to electronics.

Weber's Closeout Center

⌨ 16 West 32nd Street (between 6th and 7th avenues)

🚊 West 34th Street-Herald Square station (B, D, F, N, Q, R, V, or W train)

✆ 212-564-4545

Weber's buys closeout lots of clothing, housewares, cosmetics, and linens and offers the goods at a fraction of the original price. These stores are also a great source of seasonal knickknacks. Recent offerings have included a popular handbag that sells for $30 on sale for $8 and terrific shoes for $5 a pair. A pair of purple suede knee-high boots was purchased for $10. You have to hunt through a lot of merchandise, but it is definitely worth it if you like that type of shopping. There are other branches in the Bronx and Brooklyn.

Woodbury Commons

⌨ 498 Red Apple Court
Central Valley, New York

✆ 845-928-4000

Another shopping option is to take a day trip outside the city to Woodbury Commons. This outlet mall is where many New Yorkers do their holiday shopping. There are more than 220 stores here, including favorites like Off 5th (845-928-4351); Neiman Marcus Last Call (845-928-4993), where prices are typically 30 to 65 percent off original N-M prices; and Betsey Johnson (845-928-4678), which often sells dresses for $85. At the Frette linen outlet (845-928-4866), $1,750 imported Royal Collection bedroom sets can go for $400, and Hotel Collections go for half price. The Sony store has reconditioned merchandise at bargain prices (845-928-5112). There are some fifteen outlet stores for children's merchandise—good discount shopping at Carter's, The Children's Place Outlet, OshKosh, Disney Store Outlet, and KB Toys, to name a few.

To get to Woodbury Commons, the best option is to drive. Take the New York State Thruway (I-87) to exit 16, Harriman. Another option is to take Metro-North on weekends, or the GrayLine or Shortline bus lines (845-928-4000) from the Port Authority. The trip is about an hour and a half each way.

If you take one of the buses, you get a coupon book worth the price of the bus ticket. At *www.premiumoutlets.com* you can register for a different coupon book, which you can pick up at the customer service desk in the food court area. Open every day from 10 A.M. to 9 P.M., shortened hours on some major holidays.

CHAPTER 13

Parks, Recreation, and Sports

DESPITE ITS STATUS as an urban center, New York City is a great place to spend time outdoors. Well-designed, well-maintained, and accessible parks and public spaces make it possible to get out and enjoy sports. The Hudson River, the East River, and Long Island Sound provide New Yorkers with a wealth of water activities from boating and sailing to fishing in the warmer months. New York is a great town for sports fans. There are two major league baseball teams, the Yankees and the Mets, as well as professional football, basketball, tennis, hockey, and soccer.

A Day at the Beach

New York City is surrounded by beaches, most of which are open to the public for free. The beaches get very crowded during the summer months, but it's still a lot of fun to take a break from the city and spend a day at the shore. Many beaches are flanked by a thriving boardwalk, with food, rides, and games.

TRAVEL TIP

If you're planning a beach trip out of the city, leave early. If you get there late, you'll have trouble finding a spot anywhere near the ocean to put your blanket down. For information on beach hours, call the city information number at 311 or 212-NEW-YORK (639-9675) from outside the city. The Web site is *www.nycgovparks.org*.

Brighton Beach
🚆 Brighton Beach station (B or Q train)
📞 718-946-1350

The beach is located in a wonderful Russian neighborhood (called Little Odessa) in Brooklyn with interesting restaurants and shops. Though it boasts miles of clean beach, Brighton Beach is one of the city's most crowded, so get there early to stake out your territory. The train ride will take about an hour from midtown.

FAST FACT

Legendary playwright Neil Simon's *Brighton Beach Memoirs* is the first in a semiautobiographical trilogy. It follows Eugene Jerome, a Jewish teenager growing up in Brooklyn in 1937.

Coney Island
🚆 Coney Island-Stillwell Avenue station (D, F, N, or Q train)
📞 718-946-1350

Here you'll find the legendary amusement park with the still-impressive Cyclone roller coaster and boardwalk, which has been restored. You can still get a cracklin' good hot dog from the original Nathan's Famous. (For details on Coney Island attractions, see page 184.) The waves here are mild. Like nearby Brighton Beach, Coney Island is often crowded, with slightly more families than teenagers because of the nearby amusement park and attractions. A third, much smaller beach, Manhattan Beach, is located to the east of Coney Island. Manhattan Beach can be reached via the Q train from Brighton Beach and then the B1 bus.

Rockaway Park Beach

🚇 Rockaway Park Beach-116th Street station (A or S train)
📞 718-318-4000

Because of its distance and size (at ten miles, it's the longest municipal beach in the country), Rockaway Park is one of the least crowded beaches. The nicest stretch is north of the last subway stop on the A line at 116th Street. (Note that the S train is the Rockaway Park shuttle, not the Forty-second Street train.) The trip should take about an hour and ten minutes from midtown.

TRAVEL TIP

Far Rockaway is a year-round beach community with some die-hard surfers; they're the ones in the wet suits. Beware of the rough waves here, but do take a walk along the delightfully deserted beach.

Orchard Beach

🚇 Pelham Parkway station (2 or 5 train) then the Bx12 bus to Orchard Beach (summer only)
📞 718-885-2275

Orchard Beach, a manmade beach on Long Island Sound in the Bronx, is affectionately known as "the Riviera of New York." It's in

Pelham Bay Park, close to City Island, so it's a popular beach destination. It has a boardwalk, bandshell, and sports facilities. The nature center is open 10 A.M. to 4 P.M., as are the twenty-six baseball, basketball, volleyball, and handball courts. Snack bars are run by the Parks Department. There is ample parking for a fee. If you prefer public transportation, it should take about an hour and a half from midtown.

≡ FAST FACT

The beach and parking lot were designed by Robert Moses. Explore the rest of Pelham Bay Park if you don't want to sit on the beach all day. It has a nature center and playgrounds among other features. A nearby lagoon served as the site for the 1964 Olympic rowing trials.

Jones Beach

🚆 Freeport station (Long Island Railroad) then the N88 shuttle bus to Jones Beach (summer only)

📞 718-217-5477

✎ www.nysparks.state.ny.us/parks

You must drive or take the Long Island Rail Road (LIRR) to get to Jones Beach, so it is less crowded than the city beaches. During the week, you can actually spread out and play Frisbee on this manmade beach. There are lots of attractions and amenities in this state park. The LIRR has rail/beach packages.

A Stroll in the Park

Of course, Central Park is the center of the park universe in New York City. Many New Yorkers consider it their backyard. But there are other parks that residents regard with almost equal passion.

Battery Park

🚇 South Ferry station (1 train)

📞 212-344-3491

✎ www.thebattery.org

This twenty-three-acre park is at the southern tip of Manhattan, where colonial New Amsterdam was first established. The park has been extensively renovated over the last few years. Landscaping by garden master Piet Oudolf has been installed, as has a forest grove and a sixty-foot-wide fountain. Also of importance are gardens and monuments in tribute to the victims and survivors of 9/11, AIDS victims, and veterans of World War II and the Korean War. It's also the jumping off point for ferries to the Statue of Liberty. There's a playground and food is available. The best time to go is warm weekends.

 TRAVEL TIP

A few short years ago, Battery Park was an unsightly expanse of asphalt, but thanks to the renovation it's a park you can enjoy visiting. Allow a little extra time to stroll through the park before or after you visit the Statue of Liberty and Ellis Island.

Fort Tryon Park/Inwood Hill Park

🗺 Riverside Drive to Broadway, West 192nd to Dyckman streets

🚇 West 190th Street station (A train)

📞 212-795-1388

✎ www.nycgovparks.org

Originally the site of a fort built during the American Revolution, Fort Tryon Park is located on the extreme northwest tip of Manhattan and enjoys a commanding view of the Hudson River. Designed by Frederick Law Olmsted Jr., son of Central Park's designer, Fort Tryon has achieved landmark status. Its sixty-seven acres of wooded hills and country atmosphere makes you forget you are in Manhattan. Notable features of the park, in addition to the views, are the Cloisters Museum, a medieval refuge in the big city, and the three-acre heather garden. In the Inwood section of the park, you can find a Native American trash dump, where American Indians once discarded their shells and people still find arrowheads. If you walk through the park's paths, also designed by Olmsted, you may see wild rabbits, raccoons, and pheasants. Urban park rangers give tours throughout the spring and summer.

≡FAST FACT

In the 1950s, when Frank Lloyd Wright was looking for a home for his new corkscrew-shaped museum, Fort Tryon Park was considered (and rejected) as the site for the Guggenheim. The museum now stands on Fifth Avenue and East Eighty-ninth Street, part of Museum Mile.

Riverside Park
⊡ On the Hudson River, from West 72nd to West 158th streets
🚇 West 72nd to West 157th Street stations (1, 2, or 3 trains)
📞 212-408-0264
✍ www.nycgovparks.org

The four-mile long Riverside Park is a popular place for strolling, dog walking, and bird watching. Wintertime pursuits include sledding and cross-country skiing. Designed by Frederick Law Olmsted (of Central Park fame) and opened in 1910, the long waterside park features a bird sanctuary, community garden, a marina (West Seventy-ninth Street station (1 train), and an adjacent rotunda. From posh Upper West Siders to Columbia University students to numerous joggers, the park has a wide variety of daily visitors.

Carl Schurz Park

⌨ East River between East 84th and East 90th streets

🚇 East 86th Street station (4, 5, or 6 train)

☎ 212-459-4455

🖳 *www.carlschurzparknyc.org*

This park was a fortification for the Continental Army in the American Revolution, and it was seized by the British a few months after war broke out in 1776. Today it is taken over primarily by Upper East Siders. The multilevel park features marble stairways, beautiful paths, and gardens. Playgrounds, basketball courts, and dog runs are part of this secret little gem.

Tucked away in a cozy east side corner of the city, the park is bordered on the upper tip by the mayor's residence, Gracie Mansion. The most noteworthy aspect of this inviting little park is the John Finley Walk, a wide riverside walkway with spectacular views of Roosevelt Island, Queens, and the boat traffic along the East River. The serenity and tranquility make for a delightful afternoon.

🧳 TRAVEL TIP

Let your kids wear their bathing suits to Carl Schurz Park in the summer. There is a sprinkler area where kids of all ages can play and cool off. Bring a change of clothes or let the kids dry off before you leave.

Union Square Park

⌨ Between 14th and 18th streets, and Broadway and Park Avenue

🚇 East 14th Street-Union Square station (L, N, Q, R, W, 4, 5, or 6 train)

☎ 311 (in town)

☎ 212-NEW-YORK (639-9675) (from outside the city)

🖳 *www.unionsquarenyc.org*

The popular Fourteenth Street/Union Square subway station deposits many travelers on the park's borders, and the park remains the centerpiece of Union Square. The surrounding area has been refurbished in the past several years, with cafés and trendy restaurants now highlighting the increasingly popular neighborhood. This small park is home to a giant green market every Monday, Wednesday, Friday, and Saturday year-round featuring fresh fruits and vegetables and a flea market selling a variety of craft items. There are playgrounds at the northern end. Free tours are given every Saturday at 2 P.M. starting at the Lincoln statue near the Pavilion building.

Washington Square Park

5th Avenue and West 4th Street

West 4th Street-Washington Square station (A, B, C, D, E, F, or V train)

212-360-1316

www.nycgovparks.org

At the foot of Fifth Avenue in Greenwich Village, Washington Square Park is home to a giant white marble arch built in 1892, along with two statues of George Washington that were added in the early part of the twentieth century. The nearly ten-acre park, used in the early nineteenth century for military parade drills and public hangings, is nestled between brownstones and New York University.

FAST FACT

Washington Square Park was used as a potter's field starting in 1797. A tree known as the Hangman's Elm stands in the northwest corner of the park; its name dates back to the days when public executions were held in the park.

For decades it has been a favorite stomping ground for an eclectic variety of locals. Hippies, yuppies, punks, poets, artists, bohemians,

Frisbee players, chess players, students, panhandlers, and a variety of street performers all come to enjoy themselves here. Visiting the park is a let-your-hair-down experience and has been for many decades. Outdoor art shows are very popular.

Flushing Meadows Corona Park
🖃 Main Street to Corona Avenue to 111th Street, Flushing, Queens
🚃 111th Street station (Flushing, Queens) (7 train)
📞 718-760-6565
✍ www.nycgovparks.org

This is a full-service park on the grounds of two former World's Fairs. The icon is the Unisphere, but people also come for the Hall of Science, the wildlife center, the botanical garden, and the Pitch and Putt. There's a playground for kids of all ages and abilities, an antique carousel, and ice-skating in the winter. The grounds have softball, baseball, soccer, cricket fields, and a new boathouse.

≡FAST FACT

Most of the buildings in Flushing Meadows Corona Park were constructed for the World's Fairs and have been renovated to conform to current uses. The two exceptions are Shea Stadium and Arthur Ashe Stadium. The latter is located north of the Unisphere, and the walk from one to the other takes you through a beautiful sculpture garden.

Prospect Park
🖃 Eastern Brooklyn bounded by Prospect Park West and Southwest, Parkside Avenue, and Ocean Avenue
🚃 Prospect Park station (B, Q, or S [Brooklyn's Franklin Avenue Shuttle] train) or 15th Street-Prospect Park station (F train)
📞 718-965-8951
✍ www.prospectpark.org

Prospect Park is Brooklyn's answer to Central Park. The first urban area Audubon Center in the country, it has many programs for kids. The Songbird Café, located in a bucolic setting, offers organic coffee, snacks, baked goods, and other food. The Celebrate Brooklyn Performing Arts program has events scheduled at the band shell all summer long, with fantastic performances of music, dance, and movies. The Prospect Park Zoo, the Brooklyn Museum, and the Brooklyn Botanic Garden are all here. Facilities include ice skating in the winter, tennis courts, a playground, and a pedal boat rental. The park features the only forest in Brooklyn.

 TRAVEL TIP

Prospect Park hosts numerous festivities throughout the year. Check the calendar of events to see what's going on during your visit. Annual celebrations are held for Earth Week, Halloween, and New Year's, and the park also celebrates the seasons with special activities.

Van Cortlandt Park
⌨ Bounded by Broadway, Jerome Avenue, Van Cortlandt Park South, and the city line
🚇 242nd Street station (1 train)
✆ 718-430-1890
✎ *www.nycgovparks.org*

Van Cortlandt Park is the Bronx's answer to Central Park. You'll find horseback riding, tennis courts, baseball, basketball, bocce, football, cricket, golf, soccer, playgrounds, food, and a public pool (always very crowded). The Van Cortlandt Mansion is a house museum on the premises, and it's interesting to spend an afternoon there discovering what life was like after the American Revolution. There are free concerts in the park in summer.

 RAINY DAY FUN

Spend an afternoon at Van Cortlandt Park touring the Van Cortlandt House Museum, the first Dutch Colonial house in the city. There's a nice gift shop, and colonial fairs are held in the spring and fall. For more information, call 718-543-3344 or visit *www.vancortlandthouse.org.*

Arenas and Stadiums

There's nothing like seeing Bruce Springsteen or Bob Dylan on their home turf, or watching the Yankees play at home.

Madison Square Garden

- 7th Avenue (between West 31st and West 33rd streets)
- West 34th Street-Pennsylvania Station station (1, 2, or 3 train)
- 212-465-6741 (General information)
- *www.thegarden.com*

This is home base for the Rangers, Knicks, Liberty (women's basketball), and Titans (the new pro lacrosse expansion team), and the venue also hosts unforgettable concerts and important expositions. For event tickets, contact Ticketmaster: 212-307-7171, *www.ticket master.com.*

TRAVEL TIP

Every year when the circus comes to town, the elephants march through the Midtown Tunnel and across Thirty-fourth Street to Madison Square Garden. It's the only way to get the humongous pachyderms into the city. Even though the parade takes place around midnight (so as not to disrupt traffic), crowds line the streets to welcome the animals and their handlers.

Meadowlands Sports Complex

⊡ 50 State Route 120, East Rutherford, New Jersey

🚌 Bus from the Port Authority Bus Terminal (during games and events)

✆ 201-935-8500

✆ 201-935-3900 (Event hotline)

✍ *www.meadowlands.com*

Composed of the Continental Airlines Arena, Giants Stadium, and Meadowlands Racetrack, the Meadowlands Complex is home to no fewer than five pro teams: the New Jersey Nets, New York Jets, New Jersey Devils, New York Red Bulls (soccer), and New York Giants. It is also a major entertainment and exposition venue; there are always great rock concerts in the summer months. Giants Stadium hosts a huge flea market one or two days a week and on major holidays. For more information, call 201-935-5474 or go online at *www.meadow landsfleamarket.com*.

If you can drive, take Rte. 3 and the New Jersey Turnpike to exit 16W. For public transportation information, call 1-800-772-2222.

Shea Stadium

⊡ 123-01 Roosevelt Avenue (off Grand Central Parkway) Flushing, Queens

🚌 Willets Point-Shea Stadium station (7 train)

✆ 718-507-METS (8387) (Front office)

✆ 718-507-TIXX (8499) (For tickets)

✍ *www.mets.com*

The Mets play in the stadium they once lent the Beatles, but the team won't be there for long. A new state-of-the-art stadium, called Citi Field, will replace Shea in 2009. Inspired by the old Ebbets Field, Citi Field will be an open-air stadium built with materials reminiscent of the former site of the Brooklyn Dodgers.

Meanwhile, tickets to Met games are easy to come by, but they are cheaper at the box office—there's a heavy surcharge if you order through Ticketmaster. Batting practice starts two and a half hours before the game, admission is at Gate C. Glatt kosher food is available in various locations, and nonalcohol sections are provided. Children under 32 inches tall (the height of the turnstiles) are admitted free. The Mets' Web site has a kids club.

Yankee Stadium

🏠 161st Street and River Avenue

🚆 161st Street-Yankee Stadium station (B, D, or 4 train)

📞 718-293-6000

✍ www.yankees.com

Yankee Stadium is home to the team with the most World Series victories, the New York Yankees. The facility has a lot to offer, but only temporarily. Like their crosstown rivals, the Yankees are also getting a new stadium in 2009. The new Yankee Stadium will meld tradition (same dimensions and feel) with modern reality (fewer seats but more luxury suites). Until then, enjoy the place before it becomes history. (See the full listing on page 206.)

TRAVEL TIP

For a fun day, try to get tickets to see the Staten Island Yankees (the pin-stripers' minor league team) play their arch rivals the Brooklyn Cyclones (the Mets' minor league team) in the Richmond County Bank Ballpark. The stadium is right by the (free) Staten Island Ferry Terminal overlooking the harbor and across the street from some great restaurants. There's also a rail shuttle from the ferry terminal to the ballpark on game days.

The food court serves the usual chicken and hotdogs, but Chinese food is available too. The Yankee store has been completely remodeled. There's also a Yankee Stadium tour available. Tickets can be obtained, but order ahead for special days like opening day or Red Sox/Yankee games. Batting practice starts two hours before the game. Nonalcohol family sections (including the entire bleachers) are provided, as are baby-changing areas. Children under 30 inches tall (the height of the turnstiles) are admitted free.

Billie Jean King National Tennis Center

▱ Flushing Meadows-Corona Park, Flushing, Queens

🚃 Willets Point-Shea Stadium station (7 train)

☎ 718-760-6200

✑ www.usta.com

Every September, Arthur Ashe Stadium hosts the finals of the U.S. Open, one of tennis's premier events. The U.S. Open is the final Grand Slam tournament of the season and is played on a hard court. Tickets are available through Ticketmaster (*www.ticketmaster.com*).

⟳FAST FACT

The statue of Arthur Ashe was placed near Arthur Ashe Stadium in 2000. It depicts Ashe in midserve, but hawk-eyed visitors will notice that Ashe's tennis racket is only a handle. The artist who designed the statue, Eric Fischl, did that on purpose. The tennis racket is supposed to symbolize the qualities that Ashe passes on to future generations.

You can find everything from snack food to meals here. Aces and Champions are bar and grill establishments that offer traditional American fare. Eat outdoors at the Patio Café, which offers a menu of sandwiches and salads. The Heineken Red Star Café is a sports bar within a sports venue. For the more adventurous, the Mojito Restaurant serves Cuban-inspired food. The Food Village is a collection of more than a dozen fast-food establishments.

KeySpan Park
▫ 1904 Surf Avenue, Coney Island, Brooklyn
🚇 Coney Island-Stillwell Avenue station (D, F, N, or Q train)
📞 718-449-8497
✍ *www.brooklyncyclones.com*

The Brooklyn Cyclones are a farm team for the Mets. They play seventy-six games in a season that runs from mid-June to mid-September. Their home stadium, KeySpan Park, is a beautiful new facility in a historic location on Surf Avenue in Coney Island. It overlooks Coney Island as well as the Atlantic Ocean and is right next door to Nathan's and the famous Parachute Jump.

TRAVEL TIP

Minor league baseball teams are well known for using entertaining gimmicks to keep fans coming back for more. KeySpan Park hosted a rock-paper-scissors tournament, but there are also promotions meant to draw attention to serious issues. Whether you go home with a bobblehead or not, be sure to watch out for the Cyclones' mascot, Sandy the Seagull.

The team is very popular, a league-leader in attendance every year. It has some great promotions throughout the season, and it's worth a call or log on. A game and a day at Coney Island is a lifelong memory. Children under three are admitted free.

Richmond County Bank Ballpark
▫ St. George, Staten Island
🚇 Staten Island Ferry then S. I. Railway Shuttle
📞 718-720-9265
✍ *www.siyanks.com*

The Richmond County Bank Ballpark is home to the Staten Island Yankees, a minor league farm team for the New York Yankees. The new stadium is right across from the Staten Island Ferry Terminal (now a free ride), and a Staten Island Railway shuttle from the ferry terminal to the ballpark runs on game days. The stadium has incredible views of the Statue of Liberty and lower Manhattan. The team has a Pinstripe Plan, which puts you in a special section and gives you all-you-can-eat burgers, dogs, and chicken sandwiches, washed down by never-ending soda or water.

Athletic Activities

If they're not sitting in the bleachers and cheering for their favorite team, New Yorkers are out enjoying a world of activities. If you thought the city was a bleak, gray canyon, check out the thousands who bike or play tennis or golf. Join the natives in ice skating or horseback riding, even sailing.

Bike Rides and Rentals

New Yorkers bike all over the city, from the bike paths of Central Park and Riverside Drive through Prospect Park. You can rent bikes in Central Park at the Loeb Boathouse (212-517-2233), at the Toga Bike Shop (212-799-9625) on the Upper West Side, or at Bike Central Park 917-371-6267, *www.bikecentralpark.com*. The Five Borough Bicycle Club also offers day and weekend rides—call 212-932-2300, ext. 115, or visit *www.5bbc.org*.

A Tennis Match

This is a tennis-crazed town. The Department of Parks administers eight indoor and seventy-one outdoor tennis facilities, each with up to thirty courts. The thirty public tennis courts are in Central Park (212-280-0205), and Riverside Park (212-978-0277) has ten clay courts. Permits or single-play tickets are necessary to use the public courts. The parks and recreation office will tell you where to get a permit and will give you a list of all the indoor and outdoor tennis courts in the city if you call 311 in town, or 212-NEW-YORK (639-9675) from outside the city. The information is also available at *www.nycgovparks .org*. You can even play at the site of the U.S. Open. The USTA Billy Jean King National Tennis Center, in Flushing Meadows, Queens, has courts open for public use. Best time is weekdays before 4 P.M. (classes are held after that). Call for reservations two days before at 718-760-6200. Get more information at *www.usta.com*.

A Game of Golf

There are lots of places in the outer boroughs to play golf. You'll need a nonresident permit plus greens fees to play; the fees do not amount to much. Seniors (sixty-two and over) and juniors (sixteen and under) get a cut rate. The Department of Parks maintains fifteen public golf courses and three driving ranges in all five boroughs. Even Manhattan has a golf course, on Randall's Island (212-427-5689). The best place for information, fees, availability, and tee time reservations is at *www.nycgovparks.org*.

 TRAVEL TIP

If your teens are suffering from skateboard or inline skating deprivation, there are several parks in town to welcome them. In Manhattan, Riverside Skate Park, at West 108th Street and Riverside Drive in Riverside Park (lower level), has five ramps, half-pipes, quarter-pipes, and rails. Call 212-408-9265. Open late May through the end of October.

Ice Skating

The city's outdoor ice skating rinks are open when the Parks Department determines the ice is thick enough for safety. Check the Web site for opening/closing dates and times. All facilities offer skate rentals.

There are two rinks in Central Park: Lasker Rink (917-492-3856) is located near 106th Street, and the Wollman Rink (212-439-6900) entrance is at Fifty-ninth and Sixth Avenue. Right smack in midtown, the Pond at Bryant Park lies behind the Main Library on West Forty-second Street and Fifth Avenue (866-221-5157). There are also outdoor rinks in Brooklyn and Staten Island. The World's Fair Ice Skating Rink in the New York City Building, Flushing Meadows-Corona Park (718-271-1996), is the Park Department's only indoor facility.

The world-famous Rink at Rockefeller Center (212-332-7654) is located between Forty-ninth and Fiftieth streets, just off Fifth Avenue. It is often crowded, but skating there is a classic experience.

Horseback Riding

There are a surprising number of places in all five boroughs to rent a horse and go horseback riding. The variety of terrain for a city is unbelievable. In Manhattan's Central Park, you can book a guided tour from Riverdale Equestrian Stables at 718-548-4848 (*www.river daleriding.com*). Riverdale also supplies horses for riding Van Cortlandt Park in the Bronx. Also in the Bronx is Pelham Bay Park, handled by Pelham Bit Stables, 718-885-0551.

In Queens, Forest Park has 165 acres to ride in. Call Forest Equine Center at 718-263-3500. Brooklyn's Prospect Park is a lovely setting. Call Kensington Stables at 718-972-4588.

You can ride in a variety of terrain in Staten Island. Sequine Equestrain Center is at 718-317-1121. For more information, log on to *www.nycgovparks.org* and search "horseback riding."

Visit Chelsea Piers

- 12th Avenue and West 23rd Street
- 23rd Street station (C or E train)
- 212-336-6400
- *www.chelseapiers.com*

Chelsea Piers Sports & Entertainment Complex offers thirty acres of fun along Manhattan's Hudson River. In addition to the traditional spa amenities of a sports center, Chelsea Piers also boasts the largest indoor rock-climbing wall in the Northeast, one of the few indoor Olympic pools in the city, the only indoor sand volleyball court in New York City, a quarter-mile running track, and a forty-lane bowling alley as well as the city's only all-year, indoor ice-skating rink. There is a wonderful indoor play area called the Toddler Adventure Center that is designed for children from six months to four years old. Going to Chelsea Piers is a nice way to spend an afternoon, especially if the weather turns bad and you've got to blow off some steam.

🌂 RAINY DAY FUN

Take your family to the Sky Rink, the only year-round indoor ice skating arena in New York. General skating is offered every afternoon and is priced around $13 for adults and $9.50 for children and seniors. Occasional specials are less.

The Golf Club at Chelsea Piers is a popular favorite. The 2,000-square-foot facility features hitting stalls, an indoor putting green, and a practice sand bunker. There is also virtual golfing with full-swing simulators for about $45 an hour. Players can choose from fifty-one different championship courses worldwide.

The Chelsea Brewing Company has a restaurant and microbrewery on the premises that offers a large menu of favorites: Italian food, boutique food, sandwiches, wraps, pizza, burgers, and a kid's menu, as well as a natural beer made in-house. It's an attractive place that overlooks the marina. There is also Famous Famiglia, two cafés, and Jason's Riverside Grill.

CHAPTER 14

Broadway and the Performing Arts

THE CREATIVE ARTS are the buzz that infuses New York with its energy and impatience. There is no place on earth that devotes as much real estate to creative endeavors of all sorts as this little island. Most people who visit make a point to see at least one play and maybe catch a performance of the opera or ballet, or visit the clubs—comedy, jazz, or rock. This vast cauldron of creative output is what the city is known for.

On Broadway

A Broadway musical can set a family back a few hundred dollars, but it's one of those rare treats you'll always remember. Theater in New York City is a captivating experience. The long-running *Phantom of the Opera* is classic Broadway; for story and production values, you can see *The Lion King;* and for more great family fare, you can see *The Little Mermaid.*

Finding a Show

New York magazine, among other publications, will fill you in on the shows, as will the concierge in any good hotel (incidentally, many hotels and travel Web sites offer a theater package that will save you money on your room and tickets). It's not hard to find out what shows are the talk of the town. Whether you enjoy musicals, comedies, or dramas, there's always a selection of first-rate shows on the boards.

Yes, it can be expensive, but not by any means is that the rule. If you can't afford four tickets to *The Lion King*, there are off-off-Broadway productions with tickets for $15 per person, or even summer plays at the Delacorte Theater in Central Park that are absolutely free. You can also get cut-rate tickets from various outlets, which will be covered later in the chapter.

It takes some planning, and you should go online before you arrive and see what's playing (try searching through entertainment listings of the *New York Times*, *New York*, *Time Out New York*, the *Village Voice*, and at *http://newyork.citysearch.com*). You'll also be able to find out what tickets are available and what you can afford. You won't regret planning in advance.

TRAVEL TIP

If you are dying to see a specific show, but it's sold out when you are in town, there are several ticket brokers and online services that can probably get you seats. However, be aware that some charge stiff fees for the privilege. To find them do an Internet search for "Ticket Brokers New York" and be assaulted by scores of brokers eager for your business. If you buy via StubHub.com in advance, you may pick up tickets at their location in 1440 Broadway.

Shows are always opening and closing on Broadway, but some trends persist. There is always a riveting production of some classic drama by Eugene O'Neill, Henrik Ibsen, Edward Albee, and/or Shakespeare in any given Broadway season. There are favorite musicals as well, from the revivals of *Grease*, *A Chorus Line*, and *Company* on up to the Tony Award–winning *Chicago*.

Getting Tickets

All major theaters sell through two ticket providers: Telecharge or Ticketmaster. These ticket providers work in tandem, and the Web site of one will link you to the other if it doesn't handle a specific show.

Telecharge

  ✆ 212-239-6200

  ✆ 1-800-432-7250 (outside New York City)

  ✐ *www.telecharge.com*

Ticketmaster

  ✆ 212-307-4100

  ✆ 1-800-755-4000 (outside New York City)

  ✐ *www.ticketmaster.com*

Telecharge and Ticketmaster tack a nominal surcharge onto each ticket, but it's far less than ticket brokers charge. You can get the tickets mailed to you in hard copies or electronically, or you can pick them up at the theater the night of the show. In some cases, you can still order tickets from the theater box office.

Same-day discount tickets are available at the TKTS Booth at Forty-seventh Street and Broadway (expect to wait at least an hour, perhaps two) or at the South Street Seaport at Front and John streets—this location is a better bet, but it's out of the way unless you're sightseeing downtown. Both sites sell tickets at a 25 to 50 percent discount, with a small fee per ticket, but you have to pay in cash. The Seaport booth also sells tickets for the next day's matinee performances. You can buy tickets online at the Web site *www.tdf.org/tkts*, but they are usually for the perennials and not the last-minute hot tickets. Hint: If you've never been to a Broadway show, click on the TKTS Web site's "New York Theatre 101."

Broadway Shows

Here is a list of some of the popular Broadway shows that you might consider seeing.

A Chorus Line
Schoenfeld Theatre
- 236 West 45th Street (between Broadway and 8th Avenue)
- Times Square-West 42nd Street station (N, Q, R, S, W, 1, 2, 3, or 7 train)
- *www.achorusline.com*

A second chance for you to see this record-breaking musical (the longest running when it closed) about a series of young people who want to make it big on the Great White Way. The kids will get the message that life may not be all that easy, but keep trying and you'll have a chance to play in the chorus line.

Chicago
Ambassador Theatre
- 219 West 49th Street (between Broadway and 8th Avenue)
- West 50th Street station (1 train), West 49th Street station (N, R, or W train)
- *www.chicagothemusical.com*

A razzle-dazzle production and winner of six Tony Awards, *Chicago* brings a Midwestern powerhouse to life. However, its depiction of adultery and deceit make this musical suitable for slightly older kids, twelve and up. It's the longest-running musical revival in history. Tickets are available at Telecharge.

Hairspray
Neil Simon Theatre
- 250 West 52nd Street (between Broadway and 8th Avenue)
- West 50th Street station (1 train)
- *www.hairsprayonbroadway.com*

A wonderful adaptation of the wacky John Waters cult film, this Tony Award–winning musical is fun, but some of its subject matter makes it inappropriate for younger kids. Tickets are available at Ticketmaster.

═FAST FACT

Of course, there's some interesting theater history along Broadway. The Music Box (239 West Forty-fifth Street) was built by Irving Berlin and opened in 1921. The New Amsterdam Theatre (214 West Forty-second Street), a grand theater built in 1903 with an elaborate interior, was refurbished by Disney and is now home to Mary Poppins. The Shubert Theater (225 West Forty-fifth Street), just off Shubert Alley (the famous theater stomping ground), was built in 1913. Look for ornate architectural touches.

The Lion King
Minskoff Theater
⌨ 250 West 45th Street (at Broadway)
🚇 Times Square-West 42nd Street station (N, Q, R, S, W, 1, 2, 3, or 7 train)
📞 212-307-4747
✎ *www.disneyonbroadway.com*

This is the family show to see. It's an award-winning adaptation of the groundbreaking animated Disney film, and the sets and costumes are spectacular. Your kids will be singing and dancing in the aisles. Get tickets at least a month ahead of time.

The Little Mermaid
Lunt-Fontanne Theatre
- 205 West 46th Street (between Broadway and 8th Avenue)
- 50th Street station (1 train), 49th Street station (N, R, or W train)
- 212-307-4747
- *www.disneyonbroadway.com*

This adaptation of the popular and charming movie replaced the long-running *Beauty and the Beast*. Adding to the growing Disney on Broadway reputation, this is a wonderful production. Clever and beautiful, it is appropriate for all ages and definitely worth seeing.

Mamma Mia
Winter Garden
- 1634 Broadway (between West 50th and West 51st streets)
- 50th Street station (1 train), 49th Street station (N, R, or W train)
- *www.mamma-mia.com*

A woman invites three men, any of whom might be her daughter's father, to her daughter's wedding. The musical score is comprised of ABBA's greatest hits, so this is a good option for young and old fans of the group, but it is not for young children. Tickets are available from Telecharge.

The Phantom of the Opera
Majestic Theatre
- 247 West 44th Street (between 7th and 8th avenues)
- Times Square-West 42nd Street station (N, Q, R, S, W, 1, 2, 3, or 7 train)
- *www.thephantomoftheopera.com*

This is the ultimate Broadway experience, and it's appropriate for almost all ages except the very young. If you can afford it, ask for seats under the chandelier. Tickets are available from Telecharge.

Young Frankenstein
Hilton Theatre
⌨ West 44th Street at 7th Avenue
🚇 Times Square-West 42nd Street station (N, Q, R, S, W, 1, 2, 3, or 7 train)
✍ *www.YoungFrankensteinTheMusical.com*

Replacing the venerable *Producers*, this is another musical based on the classic Mel Brooks film about Dr. Frankenstein's little boy. Already famous for charging $450 for opening night premium tickets, it's a show better for kids than its predecessor. Tickets are available from the Web site or call 1-800-755-4000 or in New York, 212-307-4100.

Off-Broadway Shows

Without the glitz and high ticket price, off-Broadway has been the spawning ground for experimental theater. Some Broadway shows get their start here, but mostly it is the showcase for less expensive productions that seek a smaller audience. As off-Broadway grew in stature (and price), off-off-Broadway took its place. Here is where you'll find some really unusual and/or quirky theater. Although some shows run for years, most are ephemeral, so look at the theater guides, especially those at *www.villagevoice.com* and *www.nytimes.com*.

Blue Man Group
Astor Place Theatre
⌨ 434 LaFayette Street (between East 4th Street and Astor Place)
🚇 East 8th Street-New York University station (N, R, or W train) or Astor Place station (6 train)
✍ *www.blueman.com*

You've never seen anything like this almost indescribable visual and aural romp of imagination. Blue Man Group shows are appropriate for children over eight. Tickets are available from Ticketmaster.

Monday Night Magic

St. Clement's Theatre

🖳 423 West 46th Street (between 9th and 10th avenues)

🚃 West 42nd Street-Port Authority station (A, C, or E train) or Times Square-West 42nd Street station (N, Q, R, S, W, 1, 2, 3, or 7 train)

📞 212-615-6432

✉ www.mondaynightmagic.com

Every Monday at 8 P.M., three performers present their own brand of prestidigitation—fun for the whole family. An additional bonus are the discounts many area restaurants will give you when you show your tickets.

TRAVEL TIP

The Radio City Christmas Spectacular has been going strong for more than seventy-five years. The fabulous Rockettes and more than a hundred costumed performers put on an exciting seasonal spectacle. If you're in town between November and December, it's a must-see. Call 212-307-1000.

National Comedy Theater

🖳 34 West 36th Street (between 8th and 9th avenues)

🚃 West 34th Street-Pennsylvania Station station (A, C, E, 1, 2, or 3 train)

📞 212-629-5203

✉ http://manhattancomedy.com

Two teams compete in an improvisational comedy show based on audience suggestion. Similar to the television show *Whose Line is it Anyway?*, cast members of that show have performed with this group at benefits. It's clean fun for the entire family, and ticket prices are modest.

Stomp
Orpheum Theater
⌧ 126 2nd Avenue (between East 7th and East 8th streets)
✎ www.stomponline.com

A talented group of young people use only found objects—sinks, garbage can lids, newspapers, and hubcaps—to make a funny, entertaining evening of noise and dance. Everybody gets caught up in the energy, rhythm, and just plain enthusiasm. About a third of the audience are kids. This show is worth every penny. Tickets are available from Ticketmaster.

Tony n' Tina's Wedding
Vinnie Black's Coliseum at the Edison Hotel
⌧ 221 West 46th Street (between Broadway and 8th Avenue)
🚇 50th Street station (1 train); 49th Street station (N, R, or W train)
✆ 212-352-3101
✎ www.tonyandtinanewyork.com

Since 1988, Tony and Tina have tied the knot with thousands of their closest friends and family, namely you. This is an interactive play that offers a pasta dinner with the spectacle. No reduced children's price.

Performing Arts

There is no thrill for you or the kids like seeing a grand musical spectacle in person. Television pales by comparison to seeing a large stage, magically lit, with the finest performers right in front of you. Do not visit the big city without a visit to the opera, ballet, or a concert of some sort.

Carnegie Hall

881 7th Avenue (at West 57th Street)

West 57th Street-7th Avenue station (N, Q, R, or W train)

212-247-7800

www.carnegiehall.org

Carnegie Hall has been the standard for performance excellence in New York City and the world for more than 100 years. Legendary musicians, vocalists, dancers, and even speakers, including authors and politicians, have graced the hallowed stage of this international institution. The history of the hall and the esteemed artists who have played in it have created a tradition greater than the building itself.

Construction began on Carnegie Hall in 1890 at an eventual cost of more than $2 million. The building opened in 1891 with five days of performances that attracted New York's high society. In the audience were the Rockefellers, Whitneys, and Fricks, all listening to Pyotr Ilyich Tchaikovsky play for them.

The six-story structure encompasses a main hall (Isaac Stern Auditorium) seating 2,800, a recital hall (Zankel Hall) seating 600, and a chamber hall (Weil Recital Hall) seating 270.

While many people associate Carnegie Hall with classical music, its performance scope over the decades has included legendary artists in every performing category, including jazz (Fats Waller, Louis Armstrong, Count Basie, Ella Fitzgerald, Miles Davis, John Coltrane, and Benny Goodman), rock (Paul McCartney and Roger Daltrey), folk (Woody Guthrie, Pete Seeger, and Arlo Guthrie), and popular (Frank Sinatra, Judy Garland, Ethel Merman, and even the Beatles). Carnegie Hall has also been the platform from which history's great orators have spoken: Winston Churchill, Mark Twain, Booker T. Washington, and Woodrow Wilson are part of the legacy. The hall also plays host to young people's concerts and radio and television broadcasts.

≡FAST FACT

Carnegie Hall was almost demolished in 1960 when the New York Philharmonic Orchestra moved uptown to Lincoln Center. Fortunately, after a great upswell of protest, fueled by the building's own singular history and acoustics ("It has been said that the hall itself is an instrument," Isaac Stern remarked) it was saved and eventually refurbished to its former architectural glory in 1986.

There is a gift shop on the premises, as well as a small exhibit at the Rose Museum (both are located at 154 West Fifty-seventh Street, on the second floor) that features noteworthy items from performers who have graced the great stage. There is no cost for admission, and it is open seven days a week from 11 A.M. to 4:30 P.M. and to ticketholders before concerts and during intermission. It is closed during the summer.

Touring Carnegie Hall

Tours of the premises are available Monday through Friday at 11:30 A.M., 2 P.M., and 3 P.M., Saturday at 11:30 A.M. and 12:30 P.M., and Sunday at 12:30 P.M. Tours are $9 for adults, $6 for seniors and students, and $3 for children under twelve. There are also tour and dining packages; for more information call 212-903-9765.

Lincoln Center

⊡ Columbus Avenue (between West 62nd and West 65th streets)

🚇 West 66th Street-Lincoln Center station (1 train); for Rose Hall use the 59th Street-Columbus Circle station (A, B, C, D, or 1 train)

✆ 212-875-5000

✍ *www.lincolncenter.org*

The premier performing arts complex in the world, Lincoln Center for the Performing Arts occupies sixteen acres of Manhattan's Upper West Side. Home to twelve performing arts companies and educational institutions, the renowned multibuilding complex attracts more than five million visitors annually at its twenty-two venues.

 TRAVEL TIP

One of the highlights of the holiday season is the annual performance of George Balanchine's *The Nutcracker,* a magical performance by the New York City Ballet you should not miss if you are in town. Tickets sell out quickly, so order a few months in advance if you are hoping to see this with your family. Call 212-875-5000 for more information.

Originally conceived in the 1950s, the complex is a result of a search for a new home for the New York Philharmonic and the Metropolitan Opera Company. It opened in the fall of 1962. On opening night, Leonard Bernstein and the Philharmonic Orchestra played in front of a live audience of 3,000 people plus a television audience of twenty-six million. The companies that call Lincoln Center home are world-renowned and include the following.

The New York Philharmonic

Avery Fisher Hall
🖼 Columbus Avenue and West 65th Street (north end of the plaza)
✆ 212-875-5656
✍ *www.nyphil.org*

The nation's oldest orchestra was founded in 1842. The New York Philharmonic plays more than 180 concerts a year to audiences totaling more than a million people. This includes the annual visit to Central Park for a special performance under the stars, where the *1812*

Overture is performed amid fireworks. The philharmonic's schedule also includes young people's concerts, Saturday matinee programs, recording sessions, and other specially scheduled performances. It has performed more concerts than any other orchestra in the world.

The New York City Ballet
New York State Theater
▦ Columbus Avenue and West 63rd Street (south side of the plaza)
✆ 212-870-5570
✉ *www.nycballet.org*

The New York City Ballet features the choreography of its founders, George Balanchine and Jerome Robbins, who started the company in 1948. It moved to Lincoln Center in 1964. The company performs for six months at Lincoln Center, spends summers at the Saratoga Performing Arts Center (in Saratoga Springs, New York), and tours the world the rest of the time. The ballet company has many programs for kids and families; go to the Web site for details.

The Metropolitan Opera
Metropolitan Opera House
▦ Columbus Avenue and West 63rd Street (west side of the plaza)
✆ 212-262-6000
✉ *www.metopera.org*

In existence since 1883, the Metropolitan Opera performs more than two dozen operas annually to an enthusiastic audience of 800,000 people. This is a good venue to introduce your kids to opera; individual screens at each seat provide subtitled translations throughout the performance. An art gallery, Schwartz Gallery Met, located in the southside lobby, is open free to the public every day during the season. The Metropolitan Opera is aggressively seeking new audiences with new ideas and outreach programs, including tours of the facility and reduced-price tickets.

The New York City Opera
New York State Theatre
Columbus Avenue and West 63rd Street (south side of the plaza)
212-870-5570
www.nycopera.com

Began as "the people's opera company," this is the city's more innovative opera organization (they introduced subtitling). The New York City Opera performs new, offbeat, and American operas at family-friendly prices. Although not as well known as the Metropolitan Opera, this in no way a second-class citizen—both Beverly Sills and Placido Domingo began their careers here. The season runs from September through November and again in March and April.

TRAVEL TIP

Lincoln Center is an ideal destination year round. During the warmer months in the evening you are likely to find outdoor entertainment under the stars, such as the fun-filled Midsummer Night Swing from mid-June to mid-July, featuring bands and dancers from around the world.

The Chamber Music Society of Lincoln Center
Alice Tully Hall
Columbus Avenue and West 65th Street
212-875-5788
www.chambermusicsociety.org

Dedicated to bringing the beauty of 300 years of chamber music to connoisseurs and newbies alike, this is one of the world's premiere societies. It performs in several venues around town, so see its Web site. If you love chamber music, this is the place to go.

The New York Public Library for the Performing Arts

⊞ Amsterdam Avenue and West 65th Street (northwest corner of the plaza)

✆ 212-870-1630

✍ *www.nypl.org/research/lpa*

The New York Public Library has one of the world's most comprehensive collections devoted to the performing and recording arts. There is an extensive collection of plays and audio recordings. The library presents free music and dance performances, lectures, play readings, and discussions throughout the year.

Other Attractions

Also on the Lincoln Center grounds are the small Walter Reade Theater, which shows award-winning independent and foreign films, run by the Film Society of Lincoln Center; the Gallery at Lincoln Center, both an art shop and gallery; the Juilliard School and its Sharp Theater; Alice Tully Hall; Lincoln Center Plaza; and the Guggenheim Band Shell at Damrosch Park, which hosts outdoor concerts and events for up to 3,000 people.

While strolling the grounds, you will see the brilliant murals in the lobby of the Metropolitan Opera House, the architecture and grandeur of these buildings, and the fountains that are the Lincoln Center's centerpiece (and a wonderful family photo op).

Most performances take place between September and May, when the opera season, Great Performances series, and ballet companies are running. Mostly Mozart takes place during the summer; other events take place throughout the year, from outdoor concerts and meet-the-artist nights to the New York Film Festival. There are events for children of all ages. For group events, such as Sea and Symphony, which includes lunch on a yacht and a meet-the-artist program, call the Lincoln Center Visitors' Services at 212-875-5370.

You can buy gifts at the Performing Arts Shop and the Gallery (concourse level under the plaza), and at gift shops at the Met, Fisher

Hall, and Juilliard. For grub, grab a light snack at the Espresso Bar in Fisher Hall, or dine there at Panevino Restaurant, the Promenade Café in the New York State Theater, or at the Met's Grand Tier Restaurant overlooking Lincoln Center.

 **RAINY DAY FUN**

TADA! Youth Theater, with slightly fewer than 100 seats, features performances for kids and their families, presented by kids ages eight through eighteen. The theater is at 15 West Twenty-eighth Street (between Fifth Avenue and Broadway), West Twenty-eighth Street station (N, R, or W train). Call 212-252-1619.

Touring Lincoln Center

Several tours are offered at Lincoln Center. The guided tour includes the Metropolitan Opera House, Avery Fisher Hall, and New York State Theater, taking you backstage where you may get a glimpse of a rehearsal in progress. A one-hour tour is given four times a day; the fee is $15 for adults, $12 for students, and $8 for children twelve and younger.

There are also specialty tours, such as the Guided Tour of Jazz at Lincoln Center, and accessible tours for persons who use wheelchairs and/or American Sign Language (conducted on the last Thursday of every month). For reservations and information call 212-875-5350. Lincoln Center is undergoing a major modernization of its concert halls and public spaces, so times and stops may be affected.

CHAPTER 15

Family Dining

THIS LITTLE ISLAND is packed with restaurants. Every neighborhood in the city has its eateries, but because you're likely to spend most of your time in midtown Manhattan, that's where this chapter begins. The restaurants listed in this chapter are for sit-down dining and are chosen for families with children who like to eat and be served. If you feel your kids are too young or energetic for the place, try any of the restaurants listed in Chapters 16 and 17, which offer more casual dining.

So Many Options

Wow! What a city to eat in! New York has between 18,000 and 20,000 restaurants, and your choices are pretty much infinite, from the ultimate in epicurean fantasies to pushcart hot dogs. World-renowned chefs open their signature restaurants here, faddish celebrity "in" places come and go with astounding regularity, and New Yorkers flock to old favorites that have been on the block for generations. There are charming and eclectic cafés and bistros, cheap ethnic places that natives cherish, and amazing fusion restaurants that could have only come about in a city of immigrants.

Most visitors to the Big Apple are either shell-shocked or happily surprised at the cost of eating out. An expensive dinner entrée runs at least $30 per person. A moderate entrée will run between $15 and $30 per person, and a reasonable entrée is under $15 per person. Remember to ask for a children's menu, and don't be ashamed to share a meal, ask for a half portion, or to order an appetizer portion for a young gourmet. New York restaurants are used to it.

Prices can change daily and without notice, and most restaurants have a range of entrées that span price categories. You can access many of the restaurants' menus and prices on the Internet. Also check out the dinner entrée price icons at the beginning of all listings:

$15 or less: ($)
$16–$30: ($$)
$31 or more: ($$$)

The Manhattan restaurant market is highly competitive with three or four—sometimes more—restaurants on a single block. With all this choice and competition, you should not have to put up with bad service, although it's often hard to determine what you'll find once inside. The nicer restaurants should afford you the finest service, but that is not always the case. Always try to call ahead to reserve, especially for dinner at hot spots.

Midtown West

Midtown Manhattan between West Thirtieth and West Fifty-ninth streets (that's west of Fifth Avenue) is the most popular section of town because so many of the big New York attractions are here, from the Empire State Building to Times Square.

B. Smith's ($$)
⌨ 320 West 46th Street (between 8th and 9th avenues)
🚇 Times Square station (A, B, or C train)
📞 212-315-1100
✎ www.bsmith.com/restaurant_ny.php

This is the flagship of a trio of notable restaurants owned by former Oil of Olay beauty Barbara Smith, now a radio and television personality, author, and successful entrepreneur. The cuisine is global eclectic, with international influences added to her exquisite American soul food. She loves her restaurant, so she may be on the premises when you come by, to say nothing of her celebrity friends and acquaintances, some of whose photos line the walls.

JUST FOR PARENTS

Food is serious business in New York. Most waiters are professionals or performers with a college degree who work the late shift. You must tip, and you should tip like a New Yorker. Since the sales tax in the city is 8.375 percent, most New Yorkers simply double the tax, which leaves your server a bit more than a 16 percent tip.

You can get as brave or down-home as you want here. The macaroni and a plethora of cheeses dish is great for both kids and adults, as are the sweet potatoes (as a side dish or in pie). People come back again and again for the crab cakes, ribs, and stuffed chicken. There are also many vegetarian dishes to choose from. If you fall in love with your meal, you can download the recipes from the Web site.

Desserts can be served as a pick-me-up later in the evening. The Sunday brunch is spectacular, with wonderful waffles and sweet potato pancakes among a huge selection of goodies.

Open seven days for lunch and dinner and Sunday brunch. All credit cards accepted.

Bubba Gump Shrimp Co. ($$)

🖃 1501 Broadway (44th Street)

🚇 42nd Street-Times Square station (N, Q, R, S, W, 1, 2, 3, or 7 train)

📞 212-391-7100

✐ www.bubbagump.com

Life might be like a box of chocolates to Forrest Gump, but this wonderful family place in the very heart of the Big Apple is warm and friendly and full of down-home southern cooking. Unpretentious to the max, everyone in the family will feel comfortable munching on po' boys, cajun shrimp, or BBQ pork. The place is based on the movie *Forrest Gump*, and the chefs know how to whip up a great fish and chips and bourbon mahi mahi. The kid's menu is full of comfort food for small souls. Join the birthday club on the Web site and get a free birthday meal at any of the many restaurants worldwide.

Open seven days for lunch and until well after midnight. Takes all credit cards.

TRAVEL TIP

The most famous concentration of restaurants in New York is along Forty-sixth Street between Eighth and Ninth avenues, known as Restaurant Row. There are at least twenty places to eat along the way, all geared toward the theater crowd. But the city also has other, more exotic restaurant rows. East Sixth Street, between First and Second avenues, has an amazing number of Indian restaurants, most at unbelievably low prices. Chinatown's Mott Street will transport you to Asia as your family explores the many cuisines of that continent.

Carmine's Midtown ($$–$$$)

⌨ 200 West 44th Street (8th Avenue and Broadway)

🚇 Times Square-42 Street (N, R, Q, S, W, 1, 2, 3, or 7 train); 42 Street-Port Authority (A,C, or E train)

✆ 212-221-3800

✎ *www.carminesnyc.com*

Carmine's is big, bold, brassy, and loud—in other words, great for kids. And the food is as big as its environment. Carmine's offers traditional Southern Italian fare in gargantuan portions you can split three ways and never go hungry—in fact, do not place a single order per person. The taste is so bold the restrooms come equipped with mouthwash.

This is an extremely popular place, so get there before 5 P.M. or be prepared to wait. Reservations are accepted only after 6 P.M. for parties of six or more only. All major credit cards are accepted.

Carnegie Deli ($-$$)

⌨ 854 7th Avenue (55th Street)

🚇 7th Avenue station (B, D, or E train)

☎ 212-757-2245

One of the last remaining authentic New York delicatessens, this famous and popular midtown icon has been around since 1937. It is often crowded and hectic, especially during lunch, but it's also a great off-hours spot (late lunch after 2:00 P.M. or even a late dinner after 9:30 P.M.). Portions are huge, so feel comfortable asking to share, and the menu is as big as the portions. Open from 6:30 A.M. to 4 A.M. Cash only.

Docks Oyster Bar ($$)

⌨ 2427 Broadway, at 89th Street

🚇 East 86th Street station (4, 5, or 6 train)

☎ 212-986-8080

This is the Upper West Side location of a New York favorite. See the full listing in the Midtown East section.

Ellen's Stardust Diner ($-$$)

⌨ 1650 Broadway, near 51st Street

🚇 West 50th Street station (1 train); West 49th Street station (N, R, or W train); 7th Avenue station (B, D, or E train)

☎ 212-956-5151

🖱 *www.ellensstardustdiner.com*

This is a great place for families. It's a re-creation of a 1950s diner with period memorabilia, including old televisions playing videos of the time. The singing wait staff performs several shows a night, and there's even the city's largest indoor train chugging around the mezzanine (kids love to wave to the conductor). The menu is huge and features familiar American fare from the 1950s supplemented with updated popular items, so every mood and taste is covered.

At the same location is the Iridium Jazz club, which has carried over the jazz tradition to a new generation. If this interests you, check the Web site of the diner or *www.iridiumjazzclub.com*.

Macy's Cellar Bar and Grill ($)

⊞ 34th Street at Herald Square (in Macy's)

🚆 West 34th Street-Herald Square station (B, D, F, N, Q, R, V, or W train)

✆ 212-868-3001

✎ *www.rapatina.com/macysCellar*

Who would believe that the famous store houses one of the best family restaurants in the city? The location is fantastic and the décor is fun—there are displays of great moments in Macy's history, from a diorama from *Miracle on 34th Street* to old ads and appliances from the turn of the century. There is a children's menu, sandwiches, salads, entrées of various kinds, old-fashioned milkshakes, and an adequate drink menu.

 TRAVEL TIP

New York is a smoke-free town. Smoking is not permitted in any public areas, including subway stations, restaurants, taxis, and bars! Cigar smoking is permitted in registered cigar bars, however.

Mickey Mantle's ($–$$)

⊡ 42 Central Park South (5th and 6th avenues)
🚇 West 59th Street-Columbus Circle station (A, B, C, D, or 1 train)
✆ 212-688-7777
✑ www.mickeymantles.com

Mickey Mantle's is host to many live sports broadcasts and is the place to go to watch the games on twenty-eight high-def plasma/LCD televisions. It is an absolute favorite among kids, and it's a popular spot for birthday parties. In the summer or spring it's really lovely to sit outside and eat your burger and fries and watch the horse-drawn carriages go up and down Central Park South. All credit cards are accepted.

Mars 2112 ($–$$)

⊡ 1633 Broadway (51st Street)
🚇 West 50th Street station (1 train)
✆ 212-582-2112
✑ www.mars2112.com

Mars 2112 is a not-to-be missed kid pleaser on any trip to New York. This is a one-of-a-kind restaurant/theme park/interactive video game that's just as much fun for the grownups. The year is 2112, Mars is colonized, and your family has decided to vacation there. You enter the premises via a "ride" to the planet Mars—there's a side entrance if your kids are easily scared or someone in your party gets motion sickness—and are seated at a table deep inside the red rock. There are a number of alien servers, and a screen shows space-related scenes. Bring a camera to take pictures with the costumed aliens who regularly make the rounds. An excellent kids' menu offers burgers and chicken fingers, and the adults will find more refined fare to suit any mood, supplemented by a full bar with cosmic concoctions. There's an arcade for the kids to play in and a gift shop with all sorts of Mars-related gizmos and gadgets.

Planet Hollywood ($$)

🖻 1540 Broadway (at West 45th Street)

🚇 West 42nd Street-Times Square station (N, Q, R, S, W, 1, 2, 3, or 7 train)

✆ 212-333-7827

✐ www.planethollywood.com

Located in the heart of Times Square, Planet Hollywood offers some imaginative takes on pastas, grilled meats, and cocktails. For kids, visiting Planet Hollywood is like going to a museum, but one that interests them. Here you may find John Travolta's black leather jacket from *Saturday Night Fever*, the shuttle *Galileo* from *Star Trek*, the original keyboard from *Big*, Julia Robert's outfit from *Pretty Woman*, Ben Affleck's senior yearbook, and original costumes from Britney Spears's music videos.

Rock Center Café ($$$)

🖻 20 West 50th Street (in Rockefeller Center)

🚇 West 47th–50th Street-Rockefeller Center station (B, D, F, or V train)

✆ 212-332-7620

✐ http://rapatina.com/rockCenterCafe/

This new, upscale incarnation of the former American Festival Café is a stunner. Located at Rockefeller Center, it is a popular spot all year round, so reservations are recommended.

The menu is contemporary Italian-influenced American. There are extensive menus for breakfast, lunch, dinner, and weekend brunch, and a kids' menu as well. Food ranges from the sublime to the standard sandwiches and salads. Special prix fixe meals are offered daily and are a bargain if you consider the à la carte prices. There are also special prix fixe meals for all the holidays—the Thanksgiving, Year-End Holiday, and Easter menus are wonderful, and the atmosphere is one of a kind. Rock Center also runs special promotions throughout the year; go to the Web site for details. All credit cards are accepted.

Seppi's ($$–$$$)

⌧ 123 West 56th Street (between 6th and 7th avenues)

🚇 West 59th Street-Columbus Circle station (A, B, C, D, or 1 train); West 57th Street station (N, Q, R, or W train)

✆ 212-708-7444

✐ *www.parkermeridien.com/seppis.htm*

Right next door to Le Parker Meridien hotel, this delightful French restaurant serves an array of creative meals in a distinctly French/ Swiss style. This is really for the big folks, but kids are welcome, albeit with limited choices—pasta, burgers, or omelets. The terrine of foie gras is perfect, as are the escargots; the shrimp and artichoke risotto is a signature dish. There are daily specials of foie gras, omelets, pasta, meats, and fish. There are even sandwiches at dinner, a rarity. On Sundays Seppi's serves a chocolate brunch, where every dish has a hint of chocolate (even chocolate mimosas). Desserts are extraordinary. The white chocolate soufflé is perfect, and the ice creams and sorbets are all homemade. There are prix fixe menus for lunch and dinner.

21 Club ($$$)

⌧ 21 West 52nd Street (between 6th Avenue and Broadway)

✆ 212-582-7200

✐ *www.21club.com*

Who would believe the site of New York's most infamous speakeasy would become one of the best restaurants to take children who know how to dine? This is one of the best and classiest restaurants in the city (jacket and ties for all men, no matter the age, and positively no jeans for either men or women). New York's families often celebrate their great moments here. Sit in the main dining room, where sports memorabilia and toys from the rich and famous hang above your head. The foie gras is among the best in the city, and the steak and chops are wonderful, but the chicken hash is absolutely divine and worth every penny. Be sure to order a Shirley Temple for the kids. If you ask (and you should ask), your server will arrange a tour of the wine cellar, where you and the kids will be shown Richard Nixon's personal stash, and you can push the big brick door that was used to hide the speakeasy during raids. This is a classic New York experience. The food is excellent, and so is the service.

Midtown East

Restaurants in this area generally depend on the business crowd, so lunchtime tends to be hectic. Off hours are a good bet.

Docks Oyster Bar ($$)
  ▢ 633 3rd Avenue (at 40th Street)
  ☒ Grand Central-East 42nd Street station (4, 5, or 6 train)
  ✆ 212-986-8080
  ✐ www.docksoysterbar.com

This establishment is a New York favorite, so, of course, it's often packed. Docks serves fresh seafood and features a raw bar and clambakes, but there are also salads, sandwiches, pasta, meats, and poultry for all. The oysters are divine, and the clam chowder's pretty good too. The atmosphere is upbeat and fashionable.

Keen's Steakhouse ($$$)
  ▢ 72 West 36th Street (between 5th and 6th avenues)
  ☒ West 34th Street-Herald Square station (B, D, F, N, Q, R, V, or W train)
  ✆ 212-947-3636
  ✐ www.keens.com

This is one of the best-kept secrets in New York. It's where New Yorkers go for steaks and chops, but it's also the perfect place for beer and snacks before or after almost any game at Madison Square Garden. Established in 1885 as a pipe-smoking club, kids will love the thousands of clay pipes on the ceiling (the largest collection of churchwarden pipes in the world; these days they are for decoration only—there is no smoking anywhere on the premises).

Keen's is very good to kids. It doesn't have a children's menu, but it is happy to serve half portions and will bend the rules for youngsters and cook up a great burger to eat in the dining room (a privilege not extended to grownups). The Bloody Marys are made according to Keen's house recipe and, kids can drink Virgin Bloody Marys. The limeade in the summer months is wonderful. All major credit cards are accepted.

Oscar's American Brasserie ($$)

- 301 Park Ave. (50th Street and Lexington in the Waldorf-Astoria Hotel)
- East 51st Street station (6 train)
- 212-872-4920
- *www.oscarsbrasserie.com*

If you think your kids would appreciate a foray to an upscale restaurant, Oscar's is a stylish but casual introduction. This surprisingly affordable restaurant is housed in the lap of luxury, the Waldorf-Astoria Hotel.

≡FAST FACT

Oscar's was named after the legendary hotel maitre d', Oscar Tschirky, who worked at the Waldorf for more than fifty years. He was such a character that everybody just referred to him as "Oscar of Waldorf."

Kids will enjoy the dessert selection, especially if you go for the lunch buffet. Signature menu items include the Waldorf salad made of apples and walnuts, and the veal Oscar, but the best bet on this menu is always the daily buffet, where you get a bit of everything.

Chelsea and the Village

There's great food in these residential neighborhoods, from the funky to the sublime. It's the haunt of New York University students and ritzy professionals alike, so there's something for everyone.

A Salt & Battery ($)
⌨ 112 Greenwich Avenue (between West 12th and West 13th streets)

🚇 West 14th Street station (A, C, E, 1, 2, or 3 train); 8th Avenue station (L train)

✆ 212-691-2713

✎ www.asaltandbattery.com

An antidote to big-city restaurants and prices, this cleverly named place is an authentic replica of a British fish and chips shop. An array of seafood fried in veggie oil, sides, drinks, and desserts is sure to please any palate. Try the homemade mushy peas and fried Mars bars.

Cowgirl Hall of Fame ($-$$)
⌨ 519 Hudson Street (at West 10th Street)

🚇 Christopher Street-Sheridan Square station (1 train)

✆ 212-633-1133

✎ www.cowgirlnyc.com

This is a kid favorite—the restaurant even features a cowgirl candy shop at the front of the store. There are paintings of cowgirls all over the walls, and the chandeliers are made of antlers. The kids' menu is excellent—breakfast items are included, and crayons are available for coloring in the cowgirls on the menu.

Cowgirl is loaded with surprises: for the grownups, the delicious frozen margaritas are arguably among the top five in the city; for the kids, the ice cream baked potato was featured on the Food Network. The chili is excellent, the taco salad is one-of-a-kind, and the pulled pork sandwiches are worth trying. Save room for the homemade blueberry peach cobbler. It's huge, so prepare to share it.

 TRAVEL TIP

Be wary if you go online to check out restaurant or hotel reviews. Some establishments pad their reviews with phony recommendations written by staff and friends. Watch for telltale clues: short and nondescriptive reviews that just say how great the food and service were; a series of reviews that sound the same; a series of reviews with similar dates; reviews that are dramatically against the majority. Also look at the most recent reviews, as establishments may go up or downhill with age.

Cafeteria ($)

119 7th Avenue (at West 17th Street)

West 18th Street station (1 train)

212-414-1717

The name comes not from the ambiance, which is science fiction modern and totally cool, but from the menu, which is directly related to diner food with some more sophisticated stuff thrown in for good measure. There's plenty for the whole family to salivate over, from burgers and mac and cheese to mussels in a wine, tarragon, and shallot sauce. The place is open twenty-four hours, and you can get the breakfast menu all day—very appropriate for the city that never sleeps.

Chat 'n Chew ($)

10 East 16th Street (between 5th Avenue and Union Square)

14th Street-Union Square station (L, N, Q, R, W, 4, 5, or 6 train)

212-243-1616

You may not have come to the big, sophisticated city to revel in American kitsch, but this place is so much fun! You can't worry about your diet while munching on a BLT made with thick-cut bacon and veggies piled high between slices of toasted five-grain bread; huge and juicy burgers (veggie too); creamy yet crusty-topped macaroni and cheese; succulent pork chops; fresh salads; and sides for all.

Gotham Bar and Grill ($$$)

⊞ 12 East 12th Street (between 5th Avenue and University Place)

🚇 East 14th Street-Union Square station (L, N, Q, R, W, 4, 5, or 6 train)

✆ 212-620-4020

✎ www.gothambarandgrill.com

Gotham Bar and Grill is one of the city's most highly rated eateries. You'll need a reservation to enjoy the superb New American cuisine designed by master chef Alfred Portale, who won the Beard Foundation Award for the Most Outstanding Chef in the Nation in 2006. Gotham itself received the Beard Foundation's Most Outstanding Restaurant Award in 2002. This is no museum piece—the menu, wine list, and décor are regularly revamped. The prix fixe lunch menu is a good deal.

Old Homestead ($$$)

⊞ 56 9th Avenue (between West 15th and West 16th streets)

🚇 West 14th Street station (A, C, E, 1, 2, or 3 train); 8th Avenue station (L train)

✆ 212-242-9040

✎ www.theoldhomesteadsteakhouse.com

What lover of steak could resist a restaurant with a giant steer above its front door? This is a classic New York steakhouse dating from 1868. Homestead prides itself on its mastery of the four major food groups: beef, beef, beef, and beef. That they do, but they also whip up some great seafood, chops, and poultry. Homestead is just the slightest bit off the restaurant path, so you can get a table without weeks of planning. The portions are huge, so sharing is strongly suggested with children.

Woo Lae Oak ($$)

⌷ 148 Mercer Street (between Prince and Houston streets)
🚇 Prince Street station (N, R, or W train)
📞 212-925-8200
🖋 www.woolaeoaksoho.com

For another New York experience, have lunch or dinner at this pretty Korean restaurant. The food is healthy and you can prepare it yourself at your table's (smokeless) grill using the best ingredients—the fish is fresh, the chicken free-range, and the vegetables crispy.

Zoë ($$)

⌷ 90 Prince Street (between Broadway and Mercer Street)
🚇 Prince Street station (N, R, or W train)
📞 212-966-6722
🖋 www.zoerest.com

This is possibly the best restaurant in the city to take your children to dine in style. The owners, a husband and wife team, have children of their own, and they understand that kids love to eat just like their parents but need some diversion too. Kids will delight in the sights, sounds, and excitement of the open kitchen. They can join the staff at the Chef's Counter, where they will learn about the food they are being served.

The signature crispy calamari is a must and can be shared (it's also featured on the fabulous kids menu, which is one of the best in town), and the pizzas and tuna burger are wonderful. Desserts are so good that many people come by for after-dinner goodies and drinks. It's a popular neighborhood place, so make reservations on the weekends.

Lower Manhattan

This is where New York started, so it's drenched in history and memories. There's great food and shopping in these neighborhoods, reflecting past waves of immigration.

Delmonico's Steak House ($$$)

⊞ 56 Beaver Street (at South William Street)

🚇 Wall Street station (2 or 3 train)

☎ 212-509-1144

🖎 www.delmonicosny.com

Abraham Lincoln and Mark Twain ate here. The cooking staff has changed, but do you need more of an endorsement to entice you here? Since 1837, Delmonico's has satisfied Americans with a solid menu of steaks and seafood. Make arrangements to have the kids served from the bar menu or share portions. This is not a public policy, but Delmonico's always tries to make families happy. Don't miss the decadent dessert menu.

Fraunces Tavern ($$$)

⊞ 54 Pearl Street (at Broad Street)

🚇 Whitehall Street-South Ferry station (R or W train)

☎ 212-968-1776

🖎 www.frauncestavern.com

This is a must-see New York attraction and dining experience. Eat in the Revolutionary War tavern where George Washington celebrated victory over the British. This is a good place to go for classic staples you won't find at many of the fancier restaurants. There's a great selection of salads, sandwiches, and entrées during the day—don't miss the clam chowder and duck sausage. There's also a great prix fixe lunch.

≡FAST FACT

Fraunces Tavern's changing exhibits tell the story of this landmark tavern that was once the war room of the revolution and the headquarters of General George Washington.

There is no children's menu and no half portions, but you can share. You'll find a museum on the premises where you can look at Revolutionary War artifacts. Classical guitar music is featured every Wednesday night.

Sequoia ($$)

🗏 Pier 17, South Street Seaport (at Fulton Street and the East River)

🚇 Fulton Street-Broadway-Nassau Street station (A, C, J, M, Z, 2, 3, 4, or 5 train)

📞 212-732-9090

💻 www.arkrestaurants.com

At Sequoia, you'll enjoy spectacular views of historic ships, the East River, and the skyline in a nautical setting reminiscent of a classic steamer. The tantalizingly complete menu is heavy on the seafood but also has just about everything else you might crave for lunch or dinner. There's terrace dining during warmer months. A children's menu is offered seasonally, but there are always plenty of kid-friendly items, and sharing is encouraged.

World Financial Center ($–$$$)

🗏 West Street (between Liberty and Vesey streets)

🚇 World Trade Center station (E train); Cortlandt Street station (R or W train); Rector Street station (1 train)

📞 212-417-7000

💻 www.worldfinancialcenter.com

Near the World Trade Center site, you might stop by the World Financial Center, a beautifully designed complex of four towers containing offices, shops, restaurants, and public gardens with great views of the Hudson River. The financial center includes everything from fine dining at the Grill Room to snack food and drinks at national chains.

Here are the places to eat at the WFC:

- Au Bon Pain French bakery/café
- Au Mandarin French Chinese
- Blockheads Burritos
- Ciao Bella Gelato
- Columbus Bakery
- Cosi
- Devon & Blakely
- Donald Sacks
- Elixir Juice Bar
- Financier Patisserie
- The Grill Room
- Johnney's Fish Grill
- P.J. Clarke's
- SouthWest NY
- Starbucks Coffee
- Yushi

The World Financial Center is a site in itself, but it's also a convenient point to break for lunch when you explore the nearby landmarks.

Upper East Side

Some of the best restaurants in the city are located in this part of Manhattan because it's also the site of some of the most expensive housing in the city. After shopping and touring Museum Mile, it's time to reward yourself.

One Fish, Two Fish ($–$$)
⊡ 1399 Madison Avenue (at East 97th Street)
🚇 East 96th Street station (6 train)
📞 212-369-5677
🖃 www.onefishtwofish.com

If you find yourself uptown, this busy place is a good refuge for the kids to be themselves, even if your kids refuse to eat fish. The extensive menu includes steaks, burgers, salads, and vegetarian dishes in addition to seafood. The seven-day brunch special and early-bird menu make this a good choice. Live classical jazz Sundays from 1 P.M. to 3 P.M.

Park Avenue Autumn/Winter/Spring/ Summer ($$–$$$)

⊡ 100 East 63rd Street (at Park Avenue)

🚇 East 59th Street station (4, 5, or 6 train); Lexington Avenue-East 59th Street station (N, R, or W train)

✆ 212-644-1900

🖉 www.parkavenyc.com

This is both a neighborhood favorite and a busy business lunch restaurant. The name—and the menu—changes with the season. It serves rustic American bistro fare. The food combinations are creative (salmon pastrami), but there are items on the menu that the kids will eat (a burger with fries). The service is excellent. After 8:30 P.M., take advantage of the "pay your age" prix fixe menu from $25 to $65. It's also a favorite spot for weekend brunch.

Petrie Court Café ($$)

⊡ In the Metropolitan Museum of Art, 1000 5th Avenue (between East 82nd and East 83rd streets)

🚇 East 86th Street station (4, 5, or 6 train)

✆ 212-570-3964

🖉 www.metmuseum.org/visitor/dining_petrie.asp

This is a lovely place to rest and refresh after admiring the Met's outstanding collection. The café is located on the first floor in the European Sculpture Garden and boasts views of Central Park. Petrie's offers European-style waiter service and a full menu featuring hot and cold entrées, salads, and desserts for lunch and dinner. There is also a continental breakfast starting at 9:30 A.M. and weekend brunch. Reservations are recommended.

Serendipity 3 ($$)

⊡ 225 East 65th Street (between 2nd and 3rd avenues)

🚇 East 68th Street-Hunter College station (6 train)

✆ 212-838-3531

🖉 www.serendipity3.com

This kid-oriented place deserves a spot at the top of your list. There are cheddar burgers to die for, and the frozen hot chocolate is a signature dish. There are many other fun kid drinks, but this is a full-service restaurant as well with soups, salads, sandwiches, and entrées. The restaurant has a wonderful ambiance that reminds you of *Alice in Wonderland*, *Grease*, and a sweet-sixteen party all at once. Save room for dessert. This is a great place to go after a day of shopping at Bloomingdale's, but be prepared for a wait or try off-hours such as 2–4 P.M. Serves breakfast, lunch, and dinner.

Tony's Di Napoli ($$–$$$)

- 1606 2nd Avenue (between 83rd and 84th streets)
- East 86th Street station (4, 5, or 6 train)
- 212-861-8686
- *www.tonysdinapoli.com*

Tony's Di Napoli is a family favorite, much like Carmine's (see pages 280 and 297). Bring a big appetite and share—the food is served on platters meant for two to three people. There's a balloon man who makes balloon animals on Sundays. It's crowded, so get there before 6:00 P.M. or expect to wait. There's another branch in midtown at 147 West Forty-third Street (between Sixth and Seventh avenues).

Upper West Side

The Upper West Side is a residential area with many families living in the great old apartment houses east and west of Broadway. These are real New York folk, so there's great family dining in this neck of the city.

Barney Greengrass ($)

- 541 Amsterdam Avenue (between 86th and 87th streets)
- West 86th Street station (1 train)
- 212-724-4707
- *www.barneygreengrass.com*

This has been a popular Jewish deli since 1908, and with good reason. It serves the highest quality food and hasn't changed for decades. The menu is huge (for starters, there are twenty-five appetizers, five kinds of herrings, sixty-one sandwiches, and eleven desserts). For one hundred years, Barney Greengrass has been known as "the Sturgeon King," and New Yorkers line up for the smoked fish. Try the lox on an H&H bagel or maybe a *bissel* herring.

JUST FOR PARENTS

For something special, you can order wine and drinks with your meals, but don't forget your kids! Shirley Temples are always popular in fancy New York restaurants, and you can ask the server to serve your child's cranberry juice in a martini glass. It makes the kids feel sophisticated.

Carmine's Upper West Side ($$–$$$)

🖃 2450 Broadway (between 90th and 91st streets)

🚇 West 86th Street station (1 train) or West 96th Street station (1, 2, or 3 train)

📞 212-362-2200

✍ *www.carminesnyc.com*

In this warm, happy place, Southern Italian food is served family style, which means large platters meant for sharing. You can't go wrong with the stuffed artichokes, the fried calamari, or the shrimp scampi. Don't be put off by the rather pricy meat platters; they easily feed a family of three—and maybe four. The desserts are great (if you have room)—try the tiramisu. A solid house wine is available. There are no reservations for parties of less than six, and there's always a wait by 6:00 P.M. This is the real thing: family-style Italian, spacious, crowded, and good food. Bring your appetite! (There's a second location on West Forty-fourth Street—see page 280.)

Fiorello's ($$–$$$)

⊞ 1900 Broadway (between 64th and 65th streets)

🚇 West 66th Street station (1 train)

📞 212-595-5330

✎ www.cafefiorello.com

Almost across the street from Lincoln Center, this Italian restaurant has been serving the theater crowd for more than thirty years. It has a huge range of food (fifty kinds of antipasti alone) with an emphasis on Roman dishes. The Jerusalem artichokes, the heavenly rack of lamb, unparalleled pizzas, skillfully prepared fish, and the terrific tortellini are all highly recommended.

Reservations are a must. In the summer and spring you can sit outside and people watch. It's also a good spot for celebrity sightings. The service is speedy, and this is a great place for lunch, weekend brunch, or a late-night dinner.

Niko's Mediterranean Grill & Bistro ($$)

⊞ 2161 Broadway (at West 76th Street)

🚇 West 72nd Street station (1, 2, or 3 train) or West 79th Street station (1 train)

📞 212-873-7000

✎ www.nikosgrillnyc.com

Niko's is a very casual Greek taverna with a huge menu of authentic Greek food and comfortable fare like pizza, burgers, and pastas. (Niko also owns Big Nick's Burger and Pizza Joint down the block—see page 305). Here's your chance for some truly good Mediterranean fish dishes. Niko's serves breakfast/brunch, lunch, and dinner seven days a week.

Tavern on the Green ($$$)

⊞ Central Park West (between West 66th and West 67th streets)

🚇 West 72nd Street station (B or C train)

📞 212-873-3200

✎ www.tavernonthegreen.com

This is an unforgettable family experience. Kids are charmed by this unusual restaurant's over-the-top décor—there are lights and flowers and paintings everywhere. Ask to eat in the glass-enclosed Crystal or Terrace rooms. The chandeliers, in all colors, are beautiful. The Topiary Garden is legendary too.

Tavern on the Green serves lunch, brunch, pre-dinner, and dinner every day of the year. The seasonal menu is American and should satisfy everyone. There is a limited children's menu, but meals are so generous that you can share. The lobster bisque is an institution, and the crab cakes are fabulous. The menu changes often and features an array of artfully prepared fresh foods.

The wait staff is gracious, and they are truly pleased to serve children who appreciate the finer things. Special events are held during the year, some especially for kids. Check the Web site for details.

Brooklyn

Don't think you have to rush back to Manhattan for a trendy lunch or dinner. As Manhattan has pushed the creative and middle classes across the river, especially to Brooklyn, the once-maligned borough has blossomed into an epicurean center in its own right.

Flatbush Farm ($$)

⊡ 76 St. Marks Avenue (at Flatbush Avenue)

🚇 Bergen Street station (2 or 3 train)

📞 718-622-3276

✍ *www.flatbushfarm.com*

A changing seasonal menu uses local and fresh natural ingredients to craft deliciously different (but not crazy) offerings such as braised lamb shoulder with bubble and squeak and duck confit with lentils and frisee. They also turn out delicious grits, roasted chicken, burgers and fries, and eggs your way. Dinner and weekend brunch.

Grimaldi's Pizzeria ($)

⊡ 19 Old Fulton Street (under the Brooklyn Bridge)

🚇 Clark Street station (2 or 3 train); High Street-Brooklyn Bridge station (A or C train)

✆ 718-858-4300

✒ www.grimaldis.com

A cozy pizzeria nestled under the Brooklyn Bridge, Grimaldi's is renowned for scrumptious pies baked in its coal-burning brick oven. Kids will enjoy watching the pizzas go from lumps of dough to oven-baked pies in the open kitchen. This perennial favorite is always crowded, and it isn't uncommon to wait outside for an hour before sitting down. Avoid the line by phoning ahead to order takeout. Eat your pizza in a nearby park overlooking the river. Cash only.

Junior's ($$)

⊡ 386 Flatbush Avenue Extension (at DeKalb Avenue)

🚇 DeKalb Avenue station (B, M, Q, or R train)

✆ 718-852-5257

✒ www.juniorscheesecake.com

This iconic deli is a classic that Brooklynites have flocked to for generations. Many a celebration has been held within these orange walls and seats. The burgers are excellent (not what you'd expect in a deli), the blintzes are definitely worth traveling for, and the pastrami is classic. But save room for Junior's *pièce de résistance*, its cheesecake!

TRAVEL TIP

You can enjoy a piece of Brooklyn at home thanks to the Internet. Junior's sells its famous cheesecake online, and you can also get its terrific cookbook, which gives the story of this family-owned and operated business. Peter Luger also sells its steaks and steak sauce, along with a set of steak knives on the Web.

There is a nice children's menu for an exceptionally modest price. Put this restaurant on the menu for a day alongside the Brooklyn Museum or the Botanic Garden. There are Junior's restaurants in Grand Central Terminal and on West Forty-fifth Street between Broadway and Eighth Avenue.

Peter Luger's Steakhouse ($$$)

⊡ 178 Broadway (between Bedford and Driggs avenues)
🚇 Marcy Avenue station (J, M, or Z train)
📞 718-387-4700
✎ *www.peterluger.com*

Peter Luger's is the Taj Mahal of steakhouses—the best! The regulars will tell you not to look at the menu—just order a porterhouse, onion and tomato salad, creamed spinach, and fried potatoes. You can gild the lily by starting with the shrimp cocktail; Peter Luger's reputedly uses the biggest crustaceans in the city.

The restaurant is surprisingly kid-friendly, right down to the gold-covered chocolate coins that come with the bill. Be sure to make reservations, and bring a pocketful of cash; credit cards are not accepted. They do have their own Peter Luger card, which can be applied for over the Internet.

Pete's Downtown ($$)

⊡ 2 Water Street (Cadmen Plaza West, under the Brooklyn Bridge)
🚇 High Street station (A or C train)
📞 718-858-3510
✎ *http://petesdowntown.com*

This landmark establishment has been satisfying patrons since 1894 with excellent Italian food and a spectacular view of the Manhattan skyline and the Brooklyn Bridge.

River Café ($$$)
⊞ 1 Water Street (under the Brooklyn Bridge)

🚊 High Street station (A or C train)

✆ 718-522-5200

✎ www.rivercafe.com

Add great food to a spectacular view and you find perfection. The River Café turns out a menu of spectacular American food that draws crowds. This restaurant is not overly family-friendly, but don't let that stop you from treating your kids to a spectacular New York experience.

A three-course prix fixe meal is $95; lunch is considerably cheaper. River Café also serves brunch. There's usually a pianist on the premises. Don't forget to make reservations.

The Bronx

Some of the best-kept secrets of New York dining are the wonderful Italian restaurants along Arthur Avenue and the great seafood restaurants on City Island (see page 338). This is where real New Yorkers dine.

Dominick's ($–$$)
⊞ 2335 Arthur Avenue (between East 184th and 187th streets)

🚊 Not accessible by subway

✆ 718-733-2807

There is no menu. You sit in this wonderfully warm neighborhood place and tell the waiter what you want (the kitchen will make it for you), or you can ask for the day's specials. The stuffed artichoke is the best in the city (with bacon and bread crumbs), and the pastas are excellent. Meals can be shared, and the house wine is delicious. There is often a wait because it seems everyone in the city comes here if they don't feel like going downtown, even the mayor. If you go around the holidays, Dominick's gives you a pen as a keepsake. No dessert—you're expected to patronize one of the great bakeries on the block, and you should. Prices are reasonable, but only cash is accepted—no credit cards.

The Riverdale Garden ($$)
⌸ 4576 Manhattan College Parkway
🚊 Van Cortlandt Park-242 Street (1 train)
📞 718-884-5232
✍ *www.theriverdalegarden.com*

If you visit the Bronx Zoo or New York Botanical Garden, you might well have a meal in this urban garden oasis. Sculptured American regional dishes change daily according to the seasons and available raw materials as farmers send their best to the kitchen. Riverdale Garden serves the finest from New York's wineries. Various culinary events are scheduled throughout the year.

Queens

Queens is especially known for the great Greek restaurants in its Astoria neighborhood, but they aren't the only reason to eat there.

Christos Hasapo-Taverna ($$–$$$)
⌸ 41-08 23rd Street (at 41st Street)
🚊 Astoria-Ditmars Boulevard station (N or W train)
📞 718-777-8400

Christos recreates a Greek butcher shop (hasapo) with a restaurant (taverna). The specialty here is beef, and you can choose your piece from the display case.

Joe's Shanghai ($–$$)
⌸ 82-74 Broadway (between 45th Street and Whitney Avenue)
🚊 46th Street station (G, R, or V train)
📞 718-539-3838
✍ *www.joeshanghairestaurants.com*

The restaurant is famous for its soup dumplings (yes, the soup is inside the dumplings) with pork or crabmeat. There are branches at 136-21 Thirty-seventh Avenue in Flushing, Queens; 24 West Fifty-sixth Street in Manhattan; and 9 Pell Street in Chinatown. (How do they put soup inside a dumpling? It starts out jellied and melts when the dumpling is steamed!)

Staten Island

When you take the ferry to Staten Island, consider lingering for a meal in New York's final frontier.

Ruddy & Dean ($$)
⌨ 44 Richmond Terrace
✆ 718-816-4400
✎ www.ruddydean.com

Try to get to see the Staten Island Yankees (the pin-stripers' A team) play their archrivals, the Brooklyn Cyclones, for a roaring good time. Then walk across the street to this great steakhouse for pub grub in a casual atmosphere. There are great views of New York Harbor and the Statue of Liberty. Ruddy & Dean is open for lunch and dinner seven days a week.

CHAPTER 16

Breakfast, Lunch, and Beyond

THERE ARE SO MANY wonderful restaurants, diners, cafés, and cafeterias throughout New York that breakfast and lunch should never be ho-hum. In this chapter, you'll find a list of places to eat breakfast and lunch (and maybe even dinner), with most meals running between $5 and $12. Since you'll be on the go from morning until sunset, look for something along your route during the day. Another idea is to use lunch to experience some of the city's more expensive restaurants without having to pay top dollar.

Breakfast Options

There's no problem finding breakfast in New York. You can easily choose from bagel takeouts in the subway, breakfast pushcarts on the street corner, dirt-cheap specials in nontourist neighborhoods, or the most sophisticated in haute cuisine. Your best bet is likely to be in a diner around the corner. Some hotels include a continental breakfast in the price of the room, but if yours doesn't, get out and explore your options.

Big Nick's Burger and Pizza Joint ($)

▦ 2175 Broadway (between West 76th and West 77th streets)
🚊 West 79th Street station (1 train)
📞 212-362-9238
🖱 *www.bignicksnyc.com*

This small, crowded place is a true insider find. It makes the best burgers, pasta, pizza, and breakfast twenty-three (!) hours a day, seven days a week. If you really want a New York experience, this is it. Cash only, of course.

Norma's ($$)

▢ 118 West 57th Street (between 6th and 7th avenues)

🚇 West 57th Street station (F train); West 57th Street-7th Avenue station (N, Q, R, or W train)

📞 212-708-7460

Norma's is the chi-chi (but kid-friendly) breakfast/brunch/lunch restaurant at Le Parker Meridien. Don't miss such ethereal plates as the banana–macadamia nut flapjacks, the Waz-Za waffle (fruit inside and out, with a brulée topping), mango–papaya brown butter cinnamon crepes, or the foie gras brioche French toast with asparagus and mushrooms. The chef can whip you up a scrambled egg or a yogurt with fruit if you'd prefer a simpler breakfast. You'll need to reserve about a month ahead.

Sarabeth's ($)

▢ 423 Amsterdam Avenue (between West 80th and West 81st Streets)

🚇 West 79th Street station (1 train)

📞 212-496-6280

✐ www.sarabethscps.com

Celebrity chef Sarabeth Levine wows with her fabulous baking, so much so that this flagship restaurant has spawned five others—four around town and one in Key West, Florida. The pancakes, omelets, pies, and bread are wonderful. There's even a cookbook so you can try to make your own Sarabeth treats at home. All of the Sarabeth's have brunch on Saturday and Sunday. Find them at 1295 Madison Ave. (Hotel Wales at East Ninety-second Street); 945 Madison Ave. (Whitney Museum at East Seventy-fifth Street); Chelsea Market, 75

Ninth Ave. (at West Fifteenth Street); 40 Central Park South (between Fifth and Sixth avenues).

Golden Unicorn ($)

⊡ 18 East Broadway (between Catherine and Market streets)

🚇 Canal Street station (R, J, M, N, Q, R, W, Z, or 6 train); Grand Street (B or D train)

☎ 212-941-0911

How about some delicious dim sum for breakfast? If you plan on touring Chinatown, get there about 9 A.M. any day of the week and breakfast as they do in Hong Kong. Golden Unicorn is huge and popular, so try to go before noon when there is less frenzy. Service is from carts that have pictures on them to help you order. The kids will love the two huge dragons in the center with lit-up eyes.

Sunday Brunch

If you are going to be in town on Sunday and have the time for a leisurely morning, schedule a Sunday brunch at one of the city's phenomenal restaurants.

B. Smith's ($)

⊡ 320 West 46th Street (between 8th and 9th avenues)

🚇 Times Square station (A, B, or C train)

☎ 212-315-1100

Ample portions of traditional and Southern-inspired meals like sweet potato pancakes, banana and spiced pecan pancakes, and a French toasted butter crackle brioche make this a fail-safe brunch spot. There's plenty of traditional down-home stuff for the kids. See the full listing on page 278.

The Boathouse ($$)

East 72nd Street and Park Drive North (enter park at East 72nd Street and 5th Avenue)

East 68th Street-Hunter College station (6 train)

212-517-2233

www.thecentralparkboathouse.com

Take advantage of this unparalleled experience if you are in New York between April and November. Sit lakeside and watch the swans and ducks swim by while rowboats and a gondola lazily drift across the water—all in front of a backdrop of greenery, rock formations, and a spectacular city skyline. See the full listing on page 153.

Seppi's ($$)

123 West 56th Street

West 59th Street-Columbus Circle station (A, B, C, D, or 1 train); West 57th Street station (N, Q, R, or W train)

212-397-1963

Chocolate for breakfast—who could ask for more? Every meal on the Sunday brunch menu has at least a hint of chocolate. This lovely French restaurant is a treat. The prix fixe menu is $24; à la carte is also available. There's also a fantastic Saturday brunch, which is very unusual. See the full listing on page 285.

Tavern on the Green ($$)

Central Park West (between West 66th and West 67th streets)

West 72nd Street station (B or C train)

212-873-3200

Treat yourself to a real New York experience. Brunch at Tavern on the Green is memorable, especially in the Crystal Room. There's everything from Irish oatmeal to eggs Benedict to crab cakes. It's a little on the expensive side, but the experience is worth it. See the full listing on page 298.

Sylvia's

⌨ 328 Lenox Avenue (between West 126th and West 127th streets)

🚊 West 125th Street station (2 or 3 train)

📞 212-996-0660

This is simply one of the best brunch deals in town. The price varies with what you choose, but the result is an authentic gospel brunch with eggs, pork chops or sausages, black-eyed peas, sweet potatoes, and coffee. Sylvia herself shows up on many Sundays. Go to church at the Riverside Church or the Cathedral of St. John the Divine, then come here afterwards to eat. See the full listing on page 334.

Lunchtime Fare

You will most likely eat lunch on the go. If you are touring one of the city's major museums, you should consider eating in its restaurant or cafeteria. Most major attractions, such as the Metropolitan Museum of Art and the American Museum of Natural History, offer a good variety of kid-pleasing menu items. Because of security concerns, it is now almost impossible to bring food into a museum; all bags must be checked when you enter. There are plenty of dependable favorites if you are out and about in the city.

Hard Rock Cafe ($)

⌨ 1501 Broadway (at West 43rd Street)

🚊 Times Square-West 42nd Street station (N, Q, R, S, W, 1, 2, 3, or 7 train)

📞 212-343-3355

✍ *www.hardrockcafe.com*

The Hard Rock has moved to Times Square, so it's a natural place to stop for lunch or dinner while sightseeing the crossroads of the world. Expect crowds on Friday and Saturday night, but it's pretty easy to get in at lunch time. Hard Rock is famous for its high-energy atmosphere, its unparalleled collection of rock memorabilia, and, of course, its ubiquitous T-shirts. You'll find a good selection of salads, sandwiches, and burgers here.

TRAVEL TIP

Some of the major department stores have truly exceptional dining experiences, and the food court at the Manhattan Mall offers quick, inexpensive victuals. If you don't want to eat inside, pick up picnic fare from the Whole Foods Market at the Time Warner Center in Columbus Circle and head across the street to Central Park.

Mars 2112 ($–$$)
⌨ 1633 Broadway at 51st Street
🚇 West 50th Street station (1 train)
📞 212-582-2112

The décor is right out of Star Trek, with spaceship rides and aliens, and kids love it! Be prepared for a wait during busy hours, and don't be surprised if your kids don't want to leave. See the full listing on page 283.

Planet Hollywood ($)
⌨ 1540 Broadway (at West 45th Street)
🚇 West 42nd Street-Times Square station (N, Q, R, S, W, 1, 2, 3, or 7 train)
📞 212-333-7827

A nice lunch diversion during a busy midtown day, Planet Hollywood serves great wraps and burgers, and there is an excellent kids menu. You can also buy souvenir cups, magnets, and those popular baseball caps and T-shirts. See the full listing on page 284.

Jekyll and Hyde Club ($–$$)

⌨ 1409 6th Avenue (Avenue of the Americas) (between West 57th and West 58th streets)

🚉 West 57th Street station (F train)

☎ 212-541-9505

✍ *www.eerie.com*

This four-floor horror-themed restaurant is like something out of Disney's Haunted Mansion. There's a show in the middle of the restaurant and a haunted elevator ride. Be warned: this place might frighten smaller children. You can take home the canteen in which your drink was placed. It's packed on weekend nights, but it's a good bet for lunch with pub food, sandwiches, burgers, pizza, pasta for the kids, and seafood, steaks, and more than 100 beers for the grownups. There is a second location in the Village at 91 Seventh Avenue (Christopher Street); Christopher Street-Sheridan Square station (1, 2, or 3 train); 212-989-7701.

RAINY DAY FUN

New York's theme restaurants are destinations in themselves. The American Girl Place, Hard Rock Cafe, ESPN Zone, Jekyll and Hyde, Mars 2112, and Planet Hollywood all provide good food and children's menus. Who would ever want to return from New York without a Planet Hollywood New York T-shirt?

Uncle Nick's ($–$$)

⌨ 747 9th Avenue (between 50th and 51st streets)

🚉 West 50th Street station (C or E train)

☎ 212-245-7992

This is a very nice midtown Greek restaurant with an impressive selection of enticing appetizers, grilled meats, and seafood. The extensive lunch menu is a good deal. The food is good, the setting is simple, and there's a lovely outdoor garden.

Silver Star ($–$$)
⊞ 1238 2nd Avenue (between East 64th and East 65th streets)
🚊 East 68th Street station (6 train)
✆ 212-249-4250

Silver Star is a good, classic diner on the Upper East Side—but it tries to be a bit more creative than the standard. The result is an interesting menu with a good mix for every taste.

The New York Deli

Delicatessen food had its beginnings on Manhattan's Lower East Side, so eating in a real New York deli should be a must-do on your list of authentic New York experiences.

Artie's Delicatessen ($)
⊞ 2290 Broadway (between West 82nd and West 83rd streets)
🚊 West 86th Street station (1 train)
✆ 212-579-5959
✍ www.arties.com

Artie's is a re-creation of a 1930s deli, complete with heritage recipes. Salamis hang from the ceiling, the pastrami is made with a secret recipe, the hot dogs are handmade, and the knishes are grilled.

Ben's Deli ($–$$)
⊞ 209 West 38th Street (between 7th and 8th avenues)
🚊 West 42nd Street-Times Square station (N, Q, R, S, W, 1, 2, 3, or 7 train)
✆ 212-398-2367
✍ www.bensdeli.net

Ben's serves traditional deli fare amid a casual art deco décor. Although it's well-loved by garment district locals, it's not on the tourist map so you can always get a seat and a meal. There's a surprisingly full menu, from a great corned beef on hot pastrami sandwich to a platter of flavorful turkey and gravy. All baking is done on the premises. Servings are huge, so plan on sharing. There is a separate kids menu.

Katz's Deli ($-$$)
🔲 205 East Houston Street (at Ludlow Street)
🚇 Lower East Side-2nd Avenue (F or V train)
📞 212-254-2246
✍ *www.katzdeli.com*

Katz's has been serving classic delicatessen with unwavering excellence since 1888. There is simply no place like the place where Harry met Sally. The food is wonderful—the pastrami and the corned beef are hand carved, and the salami is excellent. If you've never had blintzes and knishes, consider yourself lucky because you'll be starting with the best. Portions are ridiculously huge.

Stage Deli ($$)
🔲 834 7th Avenue (between West 53rd and West 54th streets)
🚇 7th Avenue station (B, D, or E train); West 57th Street-7th
   Avenue (N, Q, R, or W train); West 50th Street station (1 train);
📞 212-245-7850
✍ *www.stagedeli.com*

This is the quintessential New York deli. It has a huge menu and serves humongous portions of classic and new recipes. It is a Stage tradition to name new combinations after the celebrities who frequent the place. It's usually crowded, but it is more kid friendly than the Carnegie Deli, Manhattan's other deli grande dame. There's food for every hour and every whim.

Out for a Burger

No matter where you are in New York, if the kids get hungry and you get tired, the instant solution is to grab a burger. There are Burger Kings and McDonald's throughout the city, but you can just as easily pop into a really good place to get a burger and fries.

Burger Joint ($)

⌨ 118 West 56th Street (in Le Parker Meridien between 6th and 7th avenues)

🚆 West 57th Street-7th Avenue station (N, Q, R, or W train); West 57th Street station (F train)

📞 212-245-5000

✎ www.parkermeridien.com/burger.htm

Did you know that there's a little burger joint hidden in the upscale Le Parker Meridien hotel? Burger Joint sells burgers, fries, milkshakes, brownies, and beer. The burgers are good, and the prices are even better. Just go into the hotel lobby and look for the floor-to-ceiling curtains in the back. Burger Joint is behind the curtains in the back.

Jackson Hole

⌨ 517 Columbus at West 85th Street

🚆 West 86th Street station (1 train)

📞 212-362-5177

✎ www.jacksonholeburgers.com

Jackson Hole is a little bit more than a burger joint, but most people come here for the burgers. It gets a little rowdy after work, but it's a great lunch spot. There's also a brunch at the location at 1270 Madison, at East Nintieth Street, 212-427-2820; East Eighty-sixth Street station (4, 5, or 6 train).

Paul's Place ($)

⌨ 131 2nd Avenue (between East 7th Street and St. Marks Place)

🚇 Astor Place station (6 train); 3rd Avenue station (L train)

📞 212-529-3033

This one's for the kids, both big and little. Paul's is a favorite Greenwich Village haunt because of its juicy, mouthwatering burgers and the crazy décor. There are many other fine eats on the menu, but the star is overwhelmingly the burger in all its iterations. Some are piled so high you'll need a knife and fork. Overhead is a never-ending show of toys, mechanical and otherwise, that entertain tirelessly and noisily.

 TRAVEL TIP

Two more family options are the New York minichains Burger Heaven and Better Burger. Both have great burgers and extended menus. Burger Heaven has a traditional American menu that will satisfy all members of the family. Better Burger uses natural and organic ingredients. Each company has a half dozen restaurants scattered around Manhattan.

Shake Shack ($)

⌨ Madison Square Park (southeast corner at Madison Avenue and East 23rd Street)

🚇 East 23rd Street station (N, R, W, or 6 train)

📞 212-889-6600

✍ *www.shakeshacknyc.com*

If you're in town during the warmer months, visit the Shake Shack, a roadside food stand nestled in an urban park in the middle of the city. You'll find award-winning burgers and hot dogs with a variety of inventive condiments and sundaes with a raft of homemade toppings. Try the smoked chicken and apple wurst. During the day, you are surrounded by lush greenery. At night, you can eat under the twinkling lights.

Only in New York

New York, a city used to good eating, has elevated the art of street vendor food to new heights. Vendors can be found all over the city, especially in front of museums and department stores, and the smell of grilling meat, sausage, and peppers often fills the air.

The mainstays of street food are the hot dog and pretzel stands. Eat the dogs with mustard and onions and everyone will think you're a native. Just about all hot dog carts have knishes, sausages, and pretzels. Staple year-round treats include fresh fruits and vegetables, honey roasted peanuts, almonds, cashews, and coconut; dry roasted chestnuts are seasonal.

Breakfast vendors sell coffee, tea, muffins, bagels, and donuts— and that's only the beginning. There is a new breed of gourmet street vendor with award-winning cuisine. Once a year, the most skilled curbside chef is presented with a "Vendy" award. Check out *www .streetvendor.org* for more information.

Gray's Papaya ($)
🖃 2090 Broadway (between 71st and 72nd streets)
🚇 72nd Street West (1, 2, or 3 train)
📞 212-799-0243

🖃 539 8th Avenue (at 37th Street)
🚇 West 34th Street-Penn Station (A, C, or E train)
📞 212-904-1588

🖃 402 6th Avenue (at Greenwich Avenue)
🚇 West 4th Street-Washington Square station (A, B, C, D, E, F, or V)
📞 212-260-3532

Join the natives in the know for the greatest hot dogs for only $1.25 a pop. Eat a couple, down the famous papaya drink, and you're an honorary New Yorker. Many former Gothamites hit the legendary Gray's Papaya right after arriving at the airport.

Papaya King ($)

▢ 179 East 86th Street (between 3rd and Lexington avenues)
🚇 East 86th Street station (4, 5, or 6 train)
📞 212-369-0648

▢ 200 West 14th Street (at Seventh Avenue)
🚇 West 14th Street station (1, 2, or 3 train)
📞 212-367-8090

▢ 121 West 125th Street (between Lenox and 7th avenues)
🚇 West 125th Street station (2 or 3 train)
📞 212-665-5732

✍ *www.papayaking.com*

Papaya King started the city's love of cheap (yet great) dogs and tropical drinks in 1932. It calls its own frankfurter formula "better than filet mignon." It may be right.

Gyro II ($)

▢ 425 7th Avenue (between West 33rd and West 34th streets)
🚇 West 34th Street-Penn Station (1, 2, or 3 train)
📞 212-239-0646

This hole-in-the-wall gyro stand has been here for at least twenty years, and it serves the best lamb or chicken gyro in the city for around six bucks. The Greek fries are pretty good too. It's a hearty meal, so young kids can share or you can order a gyro platter. It's right across from Madison Square Garden, so people often come before a concert or game.

H&H Bagels ($)

⌨ 2239 Broadway (at 80th Street)

🚇 West 79th Street station (1 train)

☎ 212-595-8003

⌨ 639 West 46th Street (between 11th Avenue and the West Side Highway)

🚇 West 50th Street station (C or E train)

☎ 212-595-8000

✎ www.handhbagel.com

H&H sets the gold standard for bagels. Ask any New Yorker; every one of them will tell you that H&H Bagels are the best in the city. If you're leaving the same day, buy a dozen for the road and take them back home with you. Once you get home and can't fathom what you did before you tried them, order from the H&H Web site. Both stores are open twenty-four hours.

Mamoun's Falafel ($)

⌨ 19 MacDougal Street (between West 3rd Street and Minetta Lane)

⌨ 22 St. Mark's Place (between 2nd and 3rd avenues)

☎ 212-674-8685

🚇 West 4th Street-Washington Square station (A, B, C, D, E, F, or V train)

✎ www.mamounsfalafel.com

Since 1971, this tiny hole-in-the-wall has been a sort of falafel heaven. A falafel sandwich consists of roasted chickpea balls in a sesame sauce with a salad of lettuce and tomatoes served in a pita. Mamoun's also has a full menu of vegetarian and nonvegetarian sandwiches and platters, none of which exceeds $10. The falafels are much less than half that. Both locations are open 365 days a year.

🧳 TRAVEL TIP

You can't travel far without finding a pizza place in New York City, especially in Manhattan. The best are the small family-run operations that bake up traditional pies. You can even stop into one of the many chains for a passable wedge, but they don't compare with the authentic pizzerias you'll find around town.

Lombardi's ($)

⌨ 32 Spring Street (at Mott Street)

🚇 Spring Street station (6 train)

📞 212-441-7994

🖊 *www.firstpizza.com*

Established in 1905, this is the oldest documented pizzeria in America, and many consider it the best. Pizza is still made the old-fashioned way, with a coal oven.

Mariella's ($)

⌨ 960 8th Avenue (between West 56th and West 57th avenues)

🚇 West 59th Street-Columbus Circle station (A, B, C, D, or 1 train)

📞 212-757-5278

Some New Yorkers agree with Oprah Winfrey that Mariella's serves up the best pizza in the city, especially if it's hot and fresh out of the oven. Also at 180 Third Avenue (between East Sixteenth and East Seventeenth streets).

Sofia Fabulous Pizza ($)

⌨ 1022 Madison Avenue (between East 78th and East 79th streets)

🚇 East 77th Street station (6 train)

📞 212-734-2676

🖊 *www.sofia-fabulous-pizza.pizzainny.com*

Sofia's is more than just a pizzeria. You can get Caesar salad and stuffed mushrooms, but everyone comes for the thin crust pizza.

≡FAST FACT

The coffee shop that George, Jerry, Elaine, and Kramer frequented in the hit series *Seinfeld* really exists—it's Tom's Restaurant, located on 112th Street and Broadway. It offers regular diner food but is now a part of the New York legend. Soup Kitchen International, which was at 259A West Fifty-fifth Street (between Broadway and Eighth Avenue) and was the inspiration for the Soup Nazi character, has closed. Al Yeganeh, who made a small fortune selling homemade soup, has franchised the tiny store and is selling his soup to stores and over the Internet.

Original Ray's Pizza ($)
⌨ 465 6th Avenue (at West 11th Street)
🚇 West 14th Street station (F, L, or V train)

Founded in 1959, this is the original and first of the famous pizzerias. Ray's is still one of the best pizzerias in the city. It built its reputation by serving extremely cheesy pizza by the slice.

CHAPTER 17

Exotic Eats

NEW YORK IS a city of immigrants, so the food is a wealth of the best and the boldest from all over the world. Every city block seems to have a Chinese, Japanese, and Latin restaurant and a pizzeria—and they all deliver. Internationally renowned chefs have come to New York to set up their kitchens and show the world what they have to offer, and the result is staggering. Most of the restaurants in this chapter are located in Manhattan below 96th Street.

Caribbean, Mexican, and Spanish

El Cid ($$)
- 322 West 15th Street (between 8th and 9th avenues)
- 14th Street station (A, C, or E train)
- 212-929-9332

People rave about the tapas in this cozy and unpretentious place. It's great for families because you can make a meal of whatever number of small portions you want of such morsels as garlic shrimp, seasoned sausages, or the wonderful Spanish torta of egg and potatoes. Full meals are also available from a small but interesting menu. Try the white sangria.

El Faro ($$)

⌨ 823 Greenwich Street (between Jane and Horatio streets)

🚇 West 14th Street station (A, C, or E train); 8th Avenue station (L train)

📞 212-929-8210

✉ www.elfaronyc.com

This place has been packing them in since 1927. It's small, but it's as close you're going to get to an authentic Spanish tapas bar in the city. El Faro uses the same recipes the founders brought from Spain almost a hundred years ago. Order tapas plates or the many delicious entrées, and don't forget the sangria. El Faro is child friendly and will make kid's half portions on request.

Francisco's Centro Vasco ($$–$$$)

⌨ 159 West 23rd Street (between 6th and 7th avenues)

🚇 West 23rd Street station (1 train)

📞 212-645-6224

✉ www.centrovasco.citysearch.com

When you want to splurge just a little on something a bit different, Francisco's is one of the best restaurants in town. This Basque restaurant specializes in shellfish, but its fish, beef, veal, and poultry dishes are great too. Its trademark is gargantuan lobsters (up to forty pounds), and the décor features huge lobster claws hanging from the ceiling. No half portions, but you can share or give the kids appetizers.

MaryAnn's ($$)

⌨ 2454 Broadway (at 90th Street)

🚇 West 86th Street station (1 train)

📞 212-877-0132

⌨ 1503 2nd Avenue (at 77th Street)

🚇 East 77th Street station (6 train)

📞 212-249-6165

⊞ 116 8th Avenue (between West 15th and West 16th streets)

🚊 West 14th Street station (A, C, or E train); 8th Avenue station (L train)

☎ 212-633-0877

An all-time favorite little Mexican restaurant in New York, Mary-Ann's is open late and very kid friendly. Your best bet is to visit during the day; people come late at night for the margaritas. The house salsa is good too.

Negril ($)

⊞ 362 West 23rd Street (between 8th and 9th avenues)

🚊 West 23rd Street station (C or E train)

☎ 212-807-6411

✎ *www.negrilvillage.com/negrilchelsea.html*

Authentic Jamaican home cooking in an unpretentious setting make this a good choice for a change of pace. A sister restaurant to the Negril Village, Negril serves solid, traditional Caribbean food. The kids will love the large fish tank. No kids menu, but half portions are available. Serves a Sunday brunch.

Negril Village ($$)

⊞ 70 West 3rd Street (between LaGuardia and Thompson

☎ 212-477-2804

🚊 West 4th Street-Washington Square station (A, B, C, D, E, F, or V train)

✎ *www.negrilvillage.com*

This pan-Islands restaurant is tastefully designed and swathed in happy colors. There's a separate kids menu and a Sunday brunch, plus good desserts.

Victor's Café 52 ($$–$$$)

▦ 236 West 52nd Street (between 8th Avenue and Broadway)

🚇 West 49th Street station (N, R, or W train)

📞 212-586-7714

✍ *www.victorscafe.com*

A New York institution since 1963, Victor's has never varied from its excellent preparation of traditional Cuban cuisine and an exciting menu of fusion recipes. There is no kids menu, but Victor's encourages sharing and waiters may suggest appetizers. It offers a three-course prix fixe lunch and dinner option. Make a reservation if you're theater-bound so you get out in time.

Chinese and Pan-Asian Cuisine

More than 100 Chinese and Asian restaurants are crammed into Chinatown. You can hop a cab, tell the driver "Chinatown," and walk into the nearest restaurant. You won't be disappointed. Here are some Chinese and Asian places on Mott Street alone:

- Buddha Bodai (5)
- Hong Ying (11)
- Sing Wong (13)
- Ajisen Noodle (14)
- Hop Kee (16)
- Wo Hop (17)
- Ping's (22)
- Peking Duck House (28)
- Green Tea (45)
- Mr. Tang (50)
- Teariffic (51)
- Wonton Garden (56)
- Mandarin Court (61)
- Amazing Restaurant (66)
- Guang Dong Yen Jia (67)
- Singapore Café (69)
- Hoy Wong (81)
- Grand Harmony (98)
- Shanghai Café (100)
- Oriental Food (103)
- Big Wing Wong (102)
- New Chao Chow (111)
- Banh Mi Saigon (138)

Other recommended Chinese restaurants include the following.

≡ FAST FACT

Dim sum consists of a variety of small dishes traditionally served with tea. You can make an entire meal out of dim sum or sample them as snacks as you explore Chinatown. Traditional dim sum offerings include fried and steamed dumplings and rice balls, but every restaurant has its own version of dim sum.

Ollie's Noodle Shop ($-$$)

⊞ 200-B West 44th Street (between 7th and 8th avenues)

🚇 Times Square-West 42nd Street station (N, Q, R, S, W, 1, 2, 3, or 7 train)

📞 212-921-5988

Ollie's is always busy, and with good reason. Favorites here are the Cantonese roast meats, filled dumplings, the sizzling platters, and, of course, the noodle dishes.

Jing Fong ($-$$)

⊞ 20 Elizabeth Street (between Bayard and Canal Street)

🚇 Canal Street station (J, M, N, Q, R, W, Z, or 6 train)

📞 212-964-5256

Jing Fong is known for its dim sum. Every member of your family will find numerous treats among the succulent carts streaming out of the kitchen. This is a vast banquet-hall-like place (the way it's done in Hong Kong), and no one cares if the kids cry, drop their food, or act like kids. Jing Fong serves dim sum from 10 A.M. to 3:30 P.M. It's best to go early for dim sum—the regular menu is forgettable.

Shun Lee Palace ($$–$$$)
⌨ 155 East 55th Street (between Lexington and 3rd avenues)
🚇 Lexington Ave.-East 53rd Street station (E or V train); East 51st Street station (6 train)
📞 212-371-8844
✐ www.shunleepalace.com/newyork

Consistently one of the best restaurants in New York, Shun Lee has an upscale menu of unusual dishes served with extravagant presentation. The meals are sharable, especially the casseroles. Some entrées are served in appetizer portions. There is a low-carb menu and a great $20 prix fixe lunch that is easily shared.

Japanese, Korean, and Thai

Nobu ($$-$$$)
⌨ 105 Hudson Street at Franklin Street
🚇 Franklin Street station (1 train)
📞 212-219-0500
✐ www.myriadrestaurantgroup.com

Nobu is a trendy and top-rated Japanese restaurant. The casual setting evokes a Japanese forest. There are lots of things to interest the kids—miso soup, tempura, kushiyaki (skewers), wraps, and desserts. Reservations are a must, and it's even a good idea to make them a week or two in advance.

The appropriately named Nobu Next Door runs on a no-reservation policy. Go early on a weeknight to get a table or order takeout at 212-334-4445 after 5:45 P.M.

Nobu Fifty Seven is an uptown location that has the same innovative cuisine as the original Nobu. It is located at 40 West Fifty-seventh Street. Call 212-757-3000 for more information.

Samurai Sam's Teriyaki Grill ($)

🖃 291 7th Ave. (between 26th and 27th streets)

🚇 West 28th Street station (1 train)

📞 212-807-8810

🖋 *www.samuraisams.net*

This is part of an international franchise started in Arizona. The food is crafted to appeal to the American palate with a tasty selection of bowls, wraps, and salads that won't scare the kids off. There is also a new Sam's at 165 Chambers Street, Chambers Street station (1, 2, or 3 train), 212-227-6550.

SOY ($)

🖃 102 Suffolk Street (between Delancy and Rivington streets)

🚇 Delancy Street-Essex Street station (F, J, M, or Z train)

📞 212-253-1168

🖋 *www.soynyc.com*

This cozy, kid-friendly little place specializes in Japanese home cooking. The wide selection of meat, fish, tofu, and vegetables are fresh and healthy.

TRAVEL TIP

Trying to get the kids to go Japanese is not as hard as you might think. Kids love the miso soup and the edamame, which are steamed soy beans with salt. Tempura is deep-fried vegetables and fish, and chicken or beef teriyaki always goes over well with kids.

Cho Dang Gol ($$$)

⌨ 55 West 35th Street (between 5th and 6th avenues)

🚆 5th Avenue-53rd Street station (E or V train)

📞 212-695-8222

✐ www.chodanggolny.com

An excellent Korean restaurant with a large and mouthwatering menu that will appeal to adults and kids willing to experiment.

Woo Chon Restaurant ($$$)

⌨ 10 West 36th Street (between 5th and 6th avenues)

🚆 West 34th Street-Herald Square station (B, D, F, N, Q, R, V, or W train)

📞 212-695-0676

Adventurous kids will absolutely love the assortment of appetizers offered with every meal (some are spicy), served on a very large table.

Chili Thai ($)

⌨ 712 9th Avenue (Between West 48th and West 49th streets)

🚆 West 50th Street station (C or E train)

📞 917-472-9838

The scores of locals who eat here regularly will tell you this is the best and cheapest Thai place in town. Comfortable for kids and parents, you can't miss with anything you pick. The tom yum soup, pad thai, and salmon are especially recommended. Hours: Monday to Thursday 11:30 A.M. to 11 P.M, Friday and Saturday to midnight, Sunday noon to 11 P.M.

Pam Real Thai Food ($-$$)

⌨ 404 West 49th Street (between 9th and 10th avenues)

🚆 West 50th Street station (C or E train)

📞 212-333-7500/7240

Another unpretentious place where the food is the center of attraction and not the décor. This is a New York find that answers the question, "How can people afford to live here?" Cash only, no reservations, open Monday–Sunday 11:30 A.M.–11:00 P.M.

Jaiya ($-$$)
- 396 Third Avenue (East 28th Street)
- 28th Street station (6 train)
- 212-889-1330
- *www.jaiya.com*

Don't be put off by the slick and elegant interior, this is a place in which you'll enjoy a superb and creative meal without emptying the bank. The humongous menu will keep all of you engrossed for a while with a seemingly endless list of ingredients and combinations. Bonus: its Web site is a good source of information on Thailand for a school project. Open Monday to Friday 11:30 A.M. to midnight; Saturday open at noon; Sunday open at 5:00 P.M.

Indian Fare

There are about 200 Indian restaurants in New York City. For a unique experience, cab over to East Sixth Street between First and Second avenues in the East Village. It's known as "Curry Lane" because dozens of Indian restaurants line the perimeter of this incredible block. These restaurants are unpretentious and quite inexpensive, and Indian food makes for excellent sharing among the family.

- Brick Lane ($–$$) (306) 212-979-2900
- Taj Mahal ($) (318) 212-505-8056
- Angon ($$–$$$) (320) 212-260-8229
- Raj Mahal ($) (322) 212-982-3632
- Calcutta ($) (324) 212-982-8127
- Spice Cove ($) (326) 212-982-8884
- Sonar Gaon ($) (328) 212-677-8876

- Mitali East ($$) (334) 212-533-2508
- Banjara (344) 212-477-5956
- Gandhi ($$) (345) 212-614-9718

Here are some other kid-friendly Indian restaurants in Manhattan.

Bukhara Grill ($$)
🖃 217 East 49th Street (between 2nd and 3rd avenues)
🚈 East 51st Street station (6 train)
✆ 1-888-285-4272
✆ 212-888-2839
✐ www.bukharany.com

This attractive, rustic place specializes in Northwest Indian cuisine. Kids will enjoy sitting at the tree-trunk tables and chairs next to a real waterfall. The chef will prepare kid-sized portions.

 TRAVEL TIP

If you go to an Indian restaurant that doesn't have a kids menu, you can always share. Start with a mixed appetizer platter of foods you think your child will eat—pakoras and samosas are favorites, and make sure to get some naan. For the main course, chicken tandoori is a fail-safe option for unadventurous children and adults alike.

Hampton Chutney Co. ($)
🖃 464 Amsterdam Avenue (between 82nd and 83rd streets)
🚈 West 79th Street or West 86th Street stations (1 train)
✆ 212-362-5050

🖃 68 Prince Street (between Broadway and Lafayette Street)
🚈 Prince Street station (N, R, or W train), Spring Street station (6 train), or Broadway-Lafayette Street station (B, D, F, or V train)
✐ www.hamptonchutney.com

These unpretentious, inexpensive restaurants have a fiercely loyal clientele. The menu includes dosas (large, crispy, sourdough crepes), uttapa (pancakes), wraps, and sandwiches stuffed with a large variety of veggies, poultry, and seafood, all centered around fresh, homemade chutneys. The uptown location provides a kids menu and a kiddie corner full of books and toys.

Italian Cuisine

Il Palazzo ($$)
▫ 151 Mulberry Street (between Grand and Hester streets)
🚇 Canal Street station (J, M, N, Q, R, W, Z, or 6 train)
📞 212-343-7000
✎ www.littleitalynyc.com/ilpalazzo

This charming two-story restaurant provides a pleasant background to the sophisticated menu at moderate prices.

Vincent's ($$)
▫ 119 Mott Street, at Hester Street
🚇 Canal Street station (J, M, N, Q, R, W, Z, or 6 train)
📞 212-226-8133

In 1904, Giuseppi and Carmela Siano moved inside, from a push-cart on the corner, and the Original Vincent's Restaurant has been there ever since. The original recipe Sicilian red sauce still forms the basis of the large, typical Italian selection. This is a casual, family-friendly place, and you'll want to dine outdoors when the weather permits.

💼 TRAVEL TIP

Go to www.opentable.com. You can set up all your meals from home and make sure you have reservations at the city's best restaurants. You can search for specific restaurants or by cuisine and neighborhood.

Moroccan Food

Café Mogador ($$)

⌨ 101 St. Marks Place (between 1st Avenue and Avenue A)

🚊 Astor Place station (6 train)

✆ 212-677-2226

New Yorkers flock from all boroughs to eat here, so things get busy on the weekends. The fabulous food and fun people are worth it. Make it a night walking around the Greenwich Village neighborhood and exploring the shops. Mogador serves great Moroccan food and kids love it. Open for breakfast, lunch, and dinner, and weekend brunch from 9 A.M. to 4 P.M.

Barbes ($$)

⌨ 21 East 36th Street (between 5th and Madison avenues)

🚊 33rd Street (6 train)

✆ 212-684-0215

✍ www.barbesrestaurantnyc.com

For the semi-venturous kid and non-too-venturous adult, this evocative restaurant will have you crooning, "Come wiz me to de Casbah." Barbes is an interesting Parisian quarter which has become home to emigrants of France's former North African colonies. The menu is a mixture of familiar French and interesting Moroccan. It's a kid-friendly place, and many of the modestly priced appetizers will serve them well. The adults will have a hard time choosing from a variety of fantasy meals. Great desserts, too. Reservations are recommended. Open Monday to Saturday 11:30 A.M. to midnight.

Nomad ($$)

⌨ 78 Second Avenue (between 4th and 5th streets)

🚊 Second Avenue (F or V train); Astor Place (6 train)

✆ 212-253-5410

✍ www.lanomadenyc.com

The kids will be awed by the spectacular North African/Moroccan décor. A very large menu yields enormous portions that must be shared. The mainstay, and always acceptable to kids, is the Couscous Royale, an epicurean feast for almost a pittance. Open Monday to Saturday from 4 P.M. to midnight; Sunday 11 A.M. to 11 P.M.

Soul Food

Miss Mamie's Spoonbread Too ($)
⌨ 366 West 110th Street
🚇 Cathedral Parkway (110th Street) station (B or C train)
📞 212-865-6744
✍ www.spoonbreadinc.com

The superlative southern cooking draws happy customers from all strata of society, from former President Bill Clinton to Columbia University students to neighborhood families. Try the former president's favorite meal—the "Miss Mamie Sampler," of shrimp, ribs, chicken, and veggies for $15.95 (that's as expensive as it gets). If you're on a special diet, don't let the fact that Miss Mamie's serves the best fried chicken in New York deter you; there's a fantastic vegetarian sampler at half the meat-eater's price. Some people make a meal of the side dishes only.

A second branch, Miss Maude's Spoonbread Too, has been added at 547 Lenox Avenue between West 137th and West 138th Street, West 135th Street station (2 or 3 train). The menu features real down-home Southern cooking. Call 212-690-3100.

Londel's ($$)
⌨ 2620 Frederick Douglass Boulevard (also known as 8th Avenue), between 139th and 140th streets
🚇 West 135th Street station (B or C train)
📞 212-234-6114
✍ www.londelsrestaurant.com

This is a classic Southern, Creole, and American comfort food restaurant just off Harlem's historical Striver's Row. Reservations are recommended, especially for the brunch. Londel's is closed Mondays.

Sylvia's Restaurant ($$–$$$)
⌨ 328 Lenox Avenue (between West 126th and West 127th streets)
🚇 West 125th Street station (2 or 3 train)
✆ 212-996-0660
✐ www.sylviassoulfood.com

Sylvia's has the best soul food in New York. The Sunday gospel brunch is one of the best buys in the city. Sometimes Sylvia herself shows up. Open for breakfast, lunch, and dinner.

Just for Fun

American Girl Place ($$)
⌨ 409 5th Avenue (at West 49th Street)
🚇 West 47th–50th Streets-Rockefeller Center station (B, D, F, or V train)
✆ 1-877-A G PLACE (247-5223)
✐ www.americangirl.com

Bring your daughter's American Girl doll in for a makeover, and explore the facility while you wait for her. There is a museum of Peek into the Past displays of American historical dioramas and floors of merchandise selling American Girl dolls, clothes, and accessories. There is a bookstore and a photo studio as well. When your doll is presentable, she can join you in her own little seat for a charming service for breakfast, lunch, brunch, afternoon tea, or dinner.

Basta Pasta ($$$)

⌨ 37 West 17th Street (between 5th and 6th avenues)

🚇 West 14th Street station (F train)

☎ 212-366-0888

✎ *www.bastapastanyc.com*

Who would believe you could find Italian food prepared by Japanese chefs in an open kitchen? The concept began in Tokyo in 1985 with a restaurant designed after the set of TV's *Iron Chef* cooking reality show. It came to New York in 1990 and hasn't slowed since. The food is terrific; kids can try linguine with meat sauce while you sample the sea urchin. Children absolutely love this place (they can be serenaded by a ukulele player on their birthday), and you'll find yourself thinking about this incredibly creative food for a long time. The décor is bright and popular.

ESPN Zone

⌨ 1492 Broadway (at 42nd Street in Times Square)

🚇 Times Square-West 42nd Street station (N, Q, R, S, W, 1, 2, 3, or 7 train)

☎ 212-921-3776

ESPN Zone is a mind-blowing sports immersion experience with 150 sports-tuned TVs (even in the restrooms), including a huge projection screen and 10,000 square feet of interactive games and attractions. The menu of American fare includes some seventy items and a separate kids menu to make everybody happy. Open for lunch and until midnight or later on weekends. No reservations, but MVP Club members get priority seating.

La Bonne Soupe ($-$$)

⌨ 48 West 55th Street (between 5th and 6th avenues)

🚇 West 57th Street station (F train)

☎ 212-586-7650

✎ *www.labonnesoupe.com*

Named after a popular French comedy, this popular bistro has been offering families its traditional food for more than thirty years. Kids love the fondue—cheese and the chocolate dessert—but there's also an affordable children's menu of American favorites. Some locals come for just the onion soup and memorable salad dressing and this is the place for authentic chocolate mousse. This place is a real family favorite, especially if you opt for the daily prix fixe special. Sunday brunch is served. Join in the delightful celebrations on Bastille Day (July 14).

Peanut Butter & Co. ($)

⌨ 240 Sullivan Street (between Bleeker and West 3rd streets)

🚈 West 4th Street-Washington Square station (A, B, C, D, E, F, or V train)

✆ 212-677-3995

✎ www.ilovepeanutbutter.com

This nutty little sandwich shop in the Village makes seventeen (and counting) different peanut butter combination sandwiches.

Salt & Pepper ($)

⌨ 139 West 33rd Street (between 6th and 7th avenues, near Herald Square)

🚈 West 34th Street-Herald Square station (B, D, F, N, Q, R, V, or W train)

✆ 212-268-1919

⌨ 239 East 14th Street (at 1st Avenue)

🚈 1st Avenue station (L train)

✆ 212-677-0005

✎ www.sandpon33rd.com

What's the family in the mood for? Spanish? Greek? American? Don't argue about it, head on over to either Salt & Pepper location, where you can get any and all the above and more in a welcoming, friendly environment. An incredibly diverse selection at crazy-cheap prices. Open 24/7.

Ruby Foo's ($$)

⊞ 1626 Broadway (at 49th Street)

🚇 West 50th Street station (1 train), West 49th Street station (N, R, or W train)

📞 212-489-5600

⊞ 2182 Broadway (at 77th Street)

🚇 79th Street station (1 train)

📞 212-724-6700

✒ *www.brguestrestaurants.com*

Show the kids what a Chinese restaurant of the 1950s would look like—if it were a Hollywood set. Tasseled lanterns hang from the ceiling, porcelain vases hold greenery, and red and black lacquer are everywhere. The food is pan-Asian with a nod toward American tastes. There are plenty of good things to choose from: dim sum, monster rolls, platters, and interesting main plates. There's a very good kids menu as well, and you will love the desserts, especially the bento box dessert, in which sweets are presented as fake sushi. The Ruby Foo signature drink is a perennial favorite, despite the fact that it packs a wicked punch. Make reservations, as this is a popular restaurant with the date crowd, tourists, and theatergoers at the Times Square location.

Trailer Park Lounge & Grill

⊞ 271 West 23rd Street (between 7th and 8th avenues)

🚇 West 23rd Street station (C, E, or 1 train)

📞 212-463-8000

✒ *www.trailerparklounge.com*

Named one of the five kitschiest restaurants in the country, the food matches the décor—burgers, dogs, and sloppy joes.

City Island Seafood

Crab Shanty ($$)

361 City Island Avenue (at Tier Street)

718-885-1810

www.originalcrabshanty.com

The Original Crab Shanty boasts a huge selection of seafood, meat, poultry, and pasta for lunch and dinner until late.

 **TRAVEL TIP**

There are many good restaurants on City Island. Other seafood places are City Island Lobster House (slightly upscale), Sammy's Fishbox (very casual, very good), Sea Shore Restaurant & Marina (great views), and Shrimp Box (Latino cuisine and jazz).

The Lobster Box ($$)

34 City Island Avenue

718-885-1952

www.lobsterbox.com

The Lobster Box is another fabulous seafood place with a menu that expands to meat and poultry. This one has been in business fifty years. It serves about two dozen variations of lobster and almost as many of shrimp. The views of Long Island Sound are great. Open for lunch and dinner until late.

CHAPTER 18

Where to Stay Under $200

HUNDREDS OF HOTELS, from the ultimate in posh to the cheapest of hostels, are available to your family. The average hotel room runs about $200 a day for double occupancy, so only in the big city would hotel rooms that run less than that be considered "budget." The hotel listings in this chapter include a few in each part of Manhattan, with an emphasis on midtown. The hotel reviews are organized by location, beginning with midtown, which is the most popular location.

How to Save

There are many ways to cut the cost of your hotel stay. You can use various club membership discounts, like the Automobile Association of America (AAA) or the American Association of Retired Persons (AARP) discounts, which are usually around 10 percent off of the rack rate. You can find a room that gives you free breakfast or even has a kitchenette. There are often family rates and discounts for summer and weekend specials, so ask for the lowest rate when you call for reservations or check the hotel's Web site for package deals. If you have some time flexibility, ask the hotel when its rates are the lowest—it may be only a day or two later!

The advent of travel search engines like Expedia, Travelocity, Orbitz, and Priceline have revolutionized the hotel industry. Use these original pioneers and newcomers like Sidestep and Kayak to find accommodations that fit your budget.

≡FAST FACT

Remember that sometimes it's worth spending a little more for location. Otherwise, you'll be paying to park the car all day and/or paying subway fares for the whole family, to say nothing of time wasted in traveling when you could just be walking from a downtown hotel.

Note that many hotel chains guarantee to match the lowest rate you find on the Internet, and you have the advantage of dealing with them directly, insuring you are getting the best accommodations possible for your family. Don't be afraid to bargain; asking if the hotel can do a little better may very well help them to suddenly "discover" a better deal. You can't do that with a Web site. The following is a good selection of travel-related sites:

- **Priceline** (*www.priceline.com*) works two ways. It will allow you to make bids on discounted hotel rooms, but you don't have control over the hotel that is chosen for you (you set the price and see what comes in). Priceline says all its hotels are members of major chains, and you can probably get a very good rate this way, but do your research before you book a room. Look up the hotels you're considering to make sure they are subway accessible and meet all of your criteria for location and comfort. You can also choose your hotel from a discounted list, the same way as you do with any of the following.
- **Expedia** (*www.expedia.com*), Orbitz (*www.orbitz.com*), Hotwire (*www.hotwire.com*), and Travelocity (*www.travelocity .com*) all work the same way. They will give you a listing of

hotels by location and price, along with photos. But make sure you look the hotel up elsewhere, as sometimes they are adjacent to seedier parts of town.

- **TripAdvisor** (*www.tripadvisor.com*) is a great Web site that will give you fellow-traveler reviews as well as the best price on the Web for any hotel you are searching for.
- **Preferred Hotels and Resorts Worldwide** (*www.preferred hotels.com*) is operated by Travelweb, which is a reservation system for the hotel industry.
- **Holiday Inn** (*www.holidayinn.com*) lets you use its Web site to find packages and last-minute deals.
- **Radisson Hotel** (*www.radisson.com*) is another hotel chain with possible discounts and packages offered through its Web site.

Using a site like Kayak or Sidestep can be beneficial. These sites pull rates from discount Web sites, and the hotels' Web sites, to let you find the best rates.

Location and Price

The two most important elements to choosing your accommodations in New York are location and price. You may also want to consider additional amenities like a swimming pool for the kids or a business center for keeping in touch with the office. If you are not coming by car or don't plan on renting one, try to find a hotel near a subway station.

There are many lower-priced hotels near the airports in Queens, but they are at least a half hour from the city by car or train. They are fine if you just need a place to stay overnight after you land; otherwise, get something in Manhattan.

Location

The obvious location choice is Manhattan, since you want to be in the middle of the action. Within Manhattan, you need to determine which area is to your liking. Hotels in and around Times Square are busy and certainly in the middle of the hustle and bustle. Since Times Square and Forty-second Street are now cleaned up and Disney-fied, the area is definitely more appropriate for families than it once was. Times Square is ideal for theatergoing and sightseeing. Several midtown hotels in both the east and west fifties put you in close proximity to the sights and excitement of the city, with slightly less hustle and bustle.

TRAVEL TIP

Choosing a hotel room solely off the Internet can be deceiving. If something looks too inexpensive, be careful. Some New York hotel rooms are no bigger than closets and are certainly not big enough for a family. Some are down-at-the-heels, some are in iffy neighborhoods. Double-check the hotel's reviews before making reservations.

As you approach Central Park, you'll find more lavish accommodations, particularly on Central Park South, where the Plaza and plush neighboring hotels overlook the park. These elegant hotels are in a less touristy area than Times Square and cost quite a bit more. Here, instead of the glut of souvenir shops you'd find in Times Square, you'll find elegant stores such as Tiffany's and Saks.

Heading downtown, there are many fine hotels in the thirties, on both the east and west side. Some of these are a little quieter and less expensive, since they're not smack in the middle of the excitement. Often these hotels will be surrounded by office or residential buildings. Since taxis are abundant and mass transit covers the city, it is not hard to get wherever you are going from here. Streets in the downtown thirties, however, can be quiet at night, and you may not feel as safe walking around.

Further downtown in lower Manhattan, you'll find some of the newest, most fashionable hotels in the city. While this area can be quiet at night and on weekends, it is bustling during the day. If you are planning to see the Statue of Liberty, Ellis Island, the South Street Seaport, and other lower Manhattan sights and are not as attracted to the midtown nightlife and Museum Mile, you may enjoy staying at these hotels, which are often frequented by business travelers in town for meetings in the financial district. You might appreciate more elbow room on the weekends as the business execs hit the road. On the other hand, if you plan evenings at the theater, want to spend days in Central Park and at the United Nations, and enjoy being in the heart of the action, this might not be the area for you.

Decide what you plan to do during your stay, what your price range is, and what atmosphere you are looking for, and then determine which part of town best suits your needs.

≡FAST FACT

Many factors affect the price of hotel rooms. Time of year, day of the week, and holidays and conventions all have a bearing. Hotel chains run national promotions and package deals, as do individual establishments. Doing some research online and on the phone may save you a bundle.

Other Considerations

Once you look through the hotel listings and determine those that fit your price range, consider these factors:

- Is there an extra charge per night for children staying in your room? Are there special children's rates or family packages?
- Is there a kitchenette in the room or a refrigerator or microwave?

- What kind of restaurants are in the hotel? For family dining, a casual restaurant is more practical if you want to grab a quick, inexpensive breakfast or lunch. All major hotels have room service, but the prices can be steep.
- What is the neighborhood like? Are there places for you to grab an inexpensive meal?
- Is there easy access to public transportation?
- Does the hotel have bus or van service to the airport?
- Does the hotel have a concierge? In New York City, a hotel concierge is far more common than a hotel swimming pool. It is also more practical, as the concierge can help you with directions, reservations, and all sorts of services.
- How much does the hotel charge for phone calls? Phone calls made from hotel rooms can be quite costly. It's to your advantage to make calls with a calling card or use a cellular phone.
- Is there Internet access in the hotel room? If so, is there an extra charge?
- Is there a safe in the room? Whenever you travel, it's important to know you can protect valuables.
- What is the parking situation? If you drive to the city, ask your hotel about parking availability and cost. Even some of the finest hotels don't have much to offer. Also ask what the fee is for re-entry to the lot and whether the lot is near the hotel.

Do some research by reading reviews and checking hotel Web sites. You will know what to expect from your accommodations after you've read up on the location and the hotel itself.

Midtown Listings

If you are only in town for a day or two, midtown is really where you should try to stay. You'll be close enough to everything you want to see and can travel by train or bus, or even by taxi.

Ameritania Hotel
🖃 230 West 54th Street (at Broadway)

🚆 West 59th Street-Columbus Circle station (A, B, C, D, or 1 train)

✆ 1-800-555-7555

✆ 212-247-5000

✉ *www.ameritaniahotelnewyork.com*

The Ameritania is a trendy 210-room hotel right next to the Ed Sullivan Theater, home to *The Late Show with David Letterman*, and a short walk to the Museum of Modern Art, Times Square, Central Park, the theater district, and Fifth Avenue shopping. It barely makes it into the under-$200 category, but the location and amenities justify the price tag. The interiors and guest rooms are sleek and modern, with a surprising list of amenities—marble bathrooms, free coffee, cable TV with PPV, CD player, and two-line telephones.

Hotel services include a concierge, guest laundry services, and valet parking for a fee.

The hotel features the popular Twist Lounge, where you can sit, sip, and contemplate the fireplace. There are a ton of restaurants in the neighborhood—the concierge will help with selections and reservations.

The Ameritania is one of several Amsterdam Hospitality Group Hotels around the city, all designed to provide quality accommodations at reasonable Manhattan prices. One such property, the Amsterdam Court Hotel, is very similar to the Ameritania and sits four blocks away at 226 West 50th Street (at Broadway), West 50th Street station (1 train). Contact the Amsterdam Court at 212-459-1000; *www.amsterdam courthotelnewyork.com*.

Best Western President
🖃 234 West 48th Street (between 8th Avenue and Broadway)

🚆 West 49th Street station (N, R, or W train); West 50th Street station (C, E, or 1 train)

✆ 1-800-826-4667

✆ 212-246-8800

✉ *www.bestwestern.com*

Best Western provides your standard clean, comfortable hotel room at a good price. The President is in the heart of Broadway, close to Rockefeller Center and Radio City, museums, Times Square, and the theater district. You can also stroll over to the nearby diamond district or Fifth Avenue stores for some shopping with the money you save on your room.

There are 238 nonsmoking rooms, forty-four suites, and two penthouse suites. The rooms have all the amenities you need, including in-room movies, irons, coffee/tea makers, free local telephone calls and long-distance access, and in-room safes. The hotel has a gift shop and twenty-four-hour security. Children under twelve are free in a room with one paying adult.

≡FAST FACT

Pay phones in New York are still plentiful. Calls cost thirty-five cents, which will apply to any of the boroughs (area codes 212, 646, 347, 718, or 917). Your cell phone will work throughout the city, except in the subway.

In Manhattan, where luxury and pricey amenities are abundant, this is comparatively a no-frills deal, but it fits the bill nicely for the get-up-and-go traveler who plans to get out each day and see the city. This is the least expensive of the four Best Westerns in Manhattan.

Nearby restaurants include the Saigon Café, which serves a continental breakfast daily; Saigon 48 for Vietnamese food; Aoki, a Japanese restaurant open for lunch and dinner; and the Z-Bar bar and lounge. Within a few steps of the front door are restaurants serving American, Brazilian, Japanese, Thai, French, and Mexican food, and, of course, a McDonalds.

Milford Plaza

270 West 45th Street (at Broadway)

Times Square-West 42nd Street station (N, Q, R, S, W, 1, 2, 3, or 7 train)

1-800-221-2690

212-869-3000

www.milfordplaza.com

The Milford Plaza calls itself the "Lullaby of Broadway" to appeal to the theatergoers; the hotel is smack in the middle of the theater district. You couldn't ask for a better location, and the Milford has established a presence amid several more luxurious hotels rich with amenities and designed for business travelers.

Some 1,300 rooms were refurbished in 1995; they are comfortable and safe and feature cable television and in-room movies. While they are not lavish, they are sufficient if you are planning to spend the bulk of your time seeing the sights and/or taking in the Broadway shows.

A spacious lobby complete with fountains, chandeliers, and flowers welcomes you. Once you're inside, the Milford features a theater, sightseeing, and transportation desk, a twenty-four-hour fitness center, and a gift and sundry shop.

The restaurant is Garvey's Irish Pub, serving lunch, dinner, and snacks. It has a pool table and video games. The neighborhood is chock-a-block with dining possibilities, it's one block from Restaurant Row (see page 280).

≡FAST FACT

The nickname "Big Apple" may have been coined by traveling jazz musicians. They bestowed the moniker on the city in honor of its prominence in the jazz world. Another theory says the name came from stablehands and horse trainers who dreamed of racing in the city. In both cases, playing in or racing in New York City meant success.

Super 8, Manhattan

⌨ 59 West 46th Street (between 5th and 6th avenues)

🚇 West 47th–50th Streets-Rockefeller Center station (B, D, F, or V train)

☎ 212-719-2300

✐ www.super8.com

A true bargain in New York hotels, this is a lovely facility at a rock-bottom price. There are 206 rooms in the renovated twelve-story building. You can walk to Rockefeller Center (in fact, you have to—it's where the subway is), Fifth Avenue, Broadway theaters, well, the list goes on and on. Amenities are generous, including a free daily continental breakfast. All rooms have twenty-five-inch TVs with cable, coffeemaker, free wireless Internet access, iron and board, and an in-room safe. The hotel has a concierge, fitness and business centers, and nonsmoking rooms. Children twelve and under stay free with parents. Restaurants are nearby.

 TRAVEL TIP

Remember to tip those who make your stay in New York a pleasant experience. Chambermaids should generally get $2–$5 per night, and you should give the valet, doorman, and bellman a couple of dollars for parking/retrieving your vehicle, helping you with baggage, and hailing a cab.

Travel Inn Hotel

⌨ 515 West 42nd Street (between 10th and 11th avenues)

🚇 West 42nd Street-Port Authority Bus Terminal (A, C, or E train)

☎ 1-800-869-4630

☎ 212-695-7171

✐ www.thetravelinnhotel.com

Not your typical Manhattan hotel, the Travel Inn is in a convenient location, just a few blocks from the Jacob Javits Convention Center and not far from Times Square. Broadway and the major theaters are not far away either. It is particularly handy for visiting the Intrepid Sea, Air & Space Museum or taking a ride around Manhattan on the Circle Line or another of the many water cruises available.

It's nothing too fancy but a good value, with clean rooms and two very unusual amenities: an outdoor pool with a deck and free parking. Yes, that's free parking. The hotel's 160 guest rooms are reasonably large with the standard hotel fare. A fitness center, gift shop, and tour desk are also included within.

≡FAST FACT

Not that long ago, there were eight daily newspapers in New York City. Today there are four major players: the *New York Times*, the *Daily News*, the *New York Post*, and the *Wall Street Journal*. *Newsday* is also published daily. There is a free weekly newspaper, the *Village Voice*, which is published on Wednesdays and offers an excellent events calendar.

The River West Café/Deli, located in the hotel (but not owned by it) is a pleasantly designed little coffee shop with standard American cuisine.

Traveling around is easy. Crosstown buses on Forty-second Street are frequent, and getting to the subway in the Port Authority Bus Terminal will be an education in itself. If you're not seeking luxury and, particularly, if you're driving into the city, this might be worth checking out. Kids sixteen and under stay free.

Lower Manhattan and Downtown

If you're in town for a holiday and all the midtown hotels are booked, this area is your next best bet. It's also good if you are visiting New York University, Greenwich Village, SoHo, or doing business in the Wall Street area. You might even be able to get a good weekend deal because these hotels cater to the business crowd.

JUST FOR PARENTS

The legendary Chelsea Hotel (222 West 23rd Street), where both illustrious and unknown artists and writers have worked, partied, and lived since 1905, is just not a place for families. Its current motto is "A Rest Stop for Rare Individuals," and it has lost none of the edgy quality that has made it a symbol of creative rebellion for a century.

Best Western Seaport Inn Downtown

🖃 33 Peck Slip (at Front Street)

🚇 Fulton Street-Broadway-Nassau station (A, C, J, M, Z, 2, 3, 4, or 5 train)

📞 1-800-HOTEL-NY (468-3569)

📞 212-766-6600

✍ *www.bestwestern.com/seaportinn*

You'll find the Seaport Inn tucked away in lower Manhattan, one block north of the South Street Seaport and one block south of the Brooklyn Bridge. A comfortable hotel with modern amenities and Old World charm, the Best Western features easy access to all lower Manhattan sites, obviously including the seaport. Rooms are large with quaint furnishings and modern amenities to please a family, including high-speed Internet access, Nintendo, in-room movies, two-line phones, a video library, and much more. Some rooms have whirlpools or terraces. It serves a free continental breakfast and cookies in the afternoon. The hotel has a twenty-four-hour exercise facility, concierge, and business center.

If you're looking for a lower Manhattan location and are planning to visit Chinatown, Little Italy, the Financial Center, and the World Trade Center Memorial, this is a cost-effective, clean hotel with all the basics. In the winter months, the area around the seaport can get awfully quiet, and the brisk winds from the river make walking around the shops, ships, and eateries less fun. In the warm weather, however, it's a wonderful area. Also, the hotel is not widely known, so you should get more personalized attention.

There is no on-site restaurant, but there are plenty of places to eat nearby. Kids twelve and under stay free in a parent's room.

Holiday Inn Soho

▫ 138 Lafayette Street (between Canal and Grand streets)
🚇 Canal Street station (J, M, N, Q, R, W, Z, or 6 train)
✆ 1-800-465-4329
✆ 212-966-8898
✍ *www.hidowntown-nyc.com/*

This 215-room hotel is housed in a historic Chinatown building and is one of the very few hotels in the area. The Asian décor of the lobby, smart and modern room design, and periodic special offers make it a favorite among family budget travelers and Europeans. The restaurant nods toward Little Italy, with fare by San Remo. Four people of any age can stay in a room for the same rate.

Upper Manhattan

The hotels in this section are located above Fifty-ninth Street in upper Manhattan, a good place to stay if you are planning on spending time at the American Museum of Natural History, the Frick Collection, the Metropolitan Museum of Art, or in Central Park.

Days Hotel

▦ 215 West 94th Street (at Broadway)

🚉 West 96th Street station (1 train)

📞 1-800-834-2972

📞 212-866-6400

✎ *www.dayshotelnyc.com*

North of the action, the hotel is only two subway express stops to Times Square and the theater district. A new addition to the Days Inn chain, the facility offers quality rooms at a comparatively good price.

Rooms are sizable, with free wireless access, coffeemakers, in-room safes, irons and boards, basic TV, and refrigerators available on request. There's laundry and dry-cleaning service, and an exercise room and business center on-site.

≡FAST FACT

There is a great hotel in Brooklyn Heights, so if you're staying there to see family, or you want to spend a day at the Brooklyn Museum, Botanic Garden, and Junior's, try the New York Marriott in Brooklyn (call 1-888-436-3759 for more information). It has an Olympic-length lap pool and a kosher menu available. Rooms have eleven-foot ceilings (unheard of in Manhattan), and the lobby features seats from the old Ebbets Field.

This is your standard place to stay, not elegant, not fancy, but comfortable and a good choice for the family who doesn't mind seeing a New York neighborhood up close and hopping the subway for a quick ride to the attractions. The Key West Diner is next to the hotel, and across the street is a twenty-four-hour deli.

Comfort Inn Central Park West

⌨ 31 West 71st Street (between Central Park West and Columbus Avenue)

🚇 West 72nd Street station (B or C train)

📞 877-727-5236

📞 212-721-4770

✍ *www.comfortinn.com/ires/hotel/ny209*

An inviting European-style boutique hotel with big-city amenities located in a compelling Upper West Side neighborhood, it's a short trip to the sights with judicious use of the subways. The hotel offers a free continental breakfast, concierge, guest laundry, dry-cleaning service, exercise room, and discounted parking. There are plenty of stores and eateries nearby as well.

Newton Hotel

⌨ 2528 Broadway (between West 94th and West 95th streets)

🚇 West 96th Street station (1, 2, or 3 train)

📞 212-678-6500

✍ *www.thehotelnewton.com*

An outstanding value, the Newton attracts travelers who seek good accommodations at a very low price. This is a smallish hotel, with 102 rooms and suites and nine floors. The rooms, inspected and approved by the AAA, are large and comfy with basic amenities such as cable TV with free movies, irons, and twenty-four-hour room service. Some bathrooms are shared, so make sure to specify you want a private one. There is a restaurant next door and plenty more in the neighborhood. Indoor parking is available. The hotel is on an express subway line, so it's a quick two-stop ride to Times Square.

CHAPTER 19

Moderately Priced Hotels ($200–$300)

IN NEW YORK CITY, a moderately priced hotel means a room under $300. When you're traveling with a family, you want to make sure that your accommodations are comfortable and safe. New York has been named the safest large city in the country by the FBI. It is also one of the top spots for family vacations in the United States, and it has some wonderful family hotels. With more than 80,000 hotel rooms in this city, there should be something in your budget even if you are traveling during the winter holidays, the busiest season.

Midtown West

As in the previous chapter, hotel listings are organized by location, starting with midtown west, the most sought-after location, and then covering midtown east, lower Manhattan, downtown, and upper Manhattan. Midtown includes the area between Fifty-ninth and Thirtieth streets.

The Algonquin
⌨ 59 West 44th Street (between 5th and 6th avenues)
🚇 5th Avenue station (7 train); West 42nd Street-Bryant Park station (B, D, F, or V train)
📞 1-888-304-2047
📞 212-840-6800
✏ *www.algonquinhotel.com*

This classic hotel is famous for its Algonquin Roundtable literary gatherings, which included such writers as Dorothy Parker and James Thurber. For many years it was the "in" place for writers to meet, and it housed visiting actors, playwrights, and other artistic greats, including Helen Hayes, Sinclair Lewis, Maya Angelou, and George S. Kaufman. Built in 1902, the Algonquin is now a historic New York landmark. Even if you're not staying there, it might still be worth a visit.

 **TRAVEL TIP**

The Algonquin is a great place to have a drink. If you're feeling extravagant, order the $10,000 "Martini on the Rock," the "rock" being a diamond from the in-house jeweler! Sit in large wing chairs and munch on salted nuts as waiters in traditional black suits serve you. Then there's Matilda, the hotel cat, entertaining guests as her predecessors have done since 1930.

The hotel is rich with history, and it is also fresh from a $5.5 million restoration designed to return the property to the glory of an earlier period, with furnishings from the turn of the century. The antiques that make up the Algonquin décor were carefully chosen to re-create the ambiance of a bygone era.

Today, the 174-room hotel combines the elegance and charm of the early twentieth century with the functionality of the early twenty-first century. Specialty suites are dedicated to and feature the works of Dorothy Parker, with warm, comfortable furnishings in all guest rooms, plus bathrobes, wireless Internet, movies, and safes as part of the in-room amenities. Suites also have a fully stocked refrigerator.

A small but state-of-the-art twenty-four-hour fitness center might seem out of place, but if you read while on the treadmill, you will at least maintain the literary theme of the hotel. Concierge and laundry service are available, and also on premises is (appropriately) a library on the second floor.

The Oak Room, for dining by day, becomes a cabaret at night from September to early July. The cabaret features dining and entertainment Tuesdays through Saturdays. Dinner begins at 7 P.M., the curtain goes up on first-rate entertainment at 9, and there's a second show at 11:30 P.M. on weekends. There is entertainment and dinner for minimum charge. Reservations are necessary. The Blue Bar serves cocktails and pub food, and the Round Table Room serves breakfast, lunch, dinner, and pre-theater dinner. The Lobby Restaurant is the place for elegant pub and finger food such as burgers, pizza, quesadillas, and the like.

The Algonquin offers a fabulous Family Celebration package that begins with a shuttle ride from the airport and includes sightseeing and attraction admissions with a room. You can also customize the package to your wishes.

Crowne Plaza

▣ 1605 Broadway (between West 48th and West 49th streets)
🚆 West 50th Street station (1 train)
✆ 1-800-243-6969
✆ 212-977-4000
✉ *www.manhattan.crowneplaza.com*

The Crowne Plaza enjoys a marvelous location—just north of the busy Times Square area, south of Central Park, and within a short walk of the theater district, Rockefeller Center, St. Patrick's Cathedral, and Fifth Avenue shopping. This is a forty-six-story, upscale, 770-room hotel. The views from the higher floors are terrific.

Crowne Plaza sports a friendly atmosphere and provides laundry service, a concierge, and on-site valet parking. Rooms feature video games, high-speed Internet access, CD player, coffee/tea maker, in-room pay-per-view movies, makeup mirrors, ironing boards, and in-room safes. The room charge covers up to four people of any age.

The on-site health club, run by New York Sports Clubs, is huge—nearly 30,000 square feet—and is run by fitness managers with trainers on hand. The health club has one of the city's largest hotel indoor swimming pools. The pool and wide array of fitness equipment are first class, and the hotel offers a wide variety of classes for guests who don't want to miss a workout while on vacation.

For dining, start the day with a light repast at the Lobby Bar Starbucks Station or a full breakfast at the signature Samplings Restaurant. Samplings serves breakfast, lunch, dinner, and pre- and post-theater meals. Both Samplings and the Lobby Bar double as lounges at night. In-room dining is available seven days a week.

Doubletree Guest Suites

⊡ 1568 Broadway (between 46th and 47th streets)

🚆 West 50th Street station (1 train), West 49th Street station (N, R, or W train)

✆ 1-800-325-9033

✆ 212-719-1600

✉ http://doubletree.hilton.com

"Suites" is the operative word here, with forty-five floors featuring some 460 suites. Like everything else in New York, the Doubletree offers you a wide range of choices, including king and double/double suites, executive conference suites, handicap suites, nonsmoking suites, and two presidential suites. Each suite includes private bedrooms and separate living rooms, plus sofa beds, wet bars, microwaves, refrigerators, cable television, movies, video games, wireless Internet, and more space than many New York City apartments. They all have numerous safety features and good décor. The hotel features a state-of-the-art fitness center, valet service, a gift shop, and laundry.

The Doubletree towers high above the heart of Times Square, with a glitzy, modern look and an off-the-street lobby (common in Times Square hotels) that affords privacy and safety. It is a very child-friendly hotel, and the kids love the freshly baked chocolate chip cookies they get at check-in. The suites, at essentially the same rates as comparable guest rooms in the area, provide much-needed space for family traveling.

☂ RAINY DAY FUN

> Doubletree Guest Suites offers several family-oriented packages that include visits to such favorites as American Girl Place and Build-A-Bear Workshop. They have also had shopping and museum deals as well. A call or Web visit will yield current specials.

The Center Stage Café, despite its name, is a full-service restaurant offering American cuisine from 6:30 A.M. to 11 P.M. in a Broadway theater ambiance. There is a separate children's menu. The Cabaret Lounge provides piano music in a lavish show biz setting while you sip cocktails.

Hilton New York and Towers

🏢 1335 Avenue of the Americas (between 53rd and 54th streets)

🚇 5th Avenue-53rd Street station (E or V train)

📞 1-800-HILTONS (445-8667)

📞 212-586-7000

✍ *www.newyork.hilton.com*

It's hard to go wrong with a Hilton property. This massive hotel, located in the heart of Manhattan, is a city unto itself. The Hilton provides all sorts of conveniences, including a state-of-the-art fitness center, concierge service, foreign currency exchange, self-service check-in and check-out, and ATMs.

Elevators with CNN newscasts keep you abreast of what's going on in the world during your ride. There are numerous shops located in this massive structure, including boutiques, a gift shop, a drugstore, a ticket booth, and a beauty salon/barber shop. An eight-level underground parking garage has twenty-four-hour valet parking.

Guest rooms are clean and roomy and sport a modern décor. Refreshment centers, pay movies, video games, and high-speed

Internet are among the expected amenities. The Hilton also has specially designed wheelchair-accessible rooms.

RAINY DAY FUN

Stay at the Hilton and your kids can borrow toys to play with. The 53rd Street hotel has a Vacation Station—a collection of toys for borrowing, as well as a folder of activities for kids to do around the city. The Vacation Station is open during the summer months.

The Towers is a special private sector from the thirty-fourth through forty-fourth floors, featuring a lounge for complimentary breakfast, afternoon tea, hors d'oeuvres, and more. There are various other amenities for Towers guests.

The Hilton has long been a favorite of visitors to the city because of its first-rate service, easy accessibility, and wide range of amenities. The hotels draw families in with their "children under 18 stay free" policy (providing they share a room with their parents or grandparents).

Restaurants include Etrusca, serving Tuscan cuisine in an elegant yet casual atmosphere (business attire required), and New York Marketplace, an indoor "sidewalk café" reflecting New York's cultural diversity, ideal for a family breakfast, lunch, or dinner. For drinks, the Bridges Bar and the Lobby Lounge are pleasant for drinks, wine, coffee, tea, and pastries.

Marriott Marquis

- ⌨ 1535 Broadway (between 45th and 46th streets)
- 🚇 Times Square-West 42nd Street station (1, 2, 3, 7, N, Q, R, S, or W train)
- 📞 1-800-843-4898
- 📞 212-398-1900
- ✉ *www.marriott.com/property/propertypage/NYCMQ*

In the heart of the theater district, and housing a Broadway theater within, the fifty-story Marriott Marquis is one of the premier hotels in the Times Square area. The modern skyscraper is accentuated by a thirty-seven-story open atrium with glass-enclosed elevators that provide a spectacular ride.

The 1,900 rooms are modern and spacious, with in-room safes, coffee/tea makers, videos, bathrobes, fax machines (in some), wired Internet access (wireless in public areas), and other conveniences. The hotel is a small city unto itself, with shops, six restaurants and three lounges, a beauty salon, and a health club. Amenities include laundry service, concierge, parking (limited and for a fee), babysitting, airport service, and a tour and transportation desk. The entire hotel is nonsmoking.

Marriotts are usually well run, and this big, bold, bright Broadway hotel is no exception. The energy and excitement of the theater district is prevalent throughout, but with the main lobby several floors above the street, there's also a feeling of being secure and away from the hustle and bustle of the busy area.

If the city doesn't have enough to offer, the hotel has more than its share of places to visit and to stop by for a bite to eat. The View is New York's only revolving rooftop restaurant, and the Atrium Lounge has a spectacular thirty-seven-story ceiling. Other places to dine include Encore, Katen Sushi Bar, the Broadway Lounge, and a Starbucks. While you browse the premises, you might want to pick up a map to avoid getting lost!

Sheraton New York Hotel and Towers
🖃 811 7th Avenue (between 52nd and 53rd streets)
🚇 7th Avenue station (B, D, or E train)
✆ 1-800-223-6550
✆ 212-581-1000
✉ *www.sheraton.com*

Sheraton Manhattan

790 7th Avenue (between 51st and 52nd Streets)

7th Avenue station (B, D, or E train)

1-800-223-6550

212-581-3300

www.sheraton.com

Sheraton is another highly trusted, top name in the hotel business, and these two impressive establishments are no exception. The Sheraton New York is a 1,750-room skyscraper; the 665-room Sheraton Manhattan, across the street, is much smaller by comparison. Both hotels are a few blocks north of the theater district, Times Square, Radio City Music Hall, and Rockefeller Center and just south of Carnegie Hall and Central Park. Guests of the Sheraton New York Hotel and Towers can cross the street and use the Sheraton Manhattan's fifty-foot swimming pool. In return, Sheraton Manhattan guests can make the reverse trip to benefit from the Sheraton New York's 4,000-square-foot fitness center and health club. The hotel also offers a theater desk.

In-room amenities at the Sheraton New York include coffeemakers with complimentary coffee, video games and movies, bathrobes, iron and board, and high-speed Internet. The Sheraton Towers houses the Club Level Rooms from floors forty-four to fifty, with a lounge on the forty-fourth floor.

Restaurants in the Sheraton Towers include Avenue Restaurant, a large glass-enclosed café that seats 180 people on various levels for breakfast, lunch, and dinner. Hudson Bar is home to thirty large-screen monitors, all featuring sporting events, and serves as an "information café" with data port outlets. Breakfast and lunch from Starbucks is available, as well as dinner in the bar. Breakfast and lunch is also available in the Lobby Restaurant where you are surrounded by leather, wood, and velvet. Drinks and conviviality are to be had in the clublike Library Bar. Dining at the Sheraton Manhattan is at Russo's Steak and Pasta Restaurant, featuring steaks, seafood, and pasta. It is open for breakfast and dinner only.

The Time Hotel

🖳 224 West 49th Street (between 8th Avenue and Broadway)

🚃 West 50th Street station (C or E train)

📞 212-246-5252

📧 www.thetimeny.com

One of the city's new breed of hip, modern hotels, the Time is a luxury boutique hotel in the middle of Times Square, featuring 164 rooms and twenty-eight suites.

Rooms are sleek and modern, decorated in bold colors. You'll find curtains in place of closet doors, canvas covers for the television set, and essays on the choice of color for the room—all part of this unique and somewhat eclectic Manhattan experience.

The hotel provides large-hotel amenities in a smaller setting. Basic amenities include a coffee/tea maker, an in-room safe, high-speed Internet access, a Bose Wave radio, a VCR with video loan service, an iron and board, and complimentary bathrobes. The Time also offers a concierge, fitness center, foreign currency exchange, laundry and dry-cleaning service, valet service, express checkout, and a second-floor lounge. While the designer rooms and fragrances may not be for everyone (check out the Web site for a preview), the hotel is excitingly different and modern, and its smaller size, compared to its Times Square counterparts, can be comforting.

The Oceo restaurant is, like the hotel, eclectic, with an American menu treated with international flair. The Time Lounge on the second floor offers a tapas menu, plus cocktails and specialty drinks.

Midtown East

Doubletree Metropolitan

🖳 569 Lexington Avenue (at East 51st Street)

🚃 East 51st Street (E, V, or 6 train)

📞 1-800-836-6471

📞 212-752-7000

📧 www.dtnewyork.com

Built in 1961 as the Summit Hotel and designed by the same architect as Miami's famed Fontainebleau, this landmark modernist hotel has just been restored and renovated at a cost of $35 million by its new owners, the Hilton company. The exterior, with hints of *The Jetsons* design, reflects the optimism of the 1960s. The interior has been brought up to the twenty-first century with clean, modern lines with the look of contemporary Scandinavian design. While the views aren't spectacular, the stylish east side/midtown area offers an array of shopping and restaurants. It's also convenient to all transportation.

Rooms are comfortable, carrying over the clean, simple lines of the lobby. They feature slate bathrooms, high-speed Internet connection, flat-screen TV, and in-room safes large enough for a laptop. Other amenities include a modern fitness center, a concierge for special requests, self-serve check-in, and reasonable parking (for Manhattan) at $30 a day (no in-and-out privileges). On the premises you'll find a hair salon, nail salon, and a W. H. Smith for gifts and worldwide newspapers and magazines.

 TRAVEL TIP

Remember that when traveling with children you can arrange a lot of what you'll need ahead of time, such as a crib in your room. You can also check to see if the hotel has in-room video games or if you'll need to bring your own.

The Met Grill is a popular location for American and Continental cuisine in a warm, casually elegant environment. It is open seven days a week from 6:30 A.M. to 10 P.M. The newly designed Met Lounge offers a comfortable and intimate setting for cocktails or snacks, complete with a multitude of television screens with news, sports, and videos. The hotel is kid friendly, even to the point of giving all guests checking in one of their huge chocolate chip cookies (guaranteed to have at least twenty chips each!).

Grand Hyatt New York

▣ 109 East 42nd Street (between Lexington and Park avenues, adjacent to Grand Central Terminal)

🚇 Grand Central Terminal-East 42nd Street station (4, 5, or 6 train)

☎ 1-800-233-1234

☎ 1-800-243-2546 (for instant check-in)

☎ 212-883-1234

✍ *www.grandnewyork.hyatt.com*

With more than 1,300 rooms, the Grand Hyatt is indeed grand! After all, Donald Trump built it. The hotel opened in 1980 and was later refurbished with a $100 million face-lift. It is a short walk from Grand Central Terminal, Broadway theaters, the United Nations, the finest shopping on Fifth Avenue, and other attractions. Sports fans may enjoy catching a glimpse of the ballplayers who stay at the hotel when the visiting teams are in town.

With the Hyatt Family Plan, you can get a guaranteed connecting room at a significant discount, but you must book with the hotel directly at least seventy-two hours prior to check-in, there must be at least one kid under twelve, and it doesn't work if you have certain special package deals already.

The Hyatt's rooms, including sixty-three suites, are well lit, sleek, and comfortable, with in-room movies on flat-screen TVs and other amenities. A twenty-four-hour fitness center, concierge, laundry service, and outdoor garden are all part of the Grand Hyatt, which features a sprawling plant-filled atrium lobby, complete with a cascading waterfall. It's quite impressive, but that's the typical Trump style.

Three restaurants include the glass-enclosed Manhattan Sky Restaurant, which has a great menu for families—breakfast buffet, weekend brunch, and Sweet Sensations dessert samplers—and overlooks Forty-second Street; the Commodore Grill, which serves American Continental cuisine and will serve small plates for the kids or for sharing; and the Grand Coffee Bar for coffees, teas, freshly baked goods, sandwiches, fruits, and continental breakfasts.

Marriott East Side

535 Lexington Avenue (between 49th and 50th streets)

East 51st Street station (E, V, or 6 train)

1-800-242-8684

212-755-4000

www.marriott.com/property/propertypage/NYCEA

This hotel property is a landmark Marriott hotel. Its east side location is ideal for those interested in visiting Rockefeller Center, the United Nations, and many other popular city locations. The grand lobby, complete with columns and a lavish interior, welcomes you to this fashionable—but not ostentatious—hotel.

Some 629 guest rooms and seventeen suites offer a range of amenities, including in-room movies, as part of their well-appointed, fashionable accommodations. It is family friendly, entirely nonsmoking, and can provide babysitting if needed. Special offers are available throughout the year, including family packages. The Shelton Grille features continental dining throughout the day, and the lobby lounge provides an intimate setting for cocktails and conversation.

≡FAST FACT

Once upon a time, the Marriott East Side was the Shelton Towers (built in 1924). Over the years it has been a stomping ground for many performers, including Harry Houdini, who performed escape tricks from the pool. Bandleader Xavier Cugat, Peggy Lee, and Eddie Fisher also performed there. Shelton Towers was also the first major New York City hotel to employ female bellhops.

Downtown and Lower Manhattan

There are some truly lovely small hotels below Thirty-fourth Street in lower Manhattan. Many of them have been catering to sophisticated travelers for generations.

Chelsea Savoy Hotel
🖃 204 West 23rd Street (at 7th Avenue)
🚇 West 23rd Street station (1 train)
📞 212-929-9353
✉ www.chelseasavoy.com

This is a small and funky hotel in New York's artsy district. Its ninety rooms are comfortably furnished and include wireless Internet, continental breakfast, and cable television. Several parking lots are close by.

The Millennium Hilton
🖃 55 Church Street (between Dey and Fulton Streets)
🚇 Chambers Street station (1, 2, or 3 train); Franklin Street station (1 train)
📞 1-800-HILTONS (445-5667)
📞 212-693-2001
✉ www.hilton.com

Reopened after sustaining damage in the September 11 terrorist attack, this sleek modern marvel rises fifty-eight stories into the New York sky. The 569-room Millennium has a lot to offer, including king-sized beds in most of the guest rooms, forty-two-inch plasma televisions, video games, movies, iron and board, high-speed Internet access, in-room safes, minibars, and makeup mirrors. Guest rooms are large and modern and offer a warm residential ambiance.

The spacious lobby is filled with the sounds of piano music. There is a fitness center and a glass-enclosed heated pool. A concierge, laundry service, and babysitting service are also among the various amenities offered at the Millennium, a popular hotel with both business and leisure travelers.

Church & Day Restaurant is on the third floor and offers authentic American regional cuisine for breakfast, lunch, and dinner. There is twenty-four-hour room service and special children's and diet menus. Parking is available for a fee but is quite limited. There are various specials throughout the year that make this luxury hotel very affordable.

New York Marriott Financial Center

⊞ 85 West Street (between Carlisle and Albany streets)

🚊 Rector Street station (R or W train)

📞 1-800-242-8685

📞 212-385-4900

✎ www.nymarriottfinancialcenter.com

There are two Marriotts in lower Manhattan. The Financial Center property houses 497 modern guest rooms and suites complete with pay movies, minibars, and standard in-room fare. The hotel is located a short walk from Wall Street and the ferries to Staten Island, Ellis Island, and the Statue of Liberty. Amenities include an indoor pool, exercise room, saunas, concierge, business center, and gift shop.

≡FAST FACT

Marriott has banned smoking in all of its 2,300 hotels in the United States and Canada. This includes all guest rooms, restaurants, lounges, meeting rooms, public spaces, and employee working areas. Smokers will be accommodated in specially designated areas outside the building. Guests who violate the ban will be charged a fee to cover the cost of restoring the room.

Since this is primarily a business hotel, you may find good deals on weekends and during the summer months when there are fewer business travelers. Marriott also runs family package specials throughout the year in all its hotels, so check on potential promotions.

The lower Manhattan location puts you out of the fast pace of midtown, which may be a plus or a minus depending on what you are looking for and what sights you are interested in seeing. Though the hotel is close to the numerous downtown sights, there is less nightlife, and the museums of Fifth Avenue are a bit of a walk. But with New York's excellent public transport and convenience of street-flagged taxis, it's a matter of choice. On-site valet parking is $40 a day.

For the unusual in dining (or lunching), even for New York, Roy's New York features Chef Roy Yamaguchi's Hawaiian fusion cuisine. Breakfast here is a full American buffet. For dinner only, 85 West is a lovely cocktail lounge with a surprisingly satisfying and eclectic menu for light snacking to serious dining. From pizzas and burgers to shrimp and steak to low-carb dishes, there's something for everyone. There's live entertainment every Wednesday and Thursday evenings from 7 P.M. to 10 P.M. Finally, there is a Starbucks Coffee House.

Park South

⊡ 124 East 28th Street at Park Avenue

🚃 East 28th Street station (6 train)

✆ 1-800-315-4642

✆ 212-448-0888

✍ *www.parksouthhotel.com*

This boutique hotel is housed in a restored historic 1906 building. It has 141 rooms, all newly redecorated. There is a long list of services and amenities, including a complimentary continental breakfast, concierge, fitness room, cable TV, DVD player and an extensive DVD library, bathrobes, and an in-room safe. Several very interesting and creative packages are available.

Dinner is at the Black Duck, a much-praised restaurant serving an eclectic, nonfrightening menu that will have you wondering what to order first. It is very kid friendly and will make half-portions on request. Along with the grilled seafood and meats, it has pasta and burgers. Every Sunday night it shows movies, and there is live entertainment Friday and Saturday evenings.

Washington Square Hotel

⊡ 103 Waverly Place (at MacDougal Street)

🚃 West 4th Street-Washington Square station (A, B, C, D, E, F, or V train)

✆ 1-800-222-0418

✆ 212-777-9515

✍ *www.washingtonsquarehotel.com*

Prospective New York University students and parents visiting NYU students have stayed here for generations. Nestled across from Washington Square Park, this small 165-room hotel evokes Paris of the 1930s, yet it includes all the modern amenities one has come to expect. Guests may use the free Wi-Fi service while sipping their afternoon tea. Other amenities include a continental breakfast and a gym.

Rooms are appointed with deluxe furnishings, in-room data ports, and cable television. North Square Restaurant is a beautiful little place serving imaginative meals for breakfast, lunch, dinner, weekend brunch, and afternoon tea in the Deco Room. There's also a jazz brunch every Sunday. As if that weren't enough, the famous Blue Note jazz club is just down the street.

Upper Manhattan

If you want a little quiet, hotels along the Upper East Side or Upper West Side will shield you from much of the hustle and bustle of the downtown streets while still putting you close to the action.

Hotel Bentley
⌨ 500 East 62nd Street (between 1st and York avenues)
🚆 Lexington Avenue-East 59th Street station (N, R or W train) or East 59th Street station (4, 5, or 6 train)
✆ 1-800-555-7555
✆ 212-644-6000
✉ *http://hotelbentleynewyork.com*

Until 1998, this was a modern twenty-one-story office building. The brilliant conversion left plenty of glass to allow spectacular panoramic views of the East River and New York skyline. A modern facility, the Bentley offers 197 spacious, well-designed, and comfortable rooms and suites. Amenities include a complimentary twenty-four-hour cappuccino bar, concierge, and on-site parking for a modest $25 a day. The location is easily accessible to LaGuardia Airport, just off the FDR Drive, and it's a short way from the United Nations and Central Park.

Away from other hotels, the Bentley provides an opportunity to be part of the residential Upper East Side of Manhattan, with numerous restaurants and plenty of shopping. If you don't want to stay in the middle of it all or you've been to the heart of the city before, this is a nice change of locale.

Excelsior

⌨ 45 West 81st Street (between Central Park West and Columbus Avenue)

🚇 West 81st Street-Museum of Natural History station (B or C train)

☎ 1-800-368-4575

☎ 212-362-9200

🖉 www.excelsiorhotelny.com

The Upper West Side, a trendy neighborhood with plenty of shopping and old New York charm, is also home to the Excelsior, a landmark hotel rich with atmosphere yet complete with modern amenities.

Overlooking the American Museum of Natural History and Rose Center for Earth and Space (a spectacular view at night), the Excelsior has one- and two-bedroom suites decorated in a French motif, with some of the recently refurbished 116 rooms and eighty suites sporting balconies and in-room PCs. The hotel features wireless Internet access, a concierge, a fitness room, entertainment lounge, library, and continental breakfast buffet on the second floor.

This is a hotel for those who want a small European hideaway in Manhattan. The location just north of all the action allows guests to enjoy quiet nights, afternoon strolls, or Central Park picnics.

The Lucerne

⌨ 201 West 79th Street (between Broadway and Amsterdam Avenue)

🚇 West 79th Street station (1 train)

☎ 1-800-492-8122

☎ 212-875-1000

🖉 www.thelucernehotel.com

A treasured landmark, the recently restored Lucerne was originally built in 1904. It is nestled among the shops and cafés on the Upper West Side and is a short walk from Central Park, the American Museum of Natural History, and Lincoln Center. Since you're away from the bustle of midtown, and the hotel is relatively small, service is more personalized.

Its 250 large rooms and suites feature marble and granite bathrooms, wireless Internet, Nintendo, and other standard amenities; the hotel offers valet parking, a concierge and tour desk, fitness center, and twenty-four-hour room service. It is a smoke-free hotel.

The adjacent restaurant is the Nice Matin, which offers a relaxed French menu softened by Italian influences. In other words, its menus for breakfast, lunch, dinner, and Sunday brunch are huge and contain everything to satisfy any taste, even sandwiches for the kids.

Milburn

▣ 242 West 76th Street (at West End Avenue)

▣ West 79th Street station (1 train)

✆ 1-800-833-9622

✆ 212-362-1006

✑ *www.milburnhotel.com*

This Upper West Side hotel is particularly geared to families. Each room has a kitchenette with a microwave and coffeemaker. The one-bedroom suites have a separate living room with a sofa bed for the kids with their own TVs and VCRs. The hotel also provides Playstations, a library of children's books, and a selection of family movies. No wonder it's a favorite for visiting parents. It's also close to Zabar's, Central Park, and the American Museum of Natural History/Rose Center for Earth and Space. There are fifty cozy and bright rooms. There is no restaurant on the premises, but the fabulous eateries of the Upper West Side are within a few minutes walk.

CHAPTER 20

Luxury Hotels

THE SKY'S THE limit when it comes to hotel rooms in New York City. There is a $30,000-a-night suite at the Four Seasons, and the apartment suites at the Waldorf Towers are swanky enough to be home to the Hilton sisters. But they are also available to the average family, and they're even surprisingly affordable once you decide to spend a little extra (finding deals on the Internet helps, too). There's nothing like a childhood memory of a weekend at the Plaza or the Pierre, so let your imagination go!

Midtown Listings

Some of the most luxurious hotels in the city line the streets along Central Park. The view and the dining are always excellent.

Jumeirah Essex House

⌨ 160 Central Park South (between 6th and 7th avenues)

🚇 West 59th Street-Columbus Circle station (A, B, C, D, or 1 train)

📞 1-888-645-5697

📞 212-247-0300

✎ www.jumeirahessexhouse.com

A historic landmark along Central Park, the Essex House has undergone some changes since being acquired by the Dubai-based Jumeirah chain. At the time of this writing, the hotel is finishing a $70 million refurbishment intended to completely update the lobby, corridors, and the 515 rooms and suites. The redesigned hotel will embody a twenty-first century interpretation of the hotel's art deco roots. There is a business center and a fully equipped spa and fitness center with an in-house trainer. Three meals daily are served in the elegant Lobby Lounge and The Restaurant at Jumeirah Essex House. Room service is to 11 P.M. only.

≡FAST FACT

The hotels along Central Park, such as the Pierre, the Plaza, the Ritz-Carleton, and the Essex House on Central Park South, are some of the city's most luxurious and historical. But such legendary edifices as the Mayflower and Stanhope have fallen to the condo monster.

Fitzpatrick Grand Central Hotel
⌗ 141 East 44th Street (between Lexington and 3rd avenues)
🚊 Grand Central-East 42nd Street station (S, 4, 5, 6, or 7 train)
📞 1-800-367-7701
📞 212-351-6800
✎ www.fitzpatrickhotels.com/grandcentral

This is the larger of the two Manhattan east side hotels run by the Irish-based Fitzpatrick Hotel Group, with 155 rooms. Rooms feature mini fridges, Wi-Fi, twenty-four-hour room service, and bathrobes, along with more than a bit o' Dublin in look and feel.

The Grand Central Fitzpatrick is home to the Wheeltapper, a quaint Old World Irish pub with a railroad theme the whole family will love (wheeltappers were the old railroad men who tested wheels for damage). The evocative pub offers a full menu with quality pub grub, an all-day Irish breakfast, and a children's menu.

Fitzpatrick Manhattan Hotel

⌖ 687 Lexington Avenue (between East 56th and East 57th streets)

🚇 East 59th Street station (N, R, W, 4, 5, or 6 train)

☏ 1-800-367-7701

☏ 212-355-0100

✉ *www.fitzpatrickhotels.com/manhattan*

A relaxing oasis just two blocks from Bloomingdale's department store and not far from Central Park and Rockefeller Center, the second of the two Fitzpatrick hotels is a small inn in the heart of Manhattan. It consists of fifty-two one-bedroom suites and forty guest rooms.

Rooms are tastefully furnished with a distinct Irish feel and many amenities that include twenty-four-hour room service, iron and board, trouser press, coffeemaker with complimentary tea and coffee, laundry service, bathrobes, free access to a nearby health club, an in-room bicycle, and concierge service. Fitzers Restaurant is a spacious and comfortable retreat, popular with locals, serving Irish delights as well as Continental and New American cuisine. A convivial Irish pub adjoins but is separate from the restaurant. There are weekend rates and specials for children.

Four Seasons Hotel

⌖ 57 East 57th Street (between Park and Madison avenues)

🚇 5th Avenue-59th Street station (N, R, or W train)

☏ 212-758-5700

✉ *www.fourseasons.com/newyorkfs*

This is an exceptionally kid-friendly hotel. Kids get their own age-appropriate welcoming gift, bathrobe, and in-room amusements. Teens have their own full-time concierge during nonschool holidays. Baby amenities, equipment, and room childproofing items are provided. Children under eighteen stay free in parents' rooms, and they have their own menus in the restaurant and for room service. The hotel will also help plan and arrange your daily family activities.

The facility is a stopper in its own right. Internationally renowned architect I. M. Pei designed the hotel's spire, and the interior Grand Foyer is chock full of marble and onyx. The soundproofed rooms are designed in a clean, modern style and feature ten-foot ceilings, refrigerated private bar, a personal safe, high-speed Internet access, twice-daily housekeeping, bathrobes, and marble bathrooms. Families can request connecting rooms and nonsmoking floors.

There's a health club and spa on the premises, and the elegant L'Atelier de Joël Robuchon restaurant serves lunch and dinner. Parking is available for a fee, and some pets are welcome.

Hotel Mela

⌨ 120 West 44th Street (between 6th Avenue and Broadway)
🚇 West 42nd Street-Bryant Park station (B, D, F, or V train)
✆ 212-710-7000
✎ *www.hotelmela.com*

A new addition to the Times Square/theater district, the Mela strives for a modern and homey sophistication. There are 230 rooms and suites with amenities such as free in-room wireless Internet access, bathrobes, twenty-six-inch flat-screen TVs, CD/MP3 alarm clocks, and H2O products in the bathroom. There is also an in-house fitness center. Dining is at the Saju; its French-Asian fusion cuisine is a new star on Broadway.

Millennium U.N. Plaza

⌨ One United Nations Plaza (at 44th Street and 1st Avenue)
🚇 Grand Central-East 42nd Street station (S, 4, 5, 6, or 7 train)
✆ 1-800-222-8888
✆ 212-758-1234
✎ *www.millenniumhotels.com*

The U.N. Plaza, directly across from the United Nations, offers quiet elegance for an affordable price. The hotel offers standard and superior rooms and junior, full, and two-bedroom suites, all with a serene, contemporary décor. Rooms include minibars, in-room movies, and high-speed Internet. The hotel offers valet parking, a multilingual concierge staff, a heated indoor pool, fitness center, massage and sauna, indoor tennis courts, and covered parking.

Dining is at the Ambassador Grille, a casually elegant and highly acclaimed eatery with an international selection, and the Ambassador Lounge, which serves light snacks and cocktails.

The hotel can arrange for babysitting, and the restaurant has a children's menu. Children under seventeen can stay free if they share a room with their parents.

New York Palace

⌖ 455 Madison Avenue (between East 50th and East 51st streets)

🚆 East 51st Street station (6 train)

☎ 1-800-697-2522

☎ 212-888-7000

✑ www.newyorkpalace.com

Set in a refurbished 1882 landmark estate, the 900-room hotel is now a luxurious facility with lavish décor, spacious first-class accommodations, and easy access to everything midtown has to offer.

Hotel amenities are generous and increase with the class of room. All guests have use of the concierge and twenty-four-hour laundry service plus a 7,000 square-foot first-class health club complete with television monitors and headphones at each treadmill. A separate Towers section has 175 guest rooms and suites with a separate check-in, butler service, and a host of other niceties, including personalized business cards and stationery during your stay. If all this isn't enough, high atop the Tower sit the Triplex suites—three-floor accommodations with their own private elevator, marble floors, fully equipped kitchen, master bedroom, a solarium, and private outdoor terrace for sunbathing.

The Palace is home to Gilt, a new modern European restaurant and bar, and Istana, an American brasserie serving breakfast, lunch, dinner, and Sunday brunch.

Omni Berkshire Place Hotel

🖭 21 East 52nd Street (between 5th and Madison avenues)

🚇 5th Avenue-53rd Street station (E or V train)

📞 1-800-843-664

📞 212-753-5800

🖎 www.omnihotels.com

This is where NBC has sent its guests since the first showings of *Saturday Night Live* more than thirty years ago. The flagship hotel of the Omni hotel chain in New York is an award-winning, family-friendly hotel. There's an extensive kids program that starts with a welcoming gift as a prelude to a list of amenities just for them, and another group for parents that includes a safety/first-aid kit, a list of emergency numbers, and help in planning activities. The Omni even has its own Web site for kids at *www.omnikidsrule.com*. Children twelve and under stay free.

The rooms are large and well-appointed with all the technology you'd expect these days. There's a fully equipped health club and spa. Dining is at the unusual Fireside restaurant, which serves an innovative cocktail cuisine. The Omni offers many special package deals throughout the year.

The Plaza

🖭 59th Street and 5th Avenue

🚇 59th Street-Columbus Circle station (A, B, C, D, or 1 train)

📞 212-759-3000

🖎 www.fairmont.com

The grand old lady of Grand Army Plaza, at the entrance to Central Park, has just completed a two-year, $400 million renovation that has turned its 692 rooms and 112 suites (where even the smallest room had fourteen-foot ceilings and chandeliers) into 282 guestrooms and 152 time-share condominiums. The hotel fuses modern convenience with a nod to the Plaza's glorious past. Under the watchful eye of the Landmark Preservations Commission, the legendary Palm Court, the Oak Room and Oak Bar, and the Terrace Room were accurately restored. Don't miss the 1,200-square-foot stained-glass ceiling on the Palm, which was re-created after the original was lost in the 1940s.

TRAVEL TIP

After a tumultuous decade of changing owners (one was Donald Trump), the Plaza Hotel has been brought into the twenty-first century as a smaller but very luxurious hotel with its historic public rooms restored. Every child has read the children's classic *Eloise,* and every kid who has the time should go for the afternoon tea in the spectacularly restored Palm Court.

St. Regis Hotel
2 East 55th Street (between 5th and Madison avenues)
5th Avenue-53rd Street station (E or V line)
1-800-759-7550
212-753-4500
www.stregis.com

Declared a New York City landmark in 1988, the St. Regis offers guests an unparalleled level of comfort and luxury. Originally opened in 1904 and restored with a $100 million face-lift, this is the lap of luxury. All guests even have access to English-style butlers available around the clock.

There is a wide assortment of rooms and suites. Standard to all are minibars, safes, fax machines, concierge, laundry service, beauty salon, library, health club, babysitting service, and parking. Designer stores, including Bottega, Veneta, Pucci, and DeBeers, are located in the building.

Restaurants include the King Cole Bar and Lounge, featuring Maxfield Parrish's art deco mural masterpiece, *Old King Cole,* and the Astor Court, an elegant tea lounge and bistro.

Sherry-Netherland Hotel

⌨ 781 5th Avenue, at 59th Street

🚇 5th Avenue-59th Street station (N, R, or W train)

☎ 1-877-743-7710

☎ 212-355-2800

✐ www.sherrynetherland.com

The Sherry has 150 guest rooms and suites. A long list of deluxe amenities includes complimentary continental breakfast in the restaurant, soft drinks, shoeshines, fresh flowers, fitness center, and Belgian chocolates. The resident restaurant, Harry Cipriani's, has recently reopened after renovations.

The Waldorf-Astoria

⌨ 301 Park Avenue (between East 49th and East 50th streets)

🚇 East 51st Street station (6 train)

☎ 1-800-WALDORF (925-3673)

☎ 212-355-3000

✐ www.waldorf.com

Originally opened in 1893 on Thirty-third Street, the Waldorf you see today has been at its current location since October 1931. Over the years, the classic hotel has undergone some $400 million in renovations to maintain its art deco look and New York City landmark status.

The Waldorf has seen its share of dignitaries, including numerous American presidents, Jordan's King Hussein, Charles de Gaulle, and Queen Elizabeth II among others. The hotel was even the residence of three five-star generals: Douglas MacArthur, Dwight Eisenhower, and Omar Bradley. It was for many years the site where Guy Lombardo and his orchestra ushered in the new year. The Empire Room was home to great entertainment, including Frank Sinatra on a number of occasions.

Today the Waldorf has some 1,245 guest rooms, including 197 suites, each designed in a slightly different manner. The rooms have luxuries ranging from marble bathrooms to high-speed Internet (for a fee; free wireless in the lobbies and restaurants).

 JUST FOR PARENTS

You can prolong your stay at the Waldorf even when you get home. A wide variety of Waldorf merchandise can be purchased online or from a paper catalog. At *www.distinctlywaldorf.com,* you can order one of those waffle-weave bathrobes you wore in the room or the bedding you slept on. Eat in style with the Waldorf cookbook while you cook in its chef's jacket and hat (in kid sizes too), and sip tea from a duplicate tea service. There are even goodies for your pet.

The hotel also features two lobbies, one of which (on the Park Avenue side) has a 148,000-piece mosaic called *Wheel of Life.* A concierge is available, plus an international concierge service desk providing assistance in more than sixty languages. There is a theater desk, a tour desk, a transportation desk, and a Plus One fitness center with six personal trainers and full-time massage therapists, as well as a Plus One Spa (a fee is charged unless you are Hilton HHonors Silver and above or a Towers guest). When you're finished with your thirty-minute personal training session, you can treat yourself to a shopping spree at one of several posh, luxurious boutiques that are also part of the Waldorf. A gift shop and florist are also on the premises.

A highlight of the Waldorf is the dining; the restaurants are the pride of this classic hotel. The legendary Peacock Alley reopened after a four-year hiatus and a $5.5 million reconstruction as an upscale venue for breakfast, lunch, pre-theater, dinner, and sumptuous Sunday brunch. The popular Bull and Bear is known for steaks and fine seafood. You can sit at the mahogany bar and enjoy a before-dinner cocktail while watching the stock quotes pass by on an electric ticker.

Oscar's is an American brasserie serving classic American dishes in a relaxed setting; it offers an incredible buffet lunch that New Yorkers consider one of the best buys in the city. The restaurant has a children's menu and a Waldorf coloring book. For elegance, you can't beat the Afternoon Tea at the Cocktail Terrace overlooking the lobby. Inagiku is a Japanese restaurant serving a variety of classic and contemporary dishes. There is also a lounge, the Cocktail Terrace, overlooking the art deco Park Avenue lobby, featuring a Saturday tea to the strains of Cole Porter piano music from 4 to 7 P.M. The hotel conducts a Children's Tea every Saturday from 2:30 P.M. to 4:30 P.M.

The Waldorf is not only an elegant place to stay but also a sight to visit on your trip. With that in mind, the hotel offers a one-and-a-half-hour guided tour on Saturdays for $25.

Downtown and Lower Manhattan

During the weekend, lower Manhattan clears out, so it's actually a great location for both families and couples.

Soho Grand Hotel

⌧ 310 West Broadway (between Canal and Grand streets)

🚃 Canal Street station (J, N, Q, or R train)

✆ 1-800-965-3000

✆ 212-228-1500

✉ *www.sohogrand.com*

Elegant, upscale, yet not insanely so, the Soho Grand Hotel is unusually kid and pet friendly. In fact, if you are lonely for your pet, the hotel will loan you a goldfish for your room. This zest for life befits its location in the heart of the trendy neighborhood of SoHo, surrounded by Greenwich Village, Chinatown, TriBeCa, and Wall Street.

The eighteen stories, housing 365 guest rooms, sit atop a large lavish lobby with oversized sofas, tropical palm trees, pillars, lanterns, and draperies surrounding sixteen-foot-high windows. Rooms are decorated in soft, natural tones and are equipped with iPods (loaners available), Bose sound docks, Power Books, minibars with healthy foods along with the fun stuff, in-room safes, and marvelous views of the city through eight-foot windows. The hotel also has valet parking, a twenty-four-hour health club, and a special Guest Satisfaction Hotline, which essentially means good concierge service. The Gallery Restaurant, serving American fare, is in the lobby, along with the Grand Bar and Lounge.

≡ FAST FACT

Far from being intimidating, many of the upscale luxury hotels in New York go out of their way to attract families and make them feel comfortable. Some of the biggest names—the Four Seasons, the Pierre, Soho Grand, the Regency, and Omni Berkshire—have extensive amenities and programs for families with infants through teenagers.

W New York—Union Square

▢ 201 Park Avenue South (between East 17th and East 18th streets)

🚆 East 14th Street-Union Square station (L, N, Q, R, W, 4, 5, or 6 train)

✆ 212-253-9119

✍ www.whotels.com

The exterior is a Beaux-Arts building erected in 1911, but inside it's all up-to-the-minute style. This is one of Manhattan's trendier hotels with a hip sense of humor—its 270 rooms and sixteen suites have names like Wonderful, Spectacular, Mega, Fantastic, Wow, and Extreme Wow. They all feature beds decked out in sharkskin coverlets, velvet armchairs, and a list of amenities you would expect from a first-rate hotel. There is a spa and fitness center and a "Whatever/Whenever Service" that will do whatever, whenever . . . so long as it's legal.

Celebrity Chef Todd English has added the hotel restaurant, Olives New York, to his string of Olives in Boston, Washington, D.C., and Las Vegas. The food is a rustic American take on Italian and Mediterranean cuisine and has made Olives New York a trendy culinary spot. The Living Room Lounge off the lobby bar is an inviting place to read, try out the specially designed game tables, or sip a drink and gaze out at the park or the people. There are five other W hotels throughout the city.

Upper Manhattan

A hotel along Central Park is a particularly nice place for watching the Thanksgiving Day Parade or enjoying the trees in the spring. Yet this is Manhattan, and it's still convenient to all the sights.

Loews Regency

🖃 540 Park Avenue (at 61st Street)

🚇 5th Avenue-59th Street station (N, R, or W train)

📞 1-800-233-2356

📞 212-759-4100

✉ *www.loewsregency.com*

One of the city's most exclusive hotels, the Regency is located on Park Avenue in Manhattan's posh Upper East Side. The luxurious hotel, which opened in 1963 and has been thoroughly renovated, is the flagship property of the Loews Hotel chain. Celebrities are often spotted in and around the hotel, which houses some 353 guest rooms, including eighty-six suites with custom-designed furnishings. The combination of traditional décor with contemporary styling creates an atmosphere that is warm and comfortable as well as practical and functional.

The Regency loves families—to the point of giving teenagers a VIT (very important teen) backpack filled with goodies and permission to raid a special hotel closet for DVDs, game systems, and other products to use during their stay. Younger kids get a Fisher-Price welcoming gift, supervised recreation programs, and lots more. Pets are also welcome.

Guest accommodations include an in-room safe, minibar, phone with caller ID, flat-screen TV, CD player, the "Ultimate Doeskin" bathrobe by Chadsworth & Haig, and (of course) televisions in every bathroom. Suites have two bathrooms—which means yet another television. Rooms that have a kitchenette with microwave and refrigerator are available.

☂ RAINY DAY FUN

Take your kids to your hotel's in-house fitness center or pool (if available) and work off some of that energy and good food. In fact, families with an active lifestyle make it a point to do just that. Note that some hotels have an age requirement for the use of their equipment.

The hotel has a twenty-four-hour concierge, overnight valet service, complimentary Evian water and towels for morning joggers, on-site twenty-four-hour limo service (at a cost), and the Nico Salon. There is also a fitness center with state-of-the-art machines.

Singer-songwriter Michael Feinstein oversees Feinstein's at the Regency, a great restaurant and cabaret with some big-name stars (*www.feinsteinsattheregency.com*). It shares space with the 540 Park restaurant, where you can go for great breakfasts and lunch; the Sunday brunch is to die for. The Library offers a comfortable, residential-style venue for a relaxed breakfast, lunch, afternoon tea, dinner, late-night meal, and Sunday brunch. It also provides the hotel's twenty-four-hour room service. This is a Loews hotel with a wonderful family program, and there are many specials and packages offered. It pays to call or go online.

The Pierre
🖃 2 East 61st Street (between 5th and Madison avenues)
🚇 5th Avenue-59th Street station (N, R, or W train)
📞 1-800-PIERREH (743-7734)
📞 212-838-8000
✍ *www.tajhotels.com/pierre*

The Pierre radiates Old World luxury. Even the fitness center on the third floor is decorated with hand-painted murals and Italian marble. The Pierre is a very family-friendly hotel with a long list of age-appropriate amenities, including specially enhanced rooms for families with young children. It even requests you provide your children's names and ages before you arrive so it may offer whatever you may need. Currently owned by the Taj chain, there are 202 rooms and suites. There's a wonderful afternoon tea here at The Rotunda (also a children's menu) and the on-site Café Pierre serves breakfast, lunch, and dinner.

Trump International Hotel & Tower

- 1 Central Park West (between West 60th and West 61st streets)
- West 59th Street-Columbus Circle (A, B, C, D, or 1 train)
- 1-888-44-TRUMP (448-7867)
- 212-299-1000
- *www.trumpintl.com*

A latecomer in the world of luxury hotels in New York, the Trump has tried to become the last word in personal service and amenities. Upscale amenities include a cellular phone, personalized business cards and stationery, telescopes, and in-room computers. Child-care facilities are available for parents who want some alone time.

The hotel has 167 rooms and suites with views of the skyline or the park. Most rooms have a fully equipped Euro-style kitchen, marble baths and Jacuzzis, high-speed and wireless (fee charged) Internet access, entertainment center, safe, bathrobe and slippers, and lots more.

The Trump has a family special: one night for four in a two-room, park-view suite; admission to one of three children's museums; a kid's cabinet of books, DVDs, and games; a refrigerator of goodies; and milk and cookies at bedtime. It'll only set you back $2,500.

The restaurant, Jean-Georges, is top of the heap. The cuisine is fusion French, American, and Indochinese, and the kids will love the tableside chefs preparing your meal. Within the restaurant is the more casual La Nougatine.

New York's Annual Events

January

Restaurant Week

Twice a year (in January and June or July), more than 200 of New York's finest restaurants offer a prix fixe lunch and dinner menu. Prices vary by year. This is a fabulous opportunity to sample the best of the city's cuisine, but make reservations, as the best restaurants fill up within hours of the announcement of restaurant week. Find more information on the Web at *www.nycvisit.com/restaurantweek* or call 212-484-1222.

National Boat Show

This annual event is held at the Jacob K. Javits Convention Center and shows the latest in boats and other pleasure craft for the water. Kids love to crawl in and out of the boats and admission is free if they're under twelve. Call 212-216-2000 for more information, or visit the Web at *www.javitscenter.com*.

Winter Antique Show

As it has been for more than fifty years, this is the top antiques fair in the city, featuring fine and decorative art from America, Asia, and Europe. Held at the historic Seventh Regiment Armory on Park

Avenue. Call 718-292-7392 for more information, or visit the Web at *www.winterantiquesshow.com.*

February

Chinese New Year Celebration

The annual celebration is held in Chinatown over a two-week period and includes a dragon parade and special menus in most Chinatown restaurants. Visit *www.explorechinatown.com* for more information.

Westminster Kennel Club Dog Show

The quintessential dog show is held at Madison Square Garden and is the nation's second oldest continuous sporting contest. Call 212-465-6741 for more information, or visit the Web site at *www.west minsterkennelclub.org.*

March

St. Patrick's Day Parade

An annual event since 1762, this is one of the biggest and best St. Patrick's Day parades in the country. The route is Fifth Avenue from Forty-fourth to Eighty-sixth streets. Call 212-484-1222 for more information.

Art Expo New York

The world's largest fine and popular art fair hosts more than 500 galleries, dealers, and artists. Held at the Jacob K. Javits Convention Center. For a floor plan and the latest on exhibitors, visit the Web site at *www.artexpos.com.*

Greek Independence Day Parade

This joyous parade on Fifth Avenue has been taking place since the 1930s on the Sunday closest to March 25. Call 718-204-6500 or visit the Web site at *www.greekparade.org.*

April

Easter Parade

Held Easter Sunday along Fifth Avenue from Forty-ninth to Fifty-seventh streets. It's a time for New Yorkers to display their Easter finery while casually strolling the closed streets. The best viewing is around St. Patrick's Cathedral.

Easter Eggstravaganza in Central Park

Held on the Saturday before Easter, it's the world's largest egg hunt. There's also egg-dyeing and egg and spoon races. Lots of free entertainment at Central Park's Naumberg Bandshell and Mall Concert Ground. Use the Seventy-second Street entrance. Visit *www.nyc govparks.org* for more information.

New York International Auto Show

The newest and weirdest cars can be seen at this show, as well as car accessories of almost any kind imaginable. At the Jacob K. Javits Convention Center. Call 212-216-2000, or go online to *www.javitscenter .com* for more information.

Opening Day at Shea Stadium

The Mets usually kick off their baseball season the first week of April. For more information, call 718-507-8499 or visit the Web site at *www.newyorkmets.com*.

Opening Day at Yankee Stadium

Like the Mets, the Yankees welcome spring and baseball the first week of April. For more information, call 718-293-6000 or visit the Web site at *www.yankees.com*.

Ringling Brothers Barnum & Bailey Circus

New Yorkers know spring is coming when the circus posters appear all over town. The big top comes to the Big Apple every April, performing in Madison Square Garden. Call TicketMaster at 212-465-

6741 for tickets, or visit the Web site at *www.ringling.com* for hours and special offers.

Cherry Blossom Festival

Spring is spectacular at the Brooklyn Botanic Garden, Brooklyn's favorite nature spot, and it's celebrated in this annual festival. Call 718-623-7200 for more information, or visit the Web site at *www.bbg* *.org* for the special "Cherry Watch" link.

Annual Macy's Flower Show

The interior of this landmark Herald Square department store is taken over by exquisite floral displays the week before Easter. Call the annual event hotline at 212-494-4495 for more information.

New York City Ballet

The city's premier ballet troupe begins its spring repertory season in late April. For more information, leap over to the Web at *www* *.nycballet.com.*

May

Bike New York Five Boro Bike Tour

For the bicycle enthusiast, here's a chance to take a forty-two-mile bike tour of all five boroughs with 30,000 other cyclists. Ends with a festival of music, food, tour merchandise, and support facilities like medical and massage. Free Staten Island Ferry ride back to your starting point. Call 212-932-0778 for more information, or find more information on the Web at *www.bikenewyork.org.*

Fleet Week

Navy ships from all over the country and abroad gather at Pier 88 at the foot of West Forty-eighth Street in Manhattan and Homepoint Pier in Staten Island where they are open to the public for viewing. Meet sailors and see military demonstrations. Note: the Intrepid Sea,

Air & Space Museum, the usual Fleet Week anchor, is closed until the fall of 2008. Call 212-245-0072 or go to *www.fleetweek.navy.mil* for more information.

Washington Square Outdoor Art Show

Hundreds of mostly local artists display paintings, photos, sculpture, and crafts on University Place in Greenwich Village from noon till 6 P.M. Held Memorial Day weekend and the following weekend, also Labor Day weekend and the following weekend. Call 212-982-6255 for more information.

Annual AIDS Walk

This celebrity-filled 10K walkathon starts and ends in Central Park. Find more information on the Web at *www.aidswalk.net.*

June

National Puerto Rican Day Parade

One of the city's largest and most popular ethnic parades, the route runs along Fifth Avenue, from Forty-fourth to Eighty-fifth Street on the second Sunday of June. It is the nation's oldest Puerto Rican parade, first celebrated in 1958. Call 212-484-1222 or visit *www .nycvisit.com* for more information.

The Belmont Stakes

One of the major horseracing events of the year, this final jewel in the Triple Crown takes place at Belmont Race Track in Long Island. Find more information on the Web at *www.nyra.com*, or call 718-641-4700.

JVC Jazz Festival New York

More than forty venues feature the best of jazz in such places as Carnegie Hall, Lincoln Center, and other venues. For more information, go to *www.festivalproductions.net.*

Restaurant Week

This semiannual event features prix fixe meals in more than 200 fine restaurants; see full listing in January events.

New York Philharmonic Concerts in the Park

New Yorkers gather on the open meadows with picnic blankets to listen to music under the stars in Central and Van Cortlandt parks. Sometimes held in July. Find more information on the Web at *www* *.nyphil.org* (great Kidszone here), or call 212-875-5656.

Bryant Park Film Festival

The park behind the New York Public Library (at Forty-second Street and Sixth Avenue) is used as an outdoor theater for the screening of classic films. Bring a blanket (no chairs allowed on the lawn) and lounge under the stars Monday nights at sunset during June, July, and August. Find more information on the Web at *www.bryantpark* *.org* or call 212-768-4242.

July

Macy's Annual Fourth of July Fireworks Display

This spectacular display takes place over the East River. Viewing sites stretch along FDR Drive from Fourteenth Street to Forty-first Street; the Brooklyn Promenade is also a good place to watch. Call 212-494-4495 for more information.

Midsummer Night Swing at Lincoln Center

One of the most popular city summer events, this dance party takes place outdoors at the Lincoln Center's Hosie Robertson Plaza. Find more information on the Web at *www.lincolncenter.org* or call 212-875-5766.

Summerstage Concerts in Central Park

Some thirty free concerts feature a wide range of music, dance, films, and the spoken word. Takes place in the evening and on weekend afternoons at the Rumsay Playfield. Enter at Sixty-ninth Street and Fifth Avenue, or Seventy-second Street and Central Park West. Find more information on the Web at *www.summerstage.org* or call 212-360-2777.

Shakespeare in the Park

A New York institution, these free performances of Shakespearean dramas take place at the Delacorte Theater in Central Park, usually with a cast of celebrity actors. Find more information on the Web at *www.publictheater.org* or call 212-539-8500.

August

U.S. Open Tennis Championships

The final grand slam event of the tennis season draws top competitors to Flushing Meadows Corona Park in Queens. Call 1-800-GO-TENNIS (1-800-468-3664) or go online at *www.usopen.org*.

West Indian American Day Parade

Held over the Labor Day weekend in Brooklyn, this parade celebrates the traditional harvest carnival native to Trinidad and Tobago. Find more information on the Web at *www.carnaval.com*, or call 718-467-1797.

Harlem Week in Upper Manhattan

This is a day-long celebration of African American culture. Held along 125th Street, it features dancing, performances, crafts, and food. For more information, call 212-862-7200.

September

Feast of San Gennaro

New York's oldest and biggest street festival is a week-long outdoor happening with food, parades, and entertainment. The annual salute to the patron saint of Naples takes place in Little Italy on Mulberry Street. Find more information on the Web at *www.sangennaro.org* or call 212-768-1600.

Medieval Festival

On the third Sunday in September, 40,000 people head to Fort Tryon Park and the Cloisters to see a joust and dress in medieval clothing. Find more information on the Web at *www.whidc.org/home.html*, or call 212-795-1600.

October

Columbus Day Parade

On the second Monday in October, New York hosts one of the oldest and biggest Columbus Day celebrations in the country with more than 35,000 marchers traveling north along Fifth Avenue from Forty-fourth and Seventy-ninth streets. Call 212-484-1222 for more information.

Halloween Parade

This very popular and crowded costume parade, with more than fifty bands, puppets, dancers, and artists, takes place in Greenwich Village, on Sixth Avenue from Twenty-third Street to Spring Street. Find more information on the Web at *www.halloween-nyc.com*, or call 212-475-3333.

November

Veterans Day Parade

This annual parade route runs up Fifth Avenue from Twenty-sixth Street to Fifty-second Street. Call 212-484-1222, or visit *www .nycvisit.com* for information.

ING New York City Marathon

Covering 26.2 miles through all five boroughs, the runners start in Staten Island and finish in Central Park. Find more information on the Web at *www.nycmarathon.org* or call 212-423-2249.

Macy's Thanksgiving Day Parade

See the giant balloons, floats, Broadway performances, bands, and celebrities parade down Central Park West on the fourth Thursday in November, from Seventy-seventh Street to Broadway and Herald Square. Information at 212-494-4495 or *www.macys.com*.

The Radio City Christmas Spectacular

This annual performance includes the world-famous Rockettes and an array of fabulously costumed performers. Radio City Music Hall is worth a visit on its own. Find more information on the Web at *www.radiocity.com* or call 212-307-1000.

The Lighting of the Christmas Tree

A few days after Thanksgiving, thousands gather to watch the lighting of the tree at Rockefeller Center. Call 212-632-3975 or go to *www.rockefellercenter.com* for more information.

December

The Lighting of World's Largest Hanukkah Menorah

This ceremony takes place on Fifth Avenue and Fifty-ninth Street, across the street from the Plaza Hotel in Manhattan. Also, a large menorah is lit in Brooklyn's Grand Army Plaza. Both are lit nightly during Hanukkah. Call 212-736-8400 for more information.

Kwanzaa Festival

The Jacob K. Javits Convention Center plays host to this colorful celebration featuring African food and culture. Call 212-216-2000 or click on *www.javitscenter.com*.

The Nutcracker

Every year, this ballet—a children's favorite—is performed at Lincoln Center. Tickets are a hot commodity, so get them early at 212-870-5570 or *www.nycballet.com*.

The Grand Central Kaleidoscope

The beautiful sky ceiling of Grand Central Station is transformed with laser light and sound every thirty minutes in December. Be awed by one of New York's newest holiday traditions. Find more information at *www.grandcentralterminal.com* or call 212-340-2345.

Midnight Run in Central Park on New Year's Eve

Sponsored by the New York Road Runners Club, this festive run features a costume parade during the fireworks. The four-mile run is more a party than a race. Find more information on the Web at *www.nyrr.org* or call 212-860-4455.

New Year's Eve

Just like you've undoubtedly seen on television, the big crystal ball drops at midnight in Times Square, drawing 750,000 revelers each year. For more information call 212-768-1560 or visit *www.timessquarenyc.org*.

Additional Resources

Web Sites

✉ *www.nycvisit.com*

☎ 212-484-1200

☎ 1-800-692-8474 (for literature only)

This site, New York City's official tourism Web site, is essential for planning your trip. Here you will find hotel and restaurant suggestions and discounts, a local calendar of events, and suggested itineraries and ways to plan and save money. A random day's "Just For Kids" listed ninety-eight things for them to do. Ask for the *NYC Visitor's Guide*. It is also available online, at the tourist kiosks listed in the Web site, and at airports.

✉ *www.iloveny.com*

☎ 1-800-CALL-NYS (U.S. and Canada)

☎ 518-474-4116 (everywhere else)

This is the official tourist Web site of New York State. Especially good is the accommodations feature, where you can find a hotel that matches your needs by checking a list of amenities; for example, a pet-friendly place. Click on "Travel Ideas" at the top of the page for NYC Weekend suggestions. You can also request the excellent travel guide.

✑ www.nytimes.com

Like the "old Gray Lady" itself, this is a great site if you have the time to take full advantage of it. Lots of editorial and pictorial material, plus lots of nitty-gritty information. You can indulge in one of several slide shows on various New York topics, or get the show times and ticket prices for every play in town. A special kids' section will be a revelation to parents. On the home page, look to the left-hand column, and under "Travel" click on "NYC Guide."

✑ www.newyorkmetro.com

New York magazine's Web site is another tool for finding just about anything you might want in the city. The restaurant review database, with comments by readers, is extensive.

✑ www.villagevoice.com

This is the Web site of the venerable weekly alternative newspaper the *Village Voice* (now free at hundreds of locations throughout town). The events list is one of the best in the city—go to "nycguide" and click on "events."

✑ www.nyc.gov

This is the city's comprehensive Web site, which will give you everything from access to the Department of Parks and Recreation to parking regulations. It's huge but very complete, with an excellent section for visitors. While in the city, you can access this information by phone by calling 311.

✑ www.ny.com

This is an easy-to-use site for general information on New York, with an emphasis on frugality.

✑ www.nyctourist.com

Another of the many unofficial Web sites about the city, this one has fairly comprehensive information about the city and numerous links to purchase attraction and events tickets and accommodations.

✎ *www.longisland.com*

A search engine aimed at Long Island locals, this site is also crammed with resources for the visitor. There are sites for tourism, entertainment, shopping, local services, railroad schedules, and maps and directions, among many others.

✎ *www.newsday.com*

This Web site for Long Island's daily newspaper is crammed with information useful to visitors. Check out their many "Best of" lists.

Suggested Reading

Kid's Books

New York has been the subject or main character of many kids' books. The city is just as much a vast playground for the kids as for grownups.

Barracca, Debra and Sal, *The Adventures of Taxi Dog* (2000, Dial). The story of Maxi the Taxi Dog and the wild cast of New York characters who ride in his master's cab is told in rhyme. The Children's Museum of Manhattan features some of the book's art.

Fitzhugh, Louise, *Harriet the Spy* (2001, Bantam Doubleday Dell). Harriet wants to be an author, and to practice she travels her Manhattan neighborhood spying on her neighbors and friends. It's a great one to take on the trip.

Konigsburg, E. L., *From the Mixed-up Files of Mrs. Basil E. Frankweiler* (2002, Simon & Schuster). Like most twelve-year-olds do at times, Claudia wanted to run away, but to somewhere warm, inside, and beautiful. So she chose the Metropolitan Museum of Art. 1968 Newbery Medal winner.

Reingold, Faith, *Tar Beach* (1996, Bantam Doubleday Dell). The part autobiographical, part fictional story of eight-year-old Cassie, who imagines herself leaving her Harlem rooftop (the "Tar Beach") and flying over 1939 New York. Based on the author's famous quilt painting of the same name.

Selden, George, *The Cricket in Times Square* (1970, Yearling). Chester the cricket winds up entirely out of his element when he unintentionally travels to New York City. He has to meet friends and figure out how to survive in all the bustle. Newbery Honor Book.

Swift, Hildegarde and Lynd Ward, *The Little Red Lighthouse and the Great Gray Bridge* (2002, Harcourt Brace). This is a classic about the relationship between two real-life landmarks—a little red lighthouse overshadowed by the massive George Washington Bridge.

Taylor, Sydney, *All-of-a-Kind Family* (1984, Random House). Five girls find joy and drama in turn-of-the-century New York.

Thompson, Kay, *Eloise* (1959, Simon and Schuster). This is the classic tale of a little girl who grew up at the Plaza Hotel.

White, E. B., *Stuart Little* (1974, HarperCollins). This children's classic about a mouse born into a human family was made into a charming and popular motion picture.

New York City Maps

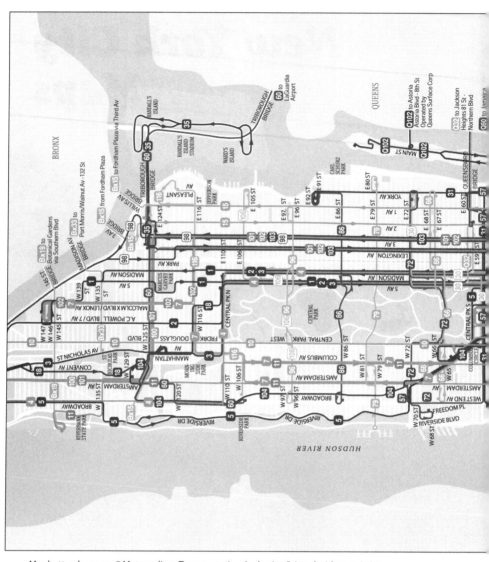

Manhattan bus map ©Metropolitan Transportation Authority. Printed with permission.

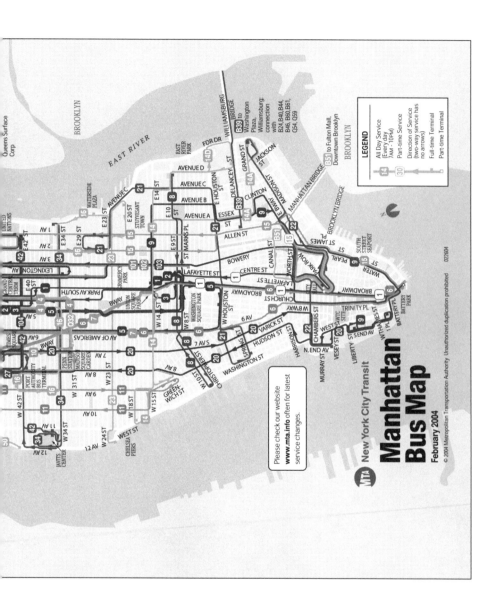

MTA New York City Transit

Manhattan Bus Map

February 2004

© 2004 Metropolitan Transportation Authority Unauthorized duplication prohibited   020604

Please check our website
www.mta.info often for latest
service changes.

QUEENS Surface Corp

BROOKLYN

EAST RIVER

B39 to Washington Plaza, Williamsburg; connection with B24, B40, B44, B46, B60, B61, Q54, Q59

B51 to Fulton Mall, Downtown Brooklyn

BROOKLYN

WILLIAMSBURG BRIDGE

MANHATTAN BRIDGE

BROOKLYN BRIDGE

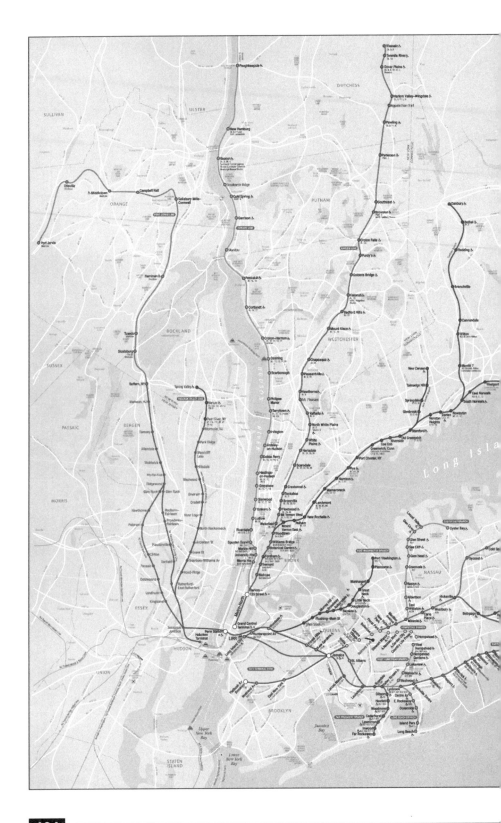

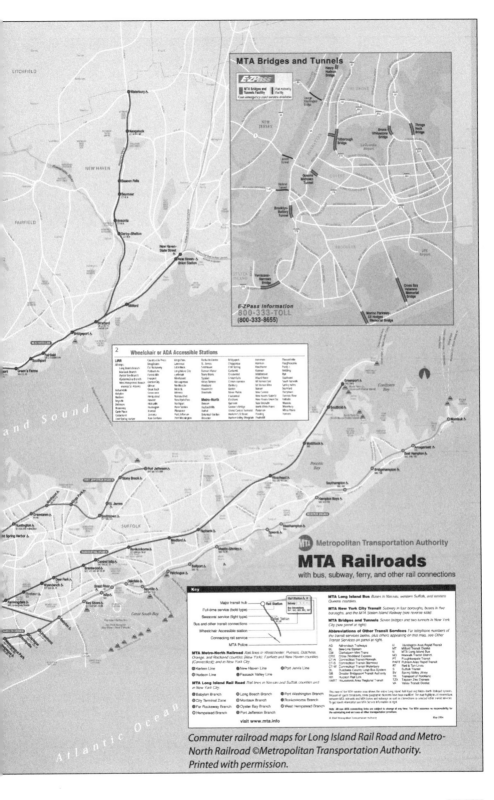

Commuter railroad maps for Long Island Rail Road and Metro-North Railroad ©Metropolitan Transportation Authority. Printed with permission.

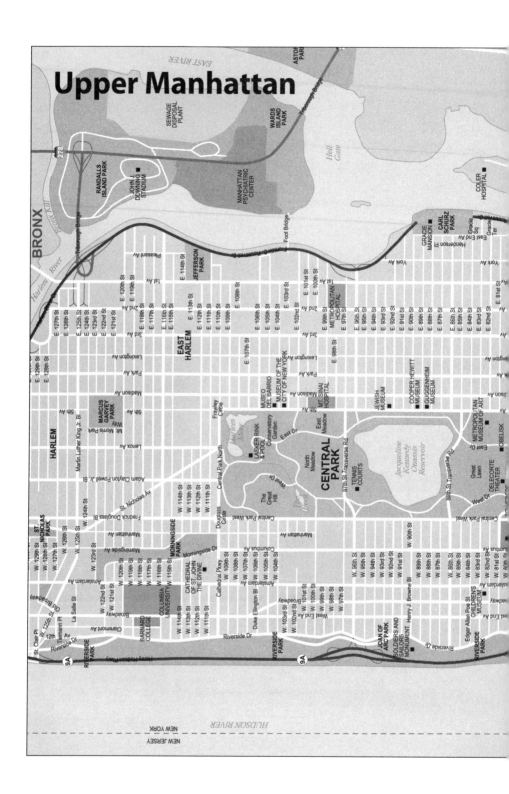

Upper Manhattan

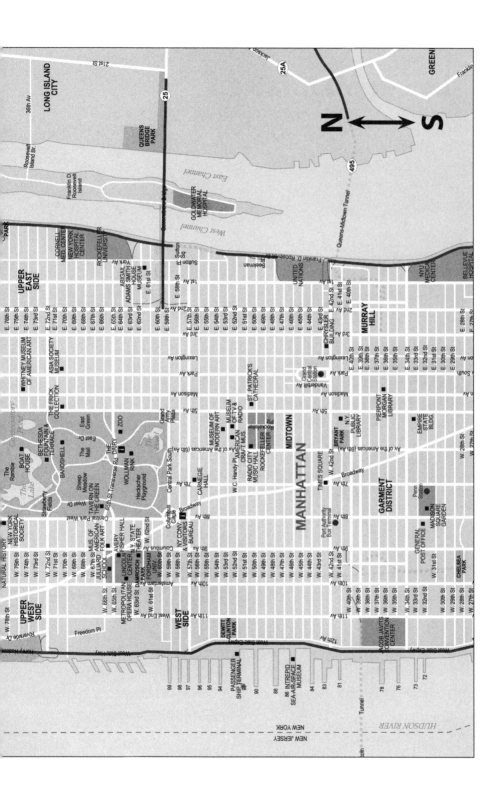

Lower Manhattan

Central Park

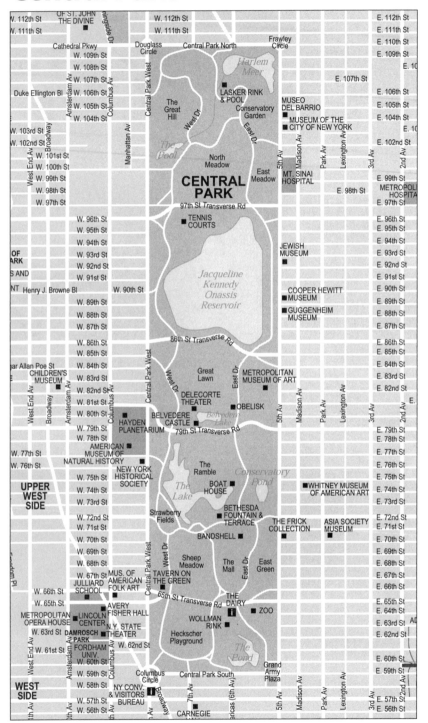

INDEX